INVOLVING PARENTS

Effective Parent-Teacher Relations

INVOLVING PARENTS

Effective Parent-Teacher Relations

Alastair Macbeth

HEINEMANN
EDUCATIONAL

Heinemann Educational,
a division of Heinemann Educational Books Ltd,
Halley Court, Jordan Hill, Oxford OX2 8EJ

OXFORD   LONDON   EDINBURGH
MELBOURNE   SYDNEY   AUCKLAND
IBADAN   NAIROBI   GABORONE   HARARE
KINGSTON   PORTSMOUTH NH (USA)
SINGAPORE   MADRID

First published 1989
Reprinted 1990

British Library Cataloguing in Publication Data
Macbeth, Alastair
    Involving parents: effective parent—teacher
    relations. — (Heinemann organisation in schools
    series).
    1. Great Britain. Schools. Relations with parents
    I. Title
    371.1′03′0941

    ISBN 0–435–80595–9

Typeset by Fakenham Photosetting Ltd., Fakenham, Norfolk
Printed in Great Britain by Biddles Ltd., Guildford and King's Lynn

CONTENTS

CONTENTS

ACKNOWLEDGEMENTS

Writing this book involved the help and advice of too many people to mention all by name. However, I am especially grateful to the following who kindly read and commented upon substantial sections of the drafts: Frank McEnroe, Alistair Marquis, John Bastiani, Neil Toppin, Elsa Davies, Bob McKay, David Harvey, Elaine Foster and, of course, Michael Marland as Editor of the Series. They, and a wide diversity of other people who advised on specific sections, brought a multiplicity of perspectives to bear on the themes of the book. My appreciation also goes to Rona Foster, not only for her typing skills but also for her patience when the advent of new educational legislation necessitated re-jigging so much of the text.

When the acknowledgement pages of so many books give credit to the long-suffering support of a spouse, how can I express the tremendous importance of my wife's constant backing without it seeming trite? When I say 'Thanks, Bud' that reflects more gratitude and appreciation of her contribution than any casual reader would realise. And lest our offspring, Ian, Rory and Kim, think that I used their education as an experiment for this book, (a), I didn't, but (b) their experiences and responses to school and home did influence my thinking; (c) if we were starting that whole process again now, I think we'd do some bits differently; (d) despite it all they've emerged as reasonable characters; and (e) they constantly tease me for writing in lists sub-divided as (a), (b), (c), (d) and (e).

INTRODUCTION

Substantially more power has been devolved to schools than ever before and schools are being held even more accountable locally in a variety of ways. Therefore, the Heinemann *Organisation in Schools Series* is adding to its support for those who carry leadership and management responsibilities in schools. The series offers practical studies of those aspects of school management that are changed by the legislation of the late eighties, especially local management of schools, the national curriculum, and the enhanced importance of parents.

Despite our efforts and considerable professional rhetoric, the United Kingdom schooling system has not been at its best in its relationships with the parents of pupils. A variety of action–research work on helping more successful learning and more successful schools through working with parents joins with legislation that gives more power to parents on Governing Bodies (School Boards in Scotland) and at the same time immensely more power to those Governing Bodies. It is therefore clear that every school will want to review the ways in which it works with the pupils' homes and will wish to seek possibilities for enhancing that work.

Alastair Macbeth has produced the most comprehensive and best researched overview of parenting and schooling. His study of all aspects of schools and their parents in the United Kingdom is enriched by his specially commissioned research on school-family relations in the countries of the European Commission. This allows him to bring fundamental thinking about the role of families in education together with the details of practical approaches of both primary and secondary schools.

Although there have been accounts of good practice in the past, this is a pioneering book in that it looks at the management and pastoral care needs of schools after the legislation of the eighties. It is designed to help middle-management and senior management of schools to develop their modes of involving parents in schooling in the changed educational world of the next decade.

Michael Marland

1 WHY PARENTS MATTER TO SCHOOLS

Parents are integral to schooling. Inevitably, by both example and instruction, usually for good but sometimes for ill, parents teach their children and through that teaching they influence the extent to which we, as teachers, can be effective. Further, parents, not teachers, are primarily responsible in law for the education of their individual child. They are therefore first-line clients of the school. They should not be lumped together with remoter interested parties, such as children's possible future employers or 'the community', which are largely outside the schooling process. The parental dimension of schooling is central to our professional performance as teachers. Yet it is often under-rated. In my view we neglect it at our peril, for our impact as teachers and our status as professionals may substantially depend upon the extent to which we take seriously the phrase 'partnership with parents'.

The Education Reform Act of 1988 for England and Wales* continued a trend to give more prominence in law to the roles of parents, a trend which had started with the 1980 and 1986 Acts. Yet much of this legislative action concentrated upon parental representation on governing bodies and upon parental rights, such as to choice of school and to information. These, of course, are important and will be discussed further in the chapters which follow, but they are less concerned with partnership between teachers and parents and ways by which parents can be involved both formally and informally in the child's education.

This book is about such involvement, as well as the recent legislative changes. Actions are generated by ideas and ideals. One cannot approach the practice of home–school relations without assessing *why* there should be partnership between parents and teachers. In the past many teachers have pursued whole careers with only minimal contact with parents, and some even now continue to do so. Reasons must be compelling if practice, involving energy, time and resources, is to be

* Scottish and Northern Irish reforms have been developing rather differently and comparisons will be made at appropriate points in this book.

1

worth changing. Before discussing the five main reasons for establishing educational partnership between family and school, consideration of the usage of the word 'education' is an essential preliminary. As teachers, we have hi-jacked the word to the point where 'education' is equated with 'schooling' in many people's minds. That is probably to the detriment of children's welfare.

Use of the Word 'Education'

There is no legal definition of 'education' and philosophers have had difficulty with the word. Peters (1966, p.23) rightly states that 'there are usages of the *term* "education" which it would be difficult to encompass in any precise definition.' Does it include only what is worthwhile, only what is deliberate, and only what is intended not to deceive? Are training, instruction, initiation and attitude-formation subsidiary parts of education? Are indoctrination or learning by accident, by experience or by copying others *not* education? Schofield (1972, p.41) refers to a 'united family of ideas' to which we give the name education; O'Connor (1957, p.5) points out that it includes techniques, theories and values, while Chambers (1983, p.33) concentrates on processes 'providing the components of a fuller personhood' which have as central elements cognitive perspective and rationality.

No matter how difficult it may be to define 'education', the word gets used daily by parents, teachers, administrators, politicians and the media. For the purposes of this book I am employing the term in a broad sense to include all the circumstances and actions leading to the child's intellectual, social, moral and physical development, while by schooling I mean related institutional provision for children. While philosophically insensitive, this approach does highlight a key point: *most of a child's education happens outside school.*

We teachers often claim to provide education, but we provide only part of it. We talk about 'the education system' when what we mean is formalised group provision. The institutional elements get emphasised in *education* Acts, by *education* authorities and by *education* officers. *Educational* administration, *educational* planning, *educational* counselling, *educational* objectives, *educational* technology, *education* vouchers and so on tend to focus on the formal system and it is not surprising that education and schooling have become almost synonymous in the minds of teachers, politicians and the general public. This is dangerous because it leads people to think that teachers are solely responsible for education and its success or failure.

Schooling is part of education and education is part of upbringing. Education happens in three main areas: school, home and community. I am aware that the word 'community' has a multitude of social and territorial implications, but I use it to embrace not only the locality, but also society, including educational facets such as the media. By this perspective we obtain the following over-simple, but still useful, formula.

Figure 1.1.

$$\text{EDUCATION} = \frac{\text{school}}{\text{learning}} + \frac{\text{home}}{\text{learning}} + \frac{\text{community}}{\text{learning}}$$

In one sense this formula is misleading, since the elements overlap with each other and perhaps it should be expressed:

Figure 1.2.

EDUCATION =

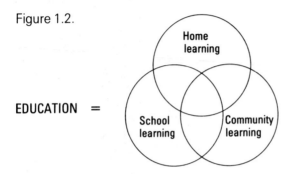

Children learn when they are awake. From birth to 16 years less than 15 per cent of a child's waking life is spent in school. Schooling is planned, structured, professionally-provided and delivered at times of day when children are alert and receptive, so that we may expect school to have more than 15 per cent of educational impact. However, a great deal of learning – especially with regard to attitudes and motivation – happens outside school, much of it in the home, particularly in the early years. To the influences of family, peer-group and neighbourhood we may add the increasing pervasiveness and sophistication of TV and other media. It is not reasonable to expect a school to counteract these influences when they are harmful, and it is often when non-school learning is disadvantageous that we teachers recognise its existence. We are perhaps less ready to accept that much, probably most, education happens outside school and is beneficial. Yet perhaps that should be the starting-point for consideration of home–school relations.

Of course, not all non-school education happens in the home. But families, especially parents, have substantial influence upon the nature of the *community learning* which a child experiences. Parents generally determine the neighbourhood in which a child grows up; what books, newspapers, television or entertainment he encounters; what sports or cultural activities he is encouraged to pursue; and even, to some extent, what friendships he will develop. Further, the huge majority of parents have a genuine, deep concern for the welfare of their children, have powerful emotional bonds with them, provide reference models which they copy, influence their attitudes (including motivation to achieve in school) and usually know more about their child than anyone else. If schools are concerned with education then parents must be viewed as key elements of it.

The Parental Dimension of Schooling

Parents are relevant to what happens *inside* school for five quite distinct reasons.

1 Parents are responsible in law for their child's education, and in that sense they may be regarded as the school's legal clients.
2 If most of a child's education happens outside school, especially in the home, and if parents are co-educators of the child with teachers, then it seems logical to make the two elements of school-learning and home-learning compatible, and for teachers to use that home-learning as a resource.
3 Research indicates that family-based learning influences the effectiveness of school on a child. It may be a significant factor among the complexity of forces associated with inequality of educational opportunity.
4 Besides providing a professional service for parents, the teacher is also an agent of the education authority and the state to some degree. There are implied functions of checking upon parents' fulfilment of duties (e.g. with regard to school attendance) and, arguably, of being an educational safety-net for pupils with incompetent or uncaring parents.
5 It seems democratically reasonable, in a decentralised system in which important decisions are made at school and class levels, that those with a stake in a school should influence (though not necessarily determine) the nature of those decisions. Parents are stakeholders on behalf of their child and should be able to influence school policy through representatives.

Each of these issues warrants separate actions. For instance, to have parents on a governing body may go some way to meeting the fifth point but is largely irrelevant to the other four; or to treat parents as clients may not necessarily do anything to make home-learning supportive of school objectives. Different reasons for partnership with parents require different sorts of responses at different levels of the system.

1. Parents' Legal Responsibility for their Child's Education

Freeman (1983, p.4), discussing the rights of children, expresses the generally-accepted principle that 'interference with a child's liberty is an inescapable consequence of the biological and physiological dependence of children'. Given that children are necessarily dependent on adults, the question becomes one of who should have responsibility for their upbringing, including education. Of course traditionally (most would say naturally) that is the family, especially parents. Yet in theory the state could take over these functions. National and international pronouncements have resisted such a radical shift. The United Nations Declaration of the Rights of the Child (1959) states:

> The best interests of the child shall be the guiding principle of those responsible for his education and guidance. That responsibility lies in the first place with his parents.

4

Churches tend to enunciate the same view. For instance, the Second Vatican Council in its Declaration of Christian Education asserted:

> Since it is the parents who have given life to their children, it is they who have the serious obligation of educating their offspring. Hence parents must be recognised as the first and foremost educators of their children.

Most national laws similarly place responsibility for the child's education upon his/her parents, granting rights commensurate with the duty. For example, the Basic Law of the Federal Republic of West Germany (1949, Article 6.2) states:

> The care and education of children are the natural right of parents and the duty is primarily theirs. The national community shall check upon their endeavours in this respect.

In Britain we do not have such a Basic Law or a Bill of Rights to enunciate fundamental principles. Our laws tend to be administrative rather than philosophical, but the same concept is clearly there. Section 36 of the 1944 Act answers the question: who, in law, is responsible for the education of the individual child?

> It shall be the duty of the parent of every child of compulsory school age to cause him to receive full-time education suitable to his age, ability, and aptitude, either by regular attendance at school or otherwise.*

It should be noted that this applies to the *individual* child, not to children in general or to the provision of facilities in general, which are central government and education authority responsibilities. That is an important distinction to which I shall refer later in this book. It may also be noted that although education is compulsory, schooling is not. Schooling may be (and normally is) used by parents to fulfil their legal duty minimally. That does not mean that schooling is the same thing as education, nor does it mean that schooling is obligatory.

Education authorities are required by Section 7 of the 1944 Act† to make educational facilities available. We may pose the question: for what purpose? If parents are responsible for their child's education, then the facilities must exist to assist parents in carrying out their legal duty. **In brief, parents may be seen as the school's prime legal clients, until the child is 16 years of age**.

That position is given emphasis by a section of the Act which is often quoted by parents, but which, in my view, is conceptually less important than the one which lays down their duty. This is Section 76‡ which requires (with qualifications about efficient instruction and the avoi-

---

* Counterpart clauses in Scotland and Northern Ireland are Section 30 of The Education (Scotland) Act, 1980, and Section 35 of The Education and Libraries (Northern Ireland) Order, 1972. Wording is not identical but is similar.
† and section 1 of the Education (Scotland) Act, 1980.
‡ and section 28 of the Education (Scotland) Act, 1980.

dance of unreasonable public expenditure) that education authorities (and therefore their school systems) are to 'have regard to the general principle that ... pupils are to be educated in accordance with the wishes of their parents.' It is interesting that here, untypically, a general principle creeps into our law. It is not clear whether it is an inviolable and overarching principle or whether the words 'have regard to' mean, in effect, 'if it happens to be convenient', but what matters here is the relationship of parental wishes to parental duty. Educational provisions according to parental wishes is a logical consequence of the fact that parents bear prime responsibility for their child's education. It reinforces parents' client-status.

Laws are man-made and they can be changed. For instance, the state (through teachers as its agents) could be made responsible for the **schooling** of the individual child, leaving out-of-school education as the responsibility of the parents. Indeed many teachers behave as if that were the case now. But what would be the implications of such a change? I consider that they would be far-reaching, for they would set a precedent affecting not just parents' rights for the upbringing of their child, but would question current assumptions about the structure of our society and individual liberties within it. At present the family is regarded as the fundamental unit of our society. Parents, as the central figures in families, are given the prime right and duty to shelter, feed, clothe, educate and secure the health of their children. The state only intervenes and takes away that prime right in cases of negligence by parents. However, it provides **services** of housing, health, education and welfare which parents can use to carry out their duties. If those services were to be **imposed**, irrespective of whether there is negligence, that would seem to be a substantial incursion into both individual liberty and the concept of the family as the fundamental unit of society. I am not saying that such a change would necessarily be wrong. I am saying that it would be a major conceptual shift, not a minor adaptation.

Professionals, presumably, must operate within the law. I shall argue later that service to a client is one criterion of professionalism. If teachers are professionals, then they owe service to parents as clients (until the child is 16 years of age), and are required by law to have regard to their wishes.

2. Parents as Co-educators of Children in Parallel with Teachers

Besides being the legal clients of teachers, parents are the co-educators of children. As already mentioned, most education happens outside school. Much of it, especially in the early years, is experienced in the family, where emotional bonds make home-learning especially effective. Parents also influence the sort of community-learning which their child will acquire.

Since parents inescapably educate their children, surely a professional teacher cannot neglect the non-professional educators. Just as the dentist relies on parents to cooperate with regard to children's dental care, so must teachers seek to guide and to draw into partnership parents' impact on educational care. Parents are co-educators of children whether that suits our professional preferences or not.

3. The Effect of Home Background on Children's School Attainment

Not only do parents largely create the nature of a child's out-of-school education, they also seem to influence (some would say determine) the extent to which their child benefits from *in*-school education. If teachers' effectiveness is linked to what families think, say and do, then an extra professional argument for collaboration with parents emerges. Unfortunately the evidence, substantial though it is, lacks the finality and precision which would enable us to define exactly which home-based initiatives would most heighten pupils' educational advance. It is therefore difficult to build closely-specified programmes of liaison based on it. Yet lack of fine detail need not deter us from action since much is already known.

Perhaps the strongest motivation for such action comes from the evidence that aspects of home background are the causes of unfulfilled potential and unequal chances in education. Equality of educational opportunity has been at the centre of educational thinking and planning for several decades, yet it has proved an elusive goal. It is difficult to define and even more difficult to attain. (See chapter 9.) Despite the abolition of 11-plus selection, the creation of comprehensive schools, the increasing deferment of separating pupils with different abilities, and other structural initiatives, certain kinds of children continue to be more successful than others. Structural steps taken within the educational system have removed some **obstacles** to attainment, but they have not sufficiently stimulated the forces which **enhance** attainment.

What are these forces? What follows in necessarily an over-simplified sketch of complex environmental processes which are still not fully understood. It should not be misinterpreted as a statement that schools make no difference. Schools *do* make a difference. Studies such as those of Rutter *et al* (1979) and Tizard *et al* (1988) have shown that school performance can be more or less professional and that its effects on children's attainment can vary accordingly. Although *Fifteen Thousand Hours* by Rutter *et al* emphasised school influence, it did not deny the impact of home, indeed, having alluded to studies of home-related factors, it stated (p.87), with tantalising brevity, 'We found the same.' It may be argued that *all* schools attain a basic level of beneficial influence and that what home learning is doing is affecting the *differences* of attainment between pupils. Yet, if equality of educational opportunity is the goal, then it is precisely those differences that matter whether they originate in homes or in schools.

The evidence of home influence on schooling began with studies which showed a general correlation between home background and in-school attainment. Home background differences often coincide with social class differences,* but researchers recognise that terms such as 'home background' and 'social class' are vague and difficult to measure. Further, there is some evidence that social class itself is not the causal factor (see Miller, 1971) and this is the foundation for optimism for it suggests that working-class children *can* do well, given the right circumstances. Questions then emerge about which elements of home background correlate with school success, whether they are causal and whether we can influence them.

What has emerged is a complex and by no means complete picture. Part of the difficulty stems from problems of measurement. Children cannot be manipulated experimentally like rats in a laboratory. Therefore controlling variables in a physical sense has to be replaced by statistical techniques to make allowances for the multiplicity of forces which might be causing an observed outcome. Even when a correlation exists between two phenomena that does not, in itself, tell us which is causing which, and indeed it does not necessarily mean that either causes the other, since a third factor may be causing both.

Further, some of the forces which researchers would like to measure are not susceptible to direct measurement and 'proxy measures' are used instead. For instance, the attitudes of parents have been advanced as a key element in pupil attainment, and it seems likely that they are; but can attitudes be measured? Since they are invisible, the best that we can do is to measure behaviour and to make assumptions about the attitudes which may trigger that behaviour. Alternatively, we can seek expressed opinions which may or may not reflect real attitudes, and these in turn have to be assessed in regard to the circumstances in which they were expressed, their strength and their persistence, all of them elusive elements. Next how do we assess educational attainment? Standardised test results and public examination grades are often used, but these tell us little about creativity, adaptability, determination and other facets of achievement. To take another example, father's occupation is often used as a measure of social class, whereas clearly it is not the same thing. Further, the involvement of researchers may itself affect the outcomes, while interpretation of results always involves value judgements.

The next problem is that the socio-psychological networks involved are intricate and variable, but as Osborn and Milbank (1987, p.189) observe, enough is known to provide some guidance.

> It is important to recognise the interrelatedness of all these factors and the complex ways in which they can combine to either support or impede a child's educational progress. Each child is unique in the particular developmental path she follows yet some general principles can be discerned in the tangle of data which help to explain how some children succeed and others fail.

* e.g. Floud *et al.*, 1957; Fraser, 1959; Mays, 1962; Douglas, 1964 and 1968; Miller, 1971; Davie *et al.*, 1972.

Thus, despite complexities, research is valuable. It provides essential indicators. Three rule-of-thumb tests may be applied which can help to decide how seriously to take a given set of findings:

(i)   Do several studies draw the same conclusions?
(ii) Is there a relative dearth of contrary evidence?
(iii) Do the findings accord with common sense and the experience of teachers?

The evidence that parents and family circumstances do influence children's educational attainments appears to meet these tests.

Besides broad correlations between home background and in-school attainment, research has suggested that particular features of background could be especially important. Attitudes such as parental interest in children's education* and aspirations† have attracted special attention, while a debate arose about the influence of language codes in coping with schooling. Later in the book I discuss evidence related to home-learning, especially with regard to parents assisting with reading (chapter 4) and interventions in areas of disadvantage (chapter 9).

One issue which has confused the picture has been the belief among some teachers that because certain (often working-class) parents do not attend school functions as avidly as do others, the former are 'apathetic'. As Mays (1980) has pointed out, 'It is dangerously easy to use a phrase such as "parental apathy" and leave it at that.' (p.63). Rather, Bridges (1981) reports that practical difficulties, deference to teachers, cynicism and a sense of alienation from the school deter parents. Some studies (e.g. Cyster et al., 1979; Johnson and Ransom, 1983) show that some parents are hesitant and unsure of themselves when confronted by the systems of schooling. But this does not necessarily mean that they lack concern for their children's welfare and there is evidence of the reverse (Lindsay, 1969). As Marland (1983, p.4) has written '... not only are the huge majority of parents not apathetic but very concerned, ... the nature of their concerns and the modes of their support have a great deal to teach us teachers', a view more recently echoed by Tizard and Hughes (1984) and Tizard et al. (1988). Yet Wolfendale (1983, p.59) is surely to some extent right when she asserts that 'between teachers' and parents' expectations and presumptions lies unexplored territory'; for there is much we still do not know about parental attitudes or actions in the home.

Several useful overviews of the evidence about the impact of homes on schooling (Marjoribanks, 1979; Sharrock, 1980; Mortimore and Blackstone, 1982; Hewison, 1985) exist and it is not the purpose of the present book to summarise the large and growing body of research into the impact of home-learning on school-learning. However, a few gener-

---

* Fraser, 1959; Wiseman, 1964; Douglas, 1964; Peaker, 1967; Miller, 1971; Osborn and Milbank, 1987.
† Rosen, 1961; McClelland, 1961; Miller 1971.

alisations do seem possible and these support (but do not determine) the practical actions discussed in later chapters.

First, Marjoribanks (1979) drew attention to the great complexity of the 'network of interrelated family environment variables that are associated with children's cognitive and affective outcomes.' However, having assessed studies from three continents he concluded 'Environments for children's learning will become more favourable when parents and teachers act as partners in the learning process.' A model which might be sustained on the basis of existing evidence could resemble that shown in Figure 1.3.

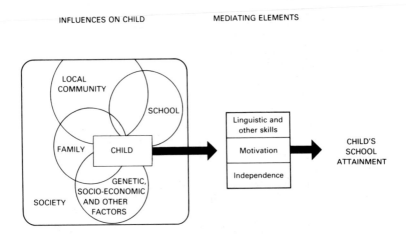

Figure 1.3.

Secondly, there are signs from several studies* that the early years of home-learning are especially important for subsequent attainment and Tizard and Hughes concluded, 'Indeed, in our opinion, it is time to shift the emphasis away from what parents should learn from professionals, and towards what professionals can learn from studying parents and children at home.' (p.267.)

The third reasonable generalisation is that, if what happens in the home does have impact on overall educational attainment, and if average differences of attainment between children from different social class groups are linked to those home experiences, then presumably the goal of equality of educational opportunity cannot be approached merely by making changes within the system of institutional education which, as we have seen, represents only about 15 per cent of a child's waking and therefore learning life to age 16. The debate will doubtless continue whether it is material circumstances or

* Wiseman, 1964; Davie *et al.* 1972; Schweinhart and Weikart, 1980; 1984; Tizard and Hughes, 1984; Osborn and Milbank, 1987.

learning circumstances which have *most* effect on that inequality; but irrespective of which is predominant, there can be no equality of educational opportunity without equality of parental input as one of the factors.

Finally, I would suggest that none of the practical steps considered in this book depends solely upon conclusions of research. Undoubtedly the studies to which I have referred have heightened educational interest in parents and have given new impetus to the quest for mechanisms of parent–teacher partnership, but parent–teacher partnership can be justified on other grounds also, irrespective of these socio-psychological findings.

4. Teachers as Agents of the Education Authority

I have argued that much of a child's education is provided in or influenced by the family, and I have outlined the ways by which legal systems consistently make parents responsible for their child's education. However, parents vary in the conscientiousness and the effectiveness with which they meet their obligations, and a small minority of parents might be described as incompetent or uncaring. The state, having delegated responsibility to parents, must still monitor parents' performance: in the words of the German Basic Law quoted earlier, 'The national community shall check upon their endeavours in this respect.' The most obvious way that teachers do this on behalf of the state is by reporting instances of truancy; for parents, if they opt to use schools to fulfil their legal duty of educating their child, must ensure regular attendance. Further, persistent misbehaviour of a child will be reported back to parents on the grounds that they are responsible for their child's education; again it is teachers who act as agents of the education authority in reporting it.

In two other important ways teachers may represent the education authority (or the state). One is by providing educational expertise (knowledge, skills, understanding) which most parents will not have. Usually this will be with relation to the formal curricula. But the second is a pastoral care function in providing an adult alternative to the parent to whom the child can turn in times of need. Marland (1980, p.157 and 1985 p.82) has drawn attention to a combination of these two in what he calls the pastoral curriculum defined as 'the school curriculum looked at for the moment solely from the point of view of the personal needs of the pupil resolving his individual problems, making informed decisions, and taking his place in his personal world.' With regard to young people over the age of 16, and therefore responsible in law for their own education, there would be less or no need for teachers to involve parents in dealing with such issues. However, parents are responsible for the education (including schooling) of under-16 children and therefore whenever teachers are, as it were, filling the gaps left by parents they presumably have an obligation to contact parents on precisely those issues.

It is possible, however, to advance a quite contrary argument, namely that the school exists, in part, to *separate* the child from the family and to provide an induction to society. Taylor (1980, p.12) has written:

> The primary school class emancipates the child from the basic emotional ties with his own family, encourages the internalization of social values and norms other than those current in the family home, and begins the process of selection and allocation relative to the adult role-system that will be continued and given great emphasis in the later stages of schooling.

This may be valid to some degree as a description of some current practice, but if rejection of family were to be an aim of the school, not only would it seem to be contrary to the spirit of current law, but it could well damage children's education. It is a major misconception, in my opinion, but a common one, to assume that being an agent of the education authority or state confers autonomy of action on the teacher. On the contrary, it implies an increased obligation to collaborate with parents.

5. Parents as Stakeholders in their Child's School

The fifth and final main reason why parents matter to schools is of an entirely different nature to the first four. It is democratic rather than educational. The principle is generally accepted in western democracies that those with a stake in an enterprise should have the opportunity to influence (though not necessarily to determine) decisions affecting that enterprise in proportion to their stake in it. We have a highly decentralised school system, and important decisions are taken at school, department and class levels. Politicians have a stake in the school as elected representatives of the community. Teachers have a stake in the school as employees, as co-educators and as taxpayers, among other criteria. Parents might claim to have a stake as clients, as co-educators and as taxpayers. I shall return to stakeholder theory and representation in chapter 8 on governing bodies (in Scotland, school boards). The governing body is the main mechanism to enable those with a stake in a school to influence decisions about the school. However, it is worth noting that the families which jointly have children in one class might also have a similar stake in that class (or group) and the decisions made for it.

In one sense a school system is like an airline: it likes to create an image of individual service in what is, essentially, a group process. Perhaps parents should have more right to discuss and influence internal school processes than has hitherto been accorded to them for, whereas in an airline the passengers choose where to go and when, in a school parents have little choice.

Levels of Parent–Teacher Liaison

In the last section there was a conceptual leap from consideration of the individual child to consideration of school policy. I could have gone further to discuss parental influence on the education authority and in national and international policy-making, and I shall do so in the chapter on voluntary parental organisations (chapter 7). At this point different levels of liaison **within** a school will be considered.

There is a tendency to visualise parent–teacher liaison as a single entity, as one particular kind of activity. When a headteacher states 'We have excellent relations with parents here because we have a flourishing PTA', he may be exhibiting such one-track thinking. Alternatively, to someone else the term 'parent–teacher liaison' may conjure up a picture of little Johnnie's parents talking to his teacher(s) about his progress. There are different **levels** of partnership between parents and teachers, and at any given level several **modes** of contact may be possible. Figure 4 suggests that in any school there are four main levels of partnership: the *individual, class, school* and *representative* levels. Above the school there are the various 'political' levels.

The danger lies in assuming that action at one level (e.g. a PTA at school level) absolves the staff from partnership at other levels. This book considers the four levels separately (chapters 3, 6, 8 and 10) but ranges between the levels with regard to parental choice (chapter 5), voluntary organisations (chapter 7), areas of disadvantage (chapter 9) and thoughts for the future (chapter 11). It seems to me that professional performance involves partnership with parents at all four levels.

Teachers' Home-based Professionalism

For some teachers liaison with parents is regarded as an optional extra, a favour bestowed on parents rather than an integral part of professional practice. In this section I shall argue that educational partnership with parents is at the very heart of teachers' professionality.* To do so it is necessary to define what constitutes a profession, to justify the view that teachers are indeed professionals, and to demonstrate that their professionalism* depends to some degree upon partnership with parents.

What is a Profession?

Although there has been change over time, the literature on professionalism suggests that four main criteria characterise a profession: **expertise** (based on theoretical knowledge and long training leading to qualification), a **code of ethical conduct** (clearly prescribed), **responsibility** (the taking of difficult decisions affecting other people's lives) and **altruistic service to others** (especially to a client). It will be noted that the list concentrates upon duties or obligations, not upon rewards such as pay, status, autonomy, monopoly or other self-interested advantages, though some authors (Lees, 1966; Millerson, 1973; Gould, 1973) have added such advantages as associated features.

---

* I employ the convention that the term 'professionalism' refers to the ideal, and the term 'professionality' refers to the practice.

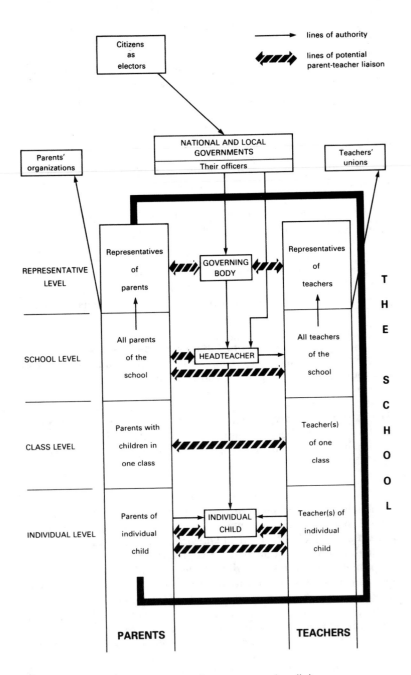

Figure 1.4. Potential elements of parent–teacher liaison.

However, we seem to be on firmer ground if we stick to obligations as the main criteria of a profession.

Yet there are difficulties in defining any given occupation as a profession because:

(a) there is variation from occupation to occupation about strengths of claims on these criteria, so that drawing a dividing line between professions and non-professions is very difficult;

(b) any one occupation may be strong on some criteria but weak on others;

(c) performance of individuals within an occupation is not a consistent standard in practice.

Thus, the professionalism (ideal) and professionality (practice) of an occupation or an individual are relative, each being at a point on a hypothetical continuum for each criterion. The question 'Is teaching a profession?' might be better phrased 'How professional is teaching?' with a recognition that individual practitioners may be more or less professional than average within the ranks of teachers.

How Professional is Teaching?

Experts have disagreed in their assessments, some (e.g. Etzioni, 1969) suggesting that primary school teaching is a 'semi-profession'. Perhaps our claim to professional status on the grounds of **expertise** is less obviously comparable to that of a doctor or an airline pilot since the **content** of what we teach, especially at primary level, may not require an exceptional degree of knowledge, and there is so much disagreement in our ranks about teaching **methods** that it is difficult for any teacher to claim to know the 'best way' to teach. For instance, it is possible to teach with less training and to continue to do so with less up-dating and re-testing than is required to fly a jumbo-jet. However, we do have a better-than-average knowledge of the educational system and have experience in handling children both individually and in groups which both increase our claim to expertise. Professor Hoyle (1974) has argued that although there is a theory of teaching, we tend not to refer to it much in our practice, and most teachers would accept that some other professions do, indeed, require a higher level of expertness.

In terms of a **code of practice**, our suit is also somewhat weakened. Where is that code of practice and what has been the impact of prolonged teachers' strikes on our public image? However, we do make important decisions affecting the lives of others, so that we can reasonably argue that **responsibility** increases our professional standing, though how professional we are depends on how carefully, how unselfishly and with what extent of consultation we make those decisions. Yet it is on the grounds of **service to others (especially to a client)** that I believe our strongest claim to professional status rests.

Service to a client requires us to be clear who our client is. Is the client the pupil (who receives instruction), the parent (who is legally responsible for the child's education and has delegated authority over the child to the teacher), the education authority (which employs the teacher) or society at large? It suits some teachers to argue that the education authority is the client since they can claim that their sole responsibility is to satisfy a generally distant bureaucracy and its less distant agent, the headteacher. Others will argue that the child is the client, not only because the child is education's direct beneficiary, but because having minors as clients leaves teachers largely free to determine their own actions unembarrassed by accountability to adults other than occupational peers.

But surely we must return to duties laid down in law (representing the public will) in order to assess who it is that teachers serve and represent. The law makes education authorities responsible for providing the facilities of the education service; a teacher is part of that and is therefore answerable to the education authority as employer for the provision of group facilities. But that education service exists to serve members of the public who are clients. When students are legally responsible for their own education – that is, over the age of 16 – then they are clearly the clients. But until the age of 16, parents have been entrusted by law with the duty of being the child's educational agents. It therefore seems that during that age span parents are the school's prime clients.

This logic suggests to me that the pupil is the *consumer*, the parent is the *client*, the education authority (or state) is the *employer* and the general public is the *indirect beneficiary*. Since this book is about parents it will concentrate on the second of these.

Quite apart from our obligation to parents-as-clients, our professional expertise suggests to us that parental influence affects the in-school attainment of pupils, so that taking action to harness that influence is also part of our professionality. In brief, it enhances rather than diminishes the professional status of teachers if there is a thorough and structured educational partnership with parents. Parents **do** matter to schools.

Note on Use of Key Terms

Since confusion is common in the world of education because people use words differently, selected key terms will be used as follows in this book:

Upbringing	All aspects of the child's development and protection, including shelter, feeding, clothing, safeguarding health and provision of education.
Education	The child's mental and moral development, including the circumstances and actions contributing to them.*
Schooling	That part of education provided in formal institutions for children and young people up to the age of 18 years.*

* Based on definitions in Macbeth *et al.*, 1984.

Instruction	Deliberate, cognitive transmission of information and skills.*
Parent	Either the natural parent or the guardian or any person who is liable to maintain or has the actual custody of a child or young person.†
Child	A person who is not over school age.†
Pupil	A child attending school.†
Young person	A person over school age who has not attained the age of 18 years.†
Education authority	The unit of government required and empowered by law to provide sufficient and efficient state provision of educational facilities for a specified area. It may be noted that I do not use the English term 'Local Education Authority (LEA)' since it seems to me that, with steps which have been taken over the past century to make political control over schools remote from the neighbourhood, the word 'local' is misleading. I therefore employ the Scottish term.
Governing body	Discussion centres on governing bodies as established in England and Wales, but reference is also made to Scottish school boards whose composition and functions are somewhat different.
Neighbourhood	Immediate social surroundings (e.g. of a school).
Community	Wider social surroundings than the neighbourhood. I use the term in a geographical sense, but with recognition that it can have cultural connotations.
Pastoral care	Personal, educational and vocational guidance and the welfare support and home–school liaison that relates to it. (I use the English term 'pastoral care' rather than the Scottish 'guidance' in the book.)

Family

Specialists have had difficulty in defining 'family'. It can be approached in **biological** terms both of genetic links and of physical needs such as for protection, shelter, food and sex; or one may emphasise **psychological** factors such as love, security, companionship and the transmission of cultural values. Alternatively, focus can be upon **place of habitation**, the home, the domestic group, often (but not necessarily) based on kinship. Then there is the question of the **extent**

* Based on definitions in Macbeth et al., 1984.
† Based on definitions in the Education (Scotland) Act, 1980, pp.95–100.

of what constitutes family, varying from a relationship between two people (husband/wife; mother/child), through the nuclear family to the extended family. The term can also be used to describe a variety of less conventional close social groupings.

Perhaps the most important criterion for the purposes of this book may be the **rearing of children**. In a recent conference Dame Mary Warnock (1985) tentatively defined the family as 'that collection of people among who it is natural to bring up children', and she gave emphasis to obligations associated with child-raising. I shall accept her provisional definition though, like her, I shall assume that the term 'family' does also relate to place of habitation, physical and emotional ties, usually (but not always) kinship, and can extend to people beyond the nuclear family.

2 A MINIMUM PROGRAMME AND A SIGNED UNDERSTANDING

There are some signs that, among teachers, proclamation of parent–teacher partnership exceeds implementation. The Plowden Report (1967, para. 104) noted this tendency:

> In the course of our visits to schools, we were almost invariably told by heads that 'we have very good relations with parents', however rudimentary the arrangements made.

Practice has improved since 1967. One sign is that the 'minimum programme' advocated by the Plowden Report itself (para. 112) now seems somewhat rudimentary: welcome to the school when a child is first admitted, at least two private consultations a year, open days, information booklets, clear written reports and some home visiting. Worthy objectives, and I shall return to them, but advances since then in our understanding of the educational importance of parents, although far from complete, suggest that rather more, both in terms of detail and of range, should be included in any minimum programme. To be fair to the Plowden Committee, they did also urge parental choice between schools (now consolidated by the 1980 and 1988 Acts), the development of the community school concept, the need to interest parents early, and the involvement of parents in extracurricular activities; but these were not part of their minimum programme.

The history of education has been one of constantly revising objectives, standards and techniques. Now, two decades after Plowden, could be the right time to consider an updated minimum programme related to current knowledge and based on techniques which have been shown to be practicable. I shall offer for consideration such a revised minimum programme, but also go beyond it with additional ideas. I am limiting myself to the compulsory education age, so that those concerned with pre-school (where parents are immensely important) may be disappointed, and I do not cover the difficulties of those who teach children with special educational needs (where, again, parents are crucial), nor the post-16 level at which young people replace parents as the school's main clients. The philosophy which informs the suggested practice is that which was outlined in the previous chapter, but the ultimate test is always: is this to the educational benefit of children?

A Revised Minimum Programme of Parent–Teacher Liaison

I consider that no school can honestly argue that it is treating its parents professionally as both clients and educational partners unless it initiates something comparable to the following 12-point programme. It will be seen that some points in the programme relate to parents individually as those responsible for their child's education, while others are concerned with the parents as a group.

1 The school might have a **welcoming system** not only when the child is first admitted, but all the time: welcoming both in the sense of being courteous and friendly and in the sense of encouraging parents to feel that they are part of the school community rather than outsiders. In terms of organisation, this might include arrangements by which parents coming to the school always receive rapid and considerate attention.

2 There should be a **written report or profile** on each child presented to his/her parents at least twice a year with thorough comments by teachers about the child's attainment, effort and behaviour, with a tear-off section containing questions about the child's progress to which parents are expected to reply. An assessment, a record and a planning document, the report should be the agenda for:

3 **a consultation**, at least twice a year, private between parent(s) and teacher(s) of the child, with the report as the starting-point, to plan the next phase of the child's learning. The reports and the consultations should not be seen as exchangeable alternatives; they are distinct, but related, actions.

4 At least termly there might be a **class meeting** to explain to those parents with children in the same class (or age-group at upper secondary level) the nature of the coming term's curriculum and how parents can reinforce it in the home.

5 **A parents' association** for the school (with class units) should be open to all parents with children in the school. It should not be run by teachers, though teachers should assist when asked by parents, especially in providing information. Its main concerns should be educational provision and parent–teacher links, its main functions consultation and information. Duplicating facilities and use of school buildings should be available free to the association at times which suit parents. Fund-raising should not be part of its remit, except to finance improved home–school liaison.

6 **A governing body (in Scotland a school board)** for each school should make accountability of parents and teachers in regard their educational obligations its main task. It should be recognised that the structure and purposes of the parents' association and the governing body are different but mutually reinforcing.

7 **Publications** by the school, to keep parents informed, should be prepared in collaboration with the parents' association.

8 Parents should have the right to see, at any reasonable time, all **official records on their child held either by the school or by the education authority** (with certain exceptions discussed in chapter 3 below); and should have a means to challenge and correct inaccuracies or misrepresentations. The child's school record/file should be available at private consultations and the attention of parents drawn to any new entries. Apart from certain confidential references, no fact, assessment or opinion about the child should be conveyed in writing or by word of mouth by any member of the education service to anyone outside the education service unless it appears on the official record. (It may be noted that proposals issued by the DES go some way towards such a system, but are more restrictive.)

9 **Education according to parental wishes** is a principle already established in statute law. That law is not limited to choice between schools, though that is important. A list of main determinant decisions (e.g. setting, streaming, subject options, remedial provision, public examinations to be taken and when, transfer to another school, etc.) might be drawn up by each school's governing body or school board. Not only should the parent(s) be consulted in regard to main determinant decisions affecting their child, but in the case of disagreement in regard to a child of school age, every effort might be made to accommodate parental wishes 'so far as is compatible with the provision of efficient instruction and training and the avoidance of unreasonable public expenditure' (Education Act, 1944, Sect. 76). After the age of 16 the young person's wishes should predominate on the same conditions.

10 A system of **home-visiting** might operate for exceptional circumstances.

11 Teachers might constantly stress that they provide **both a service and a partnership**. Service implies the dedication of teachers' specialist skills and expertise to assist parents in fulfilling their parental duty on behalf of children. That service may, on occasions, involve expressing views contrary to those of parents. Partnership recognises that much education happens in the home and that parents and teachers have differing but complementary educational functions which must operate in harmony to be most effective. Thus schooling is provided by teachers in a way which is responsive to parental wishes and in conjunction with parents' co-educative actions, but within an administrative and curricular framework informed by professional judgement.

12 Teachers should also make it clear in their dealings with parents that although they provide a professional service for parents and act as partners with them, they are also **employees of the education authority** and they must operate within the objectives, systems and constraints laid down by both national and regional democratic

processes. On occasions this may involve denying parental wishes or even checking upon parents (e.g. in regard to school attendance) on behalf of the state, for the welfare of children. It may also mean parents providing information to the school. In brief, parents should to some degree be accountable to teachers, as teachers are to them.

Several points may be noted about this minimum programme. First, it accepts the philosophy embedded in current British law and normal in Europe that parents, not schools, are primarily responsible for their child's education. The programme does not represent radical change so much as rationalisation of the existing position. Secondly, all the concepts are already operating somewhere to some degree. They are all practicable, and most are familiar to British teachers. Thirdly, the programme is a basic minimum, not a professional optimum. Schools can build upon it and, hopefully, in a decade's time it will appear to be insufficient as a basic minimum.

Fourthly, although an education authority may wish to adopt such a programme, most of the actions can be introduced by an individual school without waiting for national or regional instructions. Some details may need to be negotiated with the education authority, such as in areas where guidelines already exist about access to school records, but generally schools can take the initiatives themselves. Indeed, an individual teacher can (and some do) adopt much of the programme as personal practice. Hopefully, however, a programme of this sort may become mandatory in due time.

It was deliberate that fund-raising, the use of parents to carry out menial chores in the school, social events, speech days, extracurricular activities involving parents, open days and a variety of other activities commonly included as home–school liaison were **not** part of the minimum programme. Such activities, in my view, should be treated as peripheral and subsidiary to the main educational purposes and actions involving parents.

Impediments

A note of caution, even of pessimism, may be appropriate, for although this book seeks to advance positive suggestions to assist the growth of collaboration between parents and teachers, it must be recognised that there are problems to be faced. As Cullingford (1985, p.7) asserts,

> ... there has been a significant rise in the involvement of parents in schools, and many successful experiments. But even in the best examples it is clear that the mutual suspicion between parents and teachers continues. Beneath the surface of well-intended meetings lies misunderstanding and indifference.

Clearly the introduction of a programme such as I have outlined above in a school which does not already do these things will give rise to anxieties and difficulties. These are discussed in subsequent chapters where the proposals are dealt with in detail. But there are broader, more pervasive impediments which warrant preliminary mention. I shall consider these under four headings:

(a) Parental inhibitions and the signed understanding.
(b) Teachers' terms of service.
(c) Resources.
(d) Teachers' attitudes.

(a) Parental Inhibitions and the Signed Understanding

It is easier for parents *not* to liaise with schools than it is to do so. There are quite practical deterrents. For instance, it is usually assumed that to have contact, parents must go to teachers, not *vice versa*. To get to the school often requires time and expense of travel, and may involve finding someone to care for younger children at home. If contact is during school hours, some parents, especially fathers, may be prevented by work commitments, and if it is in the evenings or at weekends it may cut across other activities. Cultural differences, including language problems, can also deter some. School events to which they are invited may be unattractively advertised or irrelevant to their own child's schooling. Further, schools are sometimes cold, unwelcoming places and parents may retain distressing memories of their own school-days.

Some schools make great efforts to overcome these deterrents, but they may still find the parental response to be disappointing. Why? The answer must surely lie in the realm of attitudes. Attitudes are a preparedness to act or not to act; and they are learned. There can be little doubt that many parents harbour an assumption that they are irrelevant to the schooling process. There is a substantial literature on attitudes and on attitude change. To belabour it here would be unproductive. However, it is worth noting that the more firmly held is a preexisting attitude and the more often it is reinforced by those whose views are respected, the more difficult it is to change it. That parents have been on the periphery of schooling for so long, that this position is generally accepted by most parents, and that teachers, whose views are respected, reinforce this assumption – all these make a change of attitude difficult to achieve. It is therefore not just a matter of *permitting* parental involvement; the idea requires a 'hard sell' by determined teachers, supported by well-informed publicity. Indeed, such a campaign could go beyond mere exhortation (which has produced only patchy effects in the past) and aim to generate a sense of obligation. It is my view that, rather than implying to parents that liaison is optional, emphasis should be upon the responsibilities of parenthood, the legal duty of parents to provide education and the knowledge that active interest and cooperation by parents is likely to help the child to benefit from schooling. While the sales pitch by the school can be friendly, it must also be tough.

The 12-point minimum programme for liaison listed above is a set of obligations on the school. However, there might be a comparable set of obligations upon parents. Since public servants and bureaucrats are hired to provide a service, teachers can be required, as part of their conditions of employment, to fulfil obligations; but the position with parents is different. Parents fulfil obligations either because they are legally bound to do so or because they feel moral compulsion to do so, not because they are employed to do so.

Legal requirements on parents are relatively scant, apart from the one massive and fundamental duty to provide education for the child suitable to his/her age, ability and aptitude. That duty is vaguely worded and, apparently, easily satisfied by ensuring that the pupil attends school regularly. In such circumstances, how can a sense of obligation be brought home forcefully to all parents? What now follows is an attempt to answer that challenge. It is an idea which builds upon the common procedure by which parents with children in trouble, especially those who have been persistent truants or who are under threat of exclusion from school, are asked to sign documents of coop-eration. I first proposed it in a report for the EEC (Macbeth *et al.*, 1984).

In outlining this procedure I am not suggesting that it is a necessary concomitant of the 12-point minimum programme of liaison which, I believe, can stand on its own. However, as a simple formality to give emphasis to parental obligations, it may have some appeal.

The proposal starts with the prime parental duty, established by law, for parents to provide education for their child. Schooling is not compulsory, education is. Although a small number of families do successfully educate their children themselves without the aid of a school, the vast majority depend on schools to enable them to fulfil their duty. The suggestion is that, in exchange for taking a child into a school (relieving parents of the technical burden of education minimally), parents would be asked to sign an understanding that they have obligations related to that schooling process. The document might have wording along the lines of the example opposite.

I suggest that a copy is signed by the father and another by the mother (to overcome awkward 'I/we' wording) and by the one parent in the case of a lone parent family or guardian (or by whoever is legally responsible in the case of a divorced couple). While such a document would not be used as a legally-binding contract (though some authori-ties might wish to develop it into that) it could be the basis of heighten-ing awareness among all parents and of applying moral pressure on defaulting parents.

Two obvious questions arise: what would be done if parents refuse to sign, and what would happen if parents who had signed then defaulted on their undertaking? The answer to each would seem to be simple. In regard to refusal to sign, parents would be denied a place in the school for their child. The onus is on them to provide education for their individual child. The education authority's two duties are to make facilities available for children and to check that parents are carrying out their duty. Parents who refuse to sign the understanding would thus be declining a school place offered by the authority and would

I, being the parent/guardian of .... (name of child) acknowledge that **I understand**:
(1) that prime responsibility for my child's education rests with me by law;
(2) that the school will assist me to carry out that responsibility;
(3) that my active support for my child's schooling may increase his/her likelihood of gaining maximum benefit from it.

Further, **I undertake** to do the following to the best of my ability:
(a) to attend private consultations with my child's teacher(s) at mutually convenient times;
(b) to read written reports sent by the school and to respond to them;
(c) to attend class meetings or other meetings arranged to explain the curriculum and the ways in which it can be reinforced at home;
(d) to provide suitable conditions and support for my child's homework;
(e) to provide such information as the school shall require for educational purposes;
(f) to support school rules;
(g) to abide by decisions made by the headteacher and the governing body with regard to the school's management.

Signature of parent/guardian .... Date ....

either have to pay for independent schooling or educate their child at home. The latter process can be inspected and, if it is found to be unsatisfactory, proceedings relating to non-attendance and culminating in prosecution can be initiated. It is normal for other state services – medical, dental and so on – to be subject to signed conditions, so why not schools? As with those services, the vast majority will see the reasonableness of the arrangement and will sign.

What, then, if parents default on the undertakings which they have given through signature? Suppose that a parent never comes to private consultations? It is my view that persuasive rather than legal proceedings should follow. Contact could be made with the parents (if necessary at the home) and the importance of parental support and involvement would be explained in terms of benefit to the child. Where the parent speaks a minority language, an interpreter should assist. It could be added that continued failure to provide the specific support could result in details being entered on the child's school record and the matter being reported to a sub-committee of the governing body/school board before which the parents might be summoned. If contributory problems emerge they could be reported to other welfare agencies. It is not in the child's interest, in my view, to debar him/her from school in this circumstance. The parent who fails (perhaps for genuine reasons) to provide minimal educational support is different from the parent who refuses to sign the document as a matter of principle.

I am aware that the signed understanding is a leap into the unknown and may, for that reason, be unappealing at this stage. Whether or not it is employed, information and publicity of the importance of parental liaison with the school can still give emphasis to obligations.

(b) Teachers' Terms of Service

Some national documents which have advocated new or changed duties as part of teachers' normal professional practice have assumed that they would be included in that practice without special financial, contractual or timetable arrangements. The Plowden Report section on liaison with parents, for instance, concluded (para.129):

> Much depends on teachers. Every chapter could end thus – but perhaps it is even more apt here than elsewhere. Teachers are already hard pressed, and nowhere more so than in the very districts where the cooperation of parents is most needed and hardest to win. We are aware that in asking them to take on new burdens we are asking what will sometimes be next to impossible.

But ask they did. Others are prepared to relate money to professional performance, but on the assumption that professional performance is expected anyway – not as an extra. For instance, the Houghton Report on the pay of teachers in 1974 stated:

> We wish to stress that we believe the salary levels we recommend justify expectation of professional standards of performance in return. As in other professions, these salary levels are in part recognition of the fact that the job cannot be compressed within a rigid structure of prescribed duties, hours or days.

A third approach is to specify the duties of teachers in broad terms, and the Main Report on Scottish teachers' pay and conditions of service (1986) did so, and included a chapter on parents, liaison with whom was regarded as part of professional practice. It is a matter of opinion whether Main's acceptance of specified minimum hours of work in the Scottish teachers' contract was wise, for it can limit as well as extend the amount of contact with parents, which is precisely what the resulting 1987 Scottish Salaries and Conditions of Service Agreement did.

Yet the view can also be heard in some staff-rooms that 'extra' work, such as contact with parents, should be paid for *pro rata* with extra money. The dangers of this view are that teachers and administrators may continue to regard partnership with parents as not central to professional performance and therefore dispensable when cash is tight. In my view it is better for those tasks related to the minimum programme of liaison with parents to be integral to all teachers' work without ambiguity. As a separate issue, and not tied to that one element, I also consider that professional teachers should be paid a good salary. A time when the bitterness of industrial action lingers may not be ideal for seeking extra commitment; but that does not reduce the argument for building home–school liaison into thinking about teachers' conditions of service.

(c) Resources

As was indicated above, teachers' time is the most crucial resource, but we may consider others. In chapters 9 and 10 there is discussion of the value of specialised home–school link teachers, whose appearance in several cities has displayed benefits. Another advantage for any school is the presence of a senior, respected member of each school's staff who has the coordination of parent–teacher liaison as a specified duty. I use the words 'senior, respected,' since the importance of the function in the eyes of colleagues will, to some extent, be influenced by who has the task. If a raw junior or an incompetent is charged with the responsibility for relations with parents, staff will tend to see the function as having low status.

Similarly, the quality of presentation of publications for parents – report forms, handbooks, brochures, advisory booklets, newspapers – can inadvertently convey a message about the importance, or otherwise, of the communication itself. Scrappy, duplicated documents suggest that collaboration does not matter. Professionally printed, imaginatively presented and well illustrated publications are more likely to be read and respected. I discuss these more fully in chapters 3, 5 and 10. The point here is that they cost money. Having analysed report forms and school handbooks from several parts of Europe, I am convinced that expenditure on good printing and presentation is money well spent.

Schooling is a labour-intensive industry. Almost three-quarters of its cost is on personnel, and much of the rest goes on buildings. Relatively, expenditure on liaison publications is trivial. But at a time of economic cut-back, consumables always seem to be disproportionately hit. When stocks of text-books are at a dangerously low level, it is difficult to argue for expenditure on high-quality printing. An obvious plea for increased funding of the educational system generally is not the point of this book, though I do make such a plea; the choice should not be between text-books and parental liaison. Partnership should be funded by government, and funded generously because it is important. However, two practical suggestions for a time of scrimpiness are worth considering. The first is advertising. Some Continental school handbooks and the publications of most national parents' organisations offset costs by carrying advertisements. Schools can do the same. The second is delegation to the PTA/PA. In chapter 7 I argue passionately to remove the fund-raising function from parental organisations; it deters parents and diverts the PTA/PA from its educational objectives. I offer one grudging exception, and that is when a home–school liaison activity is delegated to it. If one of a PTA/PA's main reasons for existence is educational partnership, then governors or a head, (while retaining a veto and insisting on high quality,) can delegate to it authority to design and produce school report forms, handbooks, newspapers and so on, thereby ensuring that these documents contain not only what the school wants but also what parents want. That delegation can include the raising of necessary finance, though I would argue strongly against the PTA raising funds for anything else.

The cost of implementing the 12 points of my suggested minimum programme of liaison is not high. Lack of time and will rather than lack of money are the main barriers. An education authority wanting to pursue a parental partnership policy should find the returns high both educationally and, I suspect, politically, for quite a small outlay. Funding of educational partnership ought ultimately to be a government responsibility.

(d) Teachers' Attitudes

If parents' attitudes are crucial to home–school partnership, those of teachers are no less so. Despite increasing central government involvement, we have a substantially decentralised system of education, not only to education authorities but to schools and individual teachers. Marland (1985, p.68) has called it 'the most autonomous educational decision-making pattern in the world' and the official DES description of the educational system of England and Wales (1985, pp.2–3) stated,

> although local responsibility for the secular curriculum rests with the individual authority or school governing body, as the case may be, the timetabling of subjects, the choice of textbooks and the detailed content and method of day-to-day teaching are largely left to the discretion of headteachers and their staffs.

This discretion includes links with parents which is an educational and therefore to some extent a curricular issue. The extent of those links, ranging from disdain to genuine partnership, is determined by the philosophies and attitudes of headteachers and teachers. Those attitudes may have a blocking or an enabling effect, irrespective of parental attitudes.

Rutter and his team (1979) have valuably stamped the notion of school ethos on the consciousness of British education. Even though there may be variations from teacher to teacher, a school can have a character, an atmosphere, a predominant set of standards which distinguish it as a whole. Elsewhere (Macbeth *et al.*, 1984, pp.195–9) four broad stages of progression in the growth of home–school partnership have been suggested. The following is an adaptation of that.

Stage 1: the self-contained school
Stage 2: professional uncertainty
Stage 3: growing commitment
Stage 4: the school and family concordat.

The self-contained school stage is characterised by teachers assuming that the school is a closed institution neither affected by nor influencing families outside. It tends to be associated with teacher autonomy; limited and formalised contacts with parents; non-routine contacts being related to crises; little parental choice or consultation, parent associations discouraged or confined to trivia; parents denied access to school records about their child; teaching content and methods regarded defensively as the teachers' domain only.

The second stage, that of *professional uncertainty*, results from the spread of evidence about the value of home–school liaison, the growth of participatory trends and increased recognition of parents as clients. As some teachers come to acknowledge home factors, others remain entrenched, but may 'soften' to the extent of blaming home background for low pupil attainment. Administrative structures tend to remain as in Stage 1, routine contacts with parents being formalised, but with some teachers tentatively experimenting with liaison techniques individually.

The third stage, that of *growing commitment*, witnesses the school leadership increasingly encouraging liaison with parents and adapting the system. Parents are more welcome in the school and they no longer have to report to an inquisitorial head on crossing its portal. Not only the governing body, but the PTA/PA is encouraged to discuss and deal with educational issues. Emphasis is put on the value of home–school liaison, and parents are encouraged to teach their children at home, dovetailing with the school curriculum which has been explained to them. Parental choice in the school and access to their child's records increase, two-way reports are introduced and consultations become private planning sessions.

The similarity of Stage 3 to the minimum programme of liaison outlined earlier in this chapter will be obvious. What, then, is left for Stage 4? The features which characterise the ultimate stage would be an emphasis on obligation, the attempt to involve all families and a recognition that home-learning is part of education, not merely background to education. Stage 3 exhorts and permits participation with the acceptance that not all families would be involved. The shift towards obligation in Stage 4 anticipates the signed understanding which I have described in this chapter with the objective of committing all parents and teachers.

It is evident that each stage is determined by teachers, and by their attitudes – especially those of the headteacher. The leadership styles of headteachers have been the subject of research on both sides of the Atlantic (for useful summaries, *see* Nias, 1980, pp.225–73; Hughes, 1985, pp.262–90; Glatter *et al.*, 1988, pp.3–104). The extent to which a head is autocratic or democratic, defends existing structures or encourages innovation, is prepared to reassess goals and is sensitive to staff and client needs, to research evidence and to changes in society – all these can have impact on a school's home–school ethos. It is not easy for enthusiastic junior staff to initiate a different approach when the head resists it, especially since some headteachers still believe that they have a duty to act as a barrier to 'protect' teachers from parents. There is limited evidence of headteachers' attitudes differing from those of staff. Lynch and Pimlott (1976), for instance, found that Southampton teachers were more supportive of home visiting than were heads. The importance of heads finding sufficient time to read about, think about and discuss both objectives and future action cannot be over-stressed; the danger is that busy-ness stifles business, a tendency noted in a recent study of headship (Hall *et al.* 1986).

I like the anecdote told against himself by one primary headteacher who had accepted the traditional Scottish schools' indifference towards parents. One evening, having worked late, he noticed a light still burning in a classroom. Investigating, he found a probationer teacher discussing education with a group of mothers who were helping to prepare materials. Next day, prepared to indicate displeasure at the parental invasion, he quizzed her about this departure from convention. It is to the credit of both head and probationer that this discussion led to a total change of school policy.

Yet it would be wrong to suggest that the headteacher holds the key to everything. Staff, too, must be convinced. Even when the leadership of a school introduces the structures of partnership with parents (e.g. class meetings, consultations, two-way reports, and the like) their effectiveness can be substantially neutralised by hostile colleagues. Most schools have a group of staff who resist change and we should not underestimate their influence. There is a need for pre-service, in-service and in-school training and developmental work.

To some teachers the 12-point minimum programme of liaison which I outlined above will seem commonplace, tepid and lacking in originality, building as it does on the established and the conventional. To others it could seem daunting and a challenge to established routines or difficult to fit in with other demands on time. While most schools could tick off some of the twelve points as being part of their current practice, few would score 12 out of 12. Time, effort and resources are needed in order to create new routines, but staff attitudes, based on professional understanding and confidence in their own performance, are perhaps the most crucial factors.

Why should some teachers be resistant to collaboration with parents? I would suggest the following are possible elements of that resistance.

1 Some teachers may have become accustomed to functioning without parents being central to their work.
2 They may feel that they have enough child-centred work and mounting professional strains without the additional pressures of entering a genuine educational partnership with parents.
3 Some teachers may find parents threatening, especially teachers who are unaccustomed to working with parents.
4 Teachers' contracts and hours of work are not drawn up to include educational partnership with parents.

5 Few education authorities have paid much more than lip-service to the educational importance of parents. So teachers, reasonably, may tend to reflect the stance of their employers.

6 Teachers are constantly under pressure to alter the content of teaching and their working methods. Changes in technology, economic and industrial expectations, public examination systems and political demands are current examples. At a time of change, priorities have to be established for the implementation of changes. Parents tend to get low priority.

7 Some teachers may simply be unaware of all the reasons why parents are educationally central to their work.

There can be little doubt that it is easier for teachers *not* to enter into educational partnership with parents. Equally, it is easier for parents *not* to enter into educational partnership with teachers, but to 'leave it to the specialists'. The evidence suggests that such inaction is to the disadvantage of pupils and, in particular, would reinforce the inequalities of opportunity inherent in current practice.

What follows in this book is detail of practice, much of it related to the suggested minimum programme of liaison. The techniques have been selected for the most part because they have been tried and are operating successfully either in Britain or elsewhere. To the best of my knowledge the 'signed understanding' outlined earlier in this chapter has not been introduced in the form which I advocate. Otherwise I aim to portray methods which have stood the test of implementation, and many of which are relatively inexpensive to implement in terms of both effort and money.

I am aware that schooling itself could be radically different or even, as some deschoolers would like, removed. I am also aware that technology could dramatically change our approach to teaching children, but for convenience I have accepted conventional models of schools since I believe that they will be with us for some years. My relative neglect of relations between school and community does not imply that they are unimportant. The point is that contacts with 'the community' pose different problems; too often parent–teacher liaison has been seen as a sub-set of community relations and I consider that to be both misleading and educationally inappropriate. Finally, everything in this book is subject to an essential test: is this action to the educational benefit of the children?

3 COMMUNICATION ABOUT THE INDIVIDUAL CHILD

The education of the individual child is presumably the most important reason for parent–teacher cooperation. It is parents' responsibility for their individual child's education which makes them clients of the school. It is the input of the pupil's home-learning which makes liaison with parents educationally relevant to teachers' daily work. This chapter moves away from broad concepts to consider some established actions in the school, especially written school reports, personal consultations and access to school records held on the child.

Current levels of communication about the individual child seem less than impressive. In an EEC study (Macbeth *et al.*, 1984) estimates given by 1744 headteachers from nine European countries indicated that, on average, parents visit schools 2.5 times a year to discuss their child's education; receive 1.5 letters a year from the school; make 2 telephone calls to and receive 1.5 from the school; and receive just over 3 written reports a year of their child's progress. These figures suggest distance rather than educational partnership. Further, the UK average rates were below the European averages on all counts. A riposte may be offered that British report forms, while less frequent, were fuller than those normal in many European countries and that 38 per cent of them included printed invitations to parents to discuss the reports with teachers; that British schools are becoming increasingly open; and that the 1988 legislation has made them more so. It may also be argued that estimates of headteachers are likely to be imprecise and that mere numbers do not reflect quality. However, these figures do provide us with a general picture of contact between school and parents, and the level is low if educational partnership is the objective.

I use the important condition 'if educational partnership is the objective'. Conventional modes of contact were developed when educational partnership was not the objective. Traditionally parents sent their children to school and teachers received them on the assumption that home actions were largely irrelevant to school effectiveness and that school processes were mainly the business of teachers. Contacts were based on such assumptions. Courtesy, and perhaps a formal recognition of parents' legal status, led to brief and infrequent school reports and so-called 'parents' nights' when parents might queue for semi-public and brief discussions known in some staff-rooms as 'cattle markets'. Other contact was usually related to trouble. A headteacher might summon a child's parents to tell them of difficulties which had come to a point of crisis. Even a statement in the school handbook that parents can contact the headteacher in the event of a problem might be taken to imply that they should keep away unless there is a problem. Fortunately much practice has altered in recent years and the traditional approach has become rarer, though not extinct.

The idea of partnership between parents and teachers has been proclaimed by the teaching profession, but much of the practice has concentrated on fund-raising PTAs, representatives on governing bodies and the use of selected parents to carry out chores in the school. None of these activities is partnership with regard to the education of the individual child. Such communications as do concern the individual may be occasional, abbreviated, formalised and containing school information, selected by and restricted by teachers. In the present chapter I shall discuss how some of the more conventional modes of contact with regard to the individual child, especially reports, consultations and school records, might be enhanced, often simply and inexpensively. In doing so, I am assuming that the partnership approach is, indeed, the desired objective.

Written Reports

I start with written reports because they are a long-established symbol of teachers' service to parents and because the 1988 legislation is likely to affect them. Parents have entrusted their child to specialists who are employed to provide a service, and the specialists are reporting back to those who have given their trust and have delegated their authority. Written reports are more than practical devices for conveying information; they represent an accounting for stewardship.

Encouragingly, Goacher and Reid (1985, p.74), in their study of English secondary school reports, state,

> Despite the difficulties which teachers recorded relating to reports, there was virtually total acceptance that they were essential. While there was certainly evidence that teachers questioned the effectiveness of reporting in its present forms, then, there was no questioning of the need for a formal means of informing parents of their children's progress.

The EEC survey found that the number of reports received each year by an average family in nine European countries was just over three. The UK average was half that, the lowest of the countries in the survey. This accords with the average calculable from the survey by Goacher and Reid, though they show that the number of reports in English secondary schools decreases on average over the secondary span, apart from a rise in the sixth year. They also point out that 'Pupils in their third, fifth, sixth and seventh years received a spring term report more commonly than did other year groups, reflecting schools' response to pupils' need for information at major decision points.' (p.29)

There were signs from the EEC study that some British schools had reduced the frequency of reports but had increased the content, while others had only reduced the frequency from the traditional three a year without any compensating benefits to parents. Some headteachers stated that they were shifting towards more face-to-face meetings. The substitution of meetings for written reports makes the assumption that both activities fulfil the same functions. That can be questioned. The written report provides a formal record held by both family and school, and in some countries (e.g. West Germany) it can have legal status. Further, it can be an agenda for a private consultation so that such a meeting can be used to explain issues and to discuss future actions rather than wasting time reporting basic facts which are already in the report. Some schools include on report forms a simple message such as:

A meeting with your child's teacher(s) has been arranged (details separate). This report could be the basis for your discussion.

Reservations about written reports deserve mention. First, it is possible to use them as a means to evade home–school liaison rather than to enhance it. An attenuated, infrequent report placing a child in broad, unhelpful categories by ticks or grades unrelated to explained standards can be used as the basis for the claim that parents have been informed and therefore need no other contact. A written report unsupported by face-to-face discussion may be misunderstood by the recipient and may be the cause of unfounded alarm or complacency. Also, no matter how precise and scientific marks, grades, 'places' and percentages may seem on reports, they all have their foundation in judgements which are, to a greater or lesser degree, subjective. As Bastiani (1978, p.64) has written;

It also seems worth challenging the idea that most information is factual, self-contained and neutral. Information, in the end, is seldom 'value-free' and always exists in the context of a relationship between writer and reader.

However, individualised reports which give carefully-considered and personalised comments (perhaps supported by numerical data or grades), which avoid relying solely on the ticks-in-boxes approach, which have a section for the parents to complete stating how they view the child's progress over time, which are used as a basis for a parent–teacher meeting for joint future planning of the child's learning, and which provide a thorough record of the child's progress over a span of time – these can be valuable.

We may summarise the purposes of written reports as follows:

1 To enable teachers to render account for their service to parents.

2 To enable teachers and parents to exchange periodic information,

views and predictions about the development of a child, both academically and pastorally.

3 To assist and focus the assessment procedure.

4 To assist pupils to understand and assess themselves, to increase their self-sufficiency and to change their performance.

5 To provide an agenda for any of:
   (a) parent–pupil discussions,
   (b) teacher–pupil discussions,
   (c) parent–teacher discussions,
   (d) parent–teacher–pupil discussions.

6 To provide a basis for communication between the school and other parts of the education service about a pupil.

7 To furnish both school and family with a record of progress.

Goacher and Reid (p.26) suggests that reports have informing, motivating and involving functions and they point out that teachers sometimes use reports as a mechanism for conveying messages to other, usually senior, staff.

In the EEC study (p.49) we encountered six types of written report:

(i) **Periodic reports**   These are the commonest type. They summarise achievement and effort over a period of time (e.g. a month, a term or a half-year). They are usually for parents only.

(ii) **Year-end and leaving certificates and profiles**   These are public documents which may be shown to potential employers and are given to pupils. They may merely record courses completed or they may include indications of attainment, perhaps in the form of a 'profile' or a second record of attainment.

(iii) **Day-books**   In these pupils and/or teachers record homework set and other school matters to provide a means for daily liaison between school and home.

(iv) **Communication booklets**   These are similar to day-books and are carried to and from school daily by the pupil, but they are not primarily for recording homework and they have blank pages rather than being divided into days. Entries may be made whenever the teacher or parent wants to communicate with the other.

(v) **Curriculum progress reports**   In these, the broad outlines of work which should have been covered in a period are listed with indications of the child's progress. They are most commonly used in primary schools. Skills and levels expected are listed and sometimes the titles of work books used and stages in them reached by the child.

(vi) *Carnets de liaison*   These are multiple-purpose booklets containing basic information about the school; who is currently responsible for aspects of the pupil's school experience; how to contact them; timetables; and a variety of other information as well as spaces for reporting on progress and for exchange of information between parents and teachers.

A school may employ more than one kind of report. In the North Westminster Community School in London, for instance, every pupil has a School Diary which has spaces for his/her Tutor and parent(s) to comment every week, as well as the 'big bang' report once or twice a year in which subject teachers, tutor, House Year Head, Headteacher and parents all report.

Physical Features of Report Forms

Most report forms are pre-printed on single sheets of paper, usually with one or more carbon or NCR copies for file, though cards and booklets may be used. Computer print-outs are gradually appearing, though research is needed to ascertain parents' reaction to them, and they are subject to the 1984 Data Protection Act. Goacher and Reid (Ch.2) identified the most commonly used types in England and Wales as the single sheet, the report book and the slip report.

The last is perhaps the most satisfactory format, a set of paper slips (usually about postcard size) stapled together. Different staff who have responsibilities for the child, whether for subjects or for functions such as pastoral care, prepare separate slips. The considerable extent of space on each slip allows a substantive and worthwhile observation and it reduces the temptation to use unhelpful one-word comments. With a mini-page for each subject/topic, an error by one teacher does not require everyone else to re-write their observations, and mini-pages can be collated by the school office. Additional messages, perhaps pre–printed explanations of grading systems used or alerting of parents to forthcoming events relevant to particular groups, or special messages from the headteacher, can be added as extra slips. Tear-out sheets for the parent to complete and return to the school can also be included. The system is full, flexible, non-technical and non-bureaucratic. In brief it is user-friendly.

Modes of Presenting Information

Generally primary schools comment on skills such as reading, writing and calculating, while secondary schools list performance in academic subjects. A combination is possible. Attainment is almost always the central focus, but effort and behaviour are sometimes listed as discrete categories on the printed forms. Rates of attendance and punctuality can also be recorded.

More controversial is the means by which assessment is expressed. It is essential that if gradings, symbols, marks or percentages are used, an unambiguous statement of what they mean is incorporated in the report especially with the advent of national testing at seven, 11, 14 and 16. Goacher and Reid record,

> One in three parents studied felt that the information given on the school's grading policy was inadequate and a similar proportion did not know the basis on which grades were allocated.

In particular it has to be made clear whether grades relate to the standard of performance of other pupils in the class/year-group of that school, whether they relate to the pupil's previous performance, whether they relate to some external standard or whether they merely reflect some vague expectation in the teacher's mind. Wording can be quite simple; for instance, from a Hampshire school*:

> The Attainment grades (when shown) show the standard the pupil has reached within a particular teaching group; they are not necessarily related to the standards of the whole age-range. The Effort grades indicate how hard the pupil has worked compared with what is considered to be his/her potential

> (The pre-printed cover of this report also says which classes are mixed-ability and which are setted.)

Test scores should be accompanied by a statement of the types of tests, the extent to which marks are subjective or objective and what they mean. I encountered one Berkshire primary school† which encloses with its report form the following explanatory note:

> STANDARDISED TESTS
> Standardised tests in Reading and Mathematics allow us to compare the child's level of attainment and understanding with that of thousands of other children of the same age all over the country. These tests have been developed by educational researchers and age is taken into consideration on the marking scale. They are also very useful in diagnosing strengths and weaknesses.

> (This is followed by a description of the tests, including an explanation that two sets of grades appear on the report to parents, one the test score and the other referring to effort and attitude.)

The Black Report (para. 10) on national testing stated, 'In the primary phase, almost all children take such tests at some time.' It remains to be seen whether the system of national tests will replace other standardised testing or whether the two will co-exist, but in either case an explanation for parents is needed. Grading is commonly not related to an standardised tests but reflects judgements of teachers. Goacher and Reid (p.75) report their finding that 'teachers were far from achieving accurate predictive grading. Although the grades they awarded became progressively more severe from the third to the fifth year, they were optimistic when compared with pupils' examination performance. In over half the subjects studied, grades awarded in year five were significantly higher than results in public examinations and in none were the teachers' grades significantly lower.'

However, some form of referencing has value, and grades do provide a useful preliminary categorisation which can guide both pupils and parents as long as they are based on clear criteria which are then explained. Parents seem to like comparative indicators which are not as susceptible to evasive vagueness as words sometimes can be, but in my

* Testbourne Community School.
† Gorse Ride Junior School.

view they should always be accompanied by teachers' written assessments and suggestions for future action. However, the tendency for teachers to err on the optimistic side, reported above, deserves attention. A tempting but dangerous alternative is the report form which lists a very limited series of pre-printed statements, one of which is chosen by the teacher and ticked. Although it makes life easier for the teacher, it substantially fails to fulfil the purposes of the report. Even the deplorable lists of 'model phrases' for reports which are on the market are more easily defended than ticks in boxes.

Progress reports, issued between main reports, may provide detailed information of a useful short-term nature (such as the completion of specific work) and/or accompanying grade. Some schools use a 'Compliments and Complaints System' by which staff periodically report to a senior member of staff which pupils deserve special praise for effort or for attainment, or about whom parents should be alerted to problems emerging, perhaps with regard to absence, disruption, homework late or missing, or working below assessed ability. Parents of pupils thus singled out receive letters reflecting the points. While this appears to be a sensible arrangement, the system would only be appropriate if it was *in addition* to termly reports and consultations. It should certainly not replace them.

Formative or Summative?

Reports are based on assessment. There is a growing awareness of the distinction between formative, diagnostic and summative purposes of assessment. *Formative* purposes are those which look to the future in light of past attainments by the pupil so that appropriate next stages of learning can be planned and implemented. If education is a partnership, then that planning and implementation should be a joint process, and comments on reports can begin to reflect such an orientation and anticipate private consultations at which teachers and parents can formalise the next steps. Specific types of assessment may be *diagnostic* to ascertain the nature of particular difficulties to decide whether, for instance, remedial help is needed. Diagnostic assessment is therefore a specialist means of fulfilling formative aims. *Summative* purposes look backwards to record the overall achievement of a pupil in a systematic way. Thus year-end and leaving certificates, mentioned earlier, are often summative.

Most reports in the past have offered a mixture of formative and summative comments, but, with the exceptions of leaving certificates, few would doubt that they should aim to be formative, even though most of the judgements are based on past performance.

Profiles and Records of Achievement

As their names suggest, profiles and records of achievement tend to be built up over the course of time rather than completed at a given moment. Further, they may incorporate a plan of learning which is negotiated with the school by the pupil and parents so that it is a working document and a cumulative record which may include many facets of the pupil's activities and development besides performance in specified subjects or skills. Burgess and Adams (1985) describe a scheme by which a two-year programme is planned by a 14-year-old in conjunction with parents and a school tutor. This happens in four stages, the first being the negotiation, when the pupil is 14, of a learning plan to begin at the start of the year when he/she is 15. At that point comes the commitment stage. At the end of the year there is a review stage, and a year later completion. The whole process builds up a profile of attainment which can be summarised in a certificate and which, apart from conventional academic results, might include creative pursuits, community service activities, sports achievements, and recreational activities.

The Danish National Education Innovation Centre is experimenting with a teacher-pupil-parent report covering a wide range of elements other than conventional academic attainment. Bach (1988) lists 14 headings which include 'ability in problem-solving', 'judgement', 'independence', 'creativity', 'cooperation', 'initiative' and 'punctuality'. The report is completed twice a year by teachers, but identical reports are filled out by each pupil who has to evaluate his/her performance. The pupil and teachers meet to compare the two reports before they are sent to parents. The final stage is a meeting between pupil, parents and teachers to consider the implications.

The range of possible approaches is considerable and there is a danger in thinking in terms of stereotypes. Recent publications (Hitchcock, 1986; Broadfoot, 1984 and 1987) provide useful discussions, but in one of the neatest summaries, Brown and Black (1988) report that liaison with parents in regard to profiles and records of achievement has been slow because priority on this front has been given to the development work for ROAs (p.83). However, they report (p.84):

> Where parents are engaged in the developments, they have been enthusiastic. They have shown concern, however, where banks of comments have been used rather than open-ended approaches, and in cases where there have been "gaps" in their child's report. Such gaps may mean that the pupil has had little opportunity to develop those qualities, or they may reflect a reluctance to present a negative assessment.

Tone of Report Forms

Before individualised information is ever entered on a report, the nature of the form's wording, tone and layout can convey an impression of bureaucratic distance and of minimal communication, or, conversely, of friendly partnership with parents and informative concern. Indeed, the form's design may influence teachers' and parents' approach to their task of mutual reporting. Jargon and officialese in the printed text, boxes for ticks, and cramped space for comments can hamper communication. On the other hand a form which gives ample space for comment thereby encourages communication, while a thoughtful and amiable printed text can set the tone for teachers' observations. It is more difficult to be overbearing, contemptuously dismissive or unhelpfully curt on a form which itself exudes care. This is especially true if the form gives active encouragement to parents to follow up the comments, and if it contains an introductory printed statement on the educational influence of parents and the importance of regular communication and joint planning by parents and teachers. North Westminster Community School in London gives the following advice to staff in a special booklet of guidance on the use of written reports:

> ... information given in the reports must be:
> sympathetically and encouragingly put;
> clearly and simply expressed;
> objective and realistic;
> detailed and analytic;
> help pupil, parent and tutor to take action to improve.

Where a school serves linguistic minorities, the explanatory notes printed on the report form should appear in the relevant languages, with guidance about who to contact if a parent does not understand the report.

Frequency and Timing of Report Forms

If the report form does, indeed, serve the purposes outlined above then a report for each term would seem logical. Good school reports require staff time and effort. Goacher and Reid (p.45) calculate that for the secondary schools in their study 'a teacher with, say, 300 subject reports (and only one third of the teachers had more than this) would spend 28 and a half hours, or the equivalent of 43 school periods of 40 minutes, on reporting each year. Whether this is too long, too short or about right is difficult to judge.' Of course it is a matter of opinion whether one report a year, as advocated, for instance, by Mitchell (1973), is sufficient and much depends on what other communications and shared records exist, but it is my view that reporting should be more often. Competent teachers who keep systematic records of pupils' work do not find reports difficult to write. There may be grounds for expecting less frequent reports at secondary level (where a subject teacher encounters a larger number of pupils and so has to write more reports) than at primary level but the question of time must be related to the value of the task, and that is a matter of opinion.

Perhaps as important as the frequency of reports is their timing. If a report is a one-way communication, solely designed to pass information and opinions of teachers to parents without any response or planning for the future, then the end of term would be a defensible time to present it. If, however, the report is part of a two-way process of communication between educational partners, then the end of term would seem to be inappropriate. The practice of exchanging written assessments between teachers and parents as a prelude to consultation, with a view to future action, suggests that mid–term or the second half of term and immediately prior to a face-to-face meeting, is the best time for main reports.

Parental Response and Follow-up to Reports

Some school report forms include that minimal parental response, a signature denoting receipt of the report. Interpretation of that signature seems to vary from regarding it merely as administrative proof that the report arrived, to an implicit acceptance of the school's comments and judgements. While such a signature is better than no parental reaction, it does little to suggest educational partnership.

Recognising this, some schools are inviting parents to comment on the content of reports. A limited version of this leaves the real initiative to parents by printing a comment on the report form to the effect that 'Parents are welcome to discuss any aspects of this report with the school. Appointments may be made by contacting the headteacher.' Despite the claim to welcome which this makes, the message is one of permitting rather than encouraging response.

Another limited approach is when a space is left on the returned part of the report on which parents may comment if they so wish, but without any expectation that they will, or suggestion that they should do so. It is not surprising if a considerable number do not use that facility when there is no pressure from the school for them to respond or when the school in question is one which in other ways conveys the message, overtly or by implication, that parental involvement is interference. As teachers we hold most of the cards and initiative must come from us. Merely permitting response would seem to be insufficient. We could encourage and facilitate it.

One way of doing this is by making it clear that the school expects and needs a response from parents. Specific questions can be posed. A tear-out sheet which parents return to the school could look something like that on the following page.

It is obvious that such a report form is designed as a basis for discussion and planning between parents and teachers. The follow-up consultation could happen soon after the exchange of reports while the information and views are still fresh.

One practical question remains: who should receive, see and deal with the parental responses when they come back to the school? It is my view that in a primary school, no matter how large, the headteacher should receive and see all parental responses individually. This enables him to get a flavour of parental views and may also provide useful insights to the working of the school, to the confidence of parents and to the effectiveness of particular teachers. In a secondary school the headteacher may similarly wish to see them or he may prefer to delegate this to his deputy or to pastoral staff. Class teachers should, of course, receive the parental slips from the headteacher well before the

TO PARENTS/GUARDIANS

Since the education of your child is your responsibility as well as ours, we ask you to complete this slip, tear it out and return it to . . . . at the school.

This report book, and the points which you raise, will be discussed at our private consultation with you. We suggest the following date and time for that consultation . . .

If you cannot come at this time, would you please contact the school secretary to arrange another time? Thank you.

NAME OF CHILD:. CLASS: . . . .

1. What is your reaction to the comments made in this report?

2. Would you like to know more about any aspects of your child's school work in more detail? If so, what aspects?

3. You are able to observe your child's work and development in the home. How do you think he/she has progressed since the last school report?

4. Have you any hopes, worries or plans about your child's education which you would like to talk about at a private consultation? We would be pleased to discuss any ideas for increasing his/her learning at home.

Signature of Parent/Guardian . . . . Date . . . .

private consultations so that they can prepare for those meetings. Such a meeting should not involve statements from the teachers such as 'I see that you have asked about such-and-such. I shall look into this.' The point of putting the query in writing in advance is to enable the teacher to look into it *before* the consultation so that the consultation is immediately constructive.

Bearing in mind that the written report is also a record, the parental element should be filed in the child's school record folder. It is then available for either teachers or parents to return to if necessary.

The Confidentiality of Reports

Parents need to be reassured about the confidentiality of written reports, a topic to which I shall return with regard to school records. Each report could have a standard, pre-printed assurance at the start or the end:

> This is your report for you to keep. A copy is retained in the school as a record. The school copy does not have any information or comments additional to those on your copy. It is a confidential document between the school and you, and it will not be shown to any person or organisation outside the education system without your written permission.

Quite recently there were still some schools which did not provide a copy of the report for parents to retain, and comments sometimes appeared such as the following: 'Please take great care of this card and return it promptly after inspection'. Hopefully few maintain such practice. The scene is changing but if the purposes of report forms listed at the start of this section are valid, then we may still say of schools in the UK: 'There is room for improvement. Could do better.'

The National Curriculum, National Testing and Report Forms

Reporting mechanisms are bound to be influenced as the national curriculum and national testing procedures envisaged by the 1988 Education Reform Act for England and Wales and the report of the Task Group on Assessment and Testing (1987) are refined and implemented. In Parliament the Secretary of State for Education and Science stated that there were three purposes of national testing:

> . . . first to tell a parent or teacher what a child knows, is able to do and is able to understand; secondly, to identify problems which need further diagnosis and whether the child needs extra help or more demanding tasks; thirdly, to indicate through the results of assessment the achievements of schools and local education authorities generally. (House of Commons, 1st December 1987.)

Of the three purposes, the first and second anticipate reporting to parents, and the Secretary of State added, 'Parents are entitled to know how their child is doing . . .' Thus, schools will not only need to consider and involve parents as they develop systems of reports, profiles and records of achievement, but they will also need to apply the criteria discussed earlier in this chapter to the reporting of national test results. They will need especially:

(i)   to explain the meaning of the results when reporting them;
(ii)   to use that reporting as the prelude to a private consultation;
(iii) to use results formatively as a means to future planning as well as summatively;
(iv)   to ensure that parental contributions to that future planning are included.

Whatever teachers' views may be about the system of national testing – and the profession is clearly divided – over one aspect there will hopefully be consensus: that the results must be reported constructively to parents. In particular there will be a need to explain concepts upon which the tests are based and the terminology involved. In particular the following should be clarified:

1   Criteria-referencing (as constrasted with norm-referencing).
2   Formative, diagnostic and summative purposes.
3   The relationship of assessment to progression of the pupil.
4   How testing at 16 relates to GCSE or other examinations.
5   Where results are presented as 'attainment profile components' (Black Report, para.33) the nature of those components (such as skills, knowledge and exploration work in Science; writing, oracy, reading comprehension and listening skills in English).
6   Attainment targets and how they relate to profile components.
7   The types of testing devices.
8   Who does the testing and how.
9   What 'standardisation' means, and how a national item bank of standard tasks is used.
10 Levels of attainment.

It may be argued that these are technical issues with which every teacher should be familiar, but that they need not be explained to parents. Such a view might be more readily sustained with regard to the methods of moderation, arguments about reliability and validity, and aggregation techniques, but if one of the purposes of national testing is to report to parents, then explanation must accompany that reporting. The Black Report (1987, para.15) was surely right when it asserted 'Parents are interested above all in where their child stands in terms of the general progress expected at that age.' In its section on reporting to parents (paras.126–7) it argued:

> Parents require information about their child's progress in relation to the attainment targets of the national curriculum in a variety of areas and presented in such a way that the individual child's progress can be related to national performance. It is important that results communicated to parents and children should be positive – indicating what the child has achieved; and that they

should be constructive – pointing to what needs to be done if the strengths and weaknesses identified by assessment are to be dealt with appropriately. Assessment has to be designed to help all children to proceed with their schooling to the limits of their ability; weaknesses have to be recognised, and appropriate help made available.

If this is to be done, then the mechanisms (and terms) must be explained. The Black Report goes on to argue that reporting should be in terms of profile components since these give the necessary details about strengths and weaknesses in order to guide future work, (para.127). We may hope that teachers, having mastered the technicalities themselves, will not seek to use unexplained jargon in order to enhance the mystique of their occupation by confusing their clients. The Secretary of State has said that 'detailed' results of assessments must be given to parents but that the messages must be 'simple and clear'. Providing both detail and clarity will not be easy, and some professional training in the skills of communication may be needed, both in preparing written reports and, just as important, in discussing future plans with parents in personal consultations.

PERSONAL CONSULTATIONS

Informal Consultations

Obviously a private consultation must be provided when either partner – parent or teacher – feels that one is needed. Such an *ad hoc* meeting might be because the school is concerned or delighted about some aspect of a child's performance, or might be because a parent wants to discuss progress with a subject teacher or a more general (or pastoral) aspect with a specific member of staff. Such a facility should be available, of course, and its use encouraged.

It is still quite common to see in school handbooks a statement that if parents have a problem they should make an appointment to see the headteacher. Sometimes terms such as 'welcome to see the head-teacher' or 'the headteacher would be pleased' appear. At first sight this seems to be encouraging contact, but the implications often are:

1 Do not come to the school unless there is a problem.
2 The problem should be serious enough to pester the headteacher.
3 Do not approach any other staff.
4 Only enter the school with an appointment.

Some headteachers consider that they have a duty to handle contacts with 'outsiders' and especially to 'protect' teachers from parents. The notion of the head or senior teacher diverting parents, like a snarling watchdog intercepting interlopers, must surely be relegated to history along with the dunce's cap and the tawse. Yet consultations need to be subject to regulation to some extent. Interruption of classes is fair to neither teacher nor pupils, so a system of recognised consultation times each day (e.g. after classes) or each week (e.g. one evening a week), clearly listed in the school handbook, makes sense. More urgent calls can then be made between, and for these it is helpful if a duty member of staff (perhaps an assistant head with fewer timetable commitments) or a member of the pastoral staff or the school secretary can be the first point of contact, able to line up the appropriate meeting as soon as the relevant teacher is available.

A Scandinavian technique which we might emulate is the phone-in surgery. On a specified evening each week or each fortnight the teachers, or perhaps just class teachers, are available at a pre-publicised phone number (either school or home according to each teacher's preference) at a given time (say, between 7.00 p.m. and 8.00 p.m.) and parents know that they can telephone at that time. The teacher has basic records and information available. If nobody telephones, then the teacher can get on with other activities. A study of home–school relations in a Swedish municipality (Niléhn, 1976, p.250) recorded that in the course of one month:

> One fourth of the parents stated that they have telephoned the class teacher, whereas 9% answered that the teacher had telephoned them during the last month. When the parents got in touch by telephone, they usually phoned the teacher at home and not at school. This is probably due to the fact that many teachers have given their home telephone number if and when they have stated a telephone time. Their official telephone time was generally 20–30 minutes, one day per week, in certain cases during school time.

It is an interesting reflection of cultural assumptions that Niléhn considered the rate at which parents phoned in (one-quarter of them during one month) to be a disappointingly low rate, but it is my guess that such a scheme, if put to widespread use in Britain, would take time to build up to that rate. It is not usual for British teachers to make their home telephone numbers available to parents, and in the EEC study we encountered examples of schools listing staff home telephone numbers in handbooks in Denmark and the Netherlands only. Yet the system would seem to have merit, for most parents do have access to telephones. Such a system, of course, should not replace face-to-face meetings but should be supplementary.

Formal Consultations

Even if a school has a sound system to allow for *ad hoc* consultations as discussed above, it should also have regular formalised meetings by prior appointment. There are several reasons for this. The first is to provide a planning follow-up to written school reports. Earlier I outlined why written reports alone, unsupported by discussion, are limited in value. Here, then, is the second half of that consultative process. Nias (1981, p.93) found that in practice 'both parents and teachers come to consultation evenings with their own agendas', but points out that 'the lion's share of the short meetings is devoted to the teacher's agenda' with consequent stress for parents. How much more sensible it would be if agendas, in the form of written reports, were exchanged in advance.

A fixed and formal meeting has benefits. While much can be achieved through incidental contacts, such as if parents and teachers chat when the child is collected from school, such a setting is often not appropriate for in-depth discussion; it may be too public for confidential observations and too brief for full explanations. It also excludes families whose children travel to school by bus or walk. Further, a formal session planned well in advance and based on reports concentrates the issues. Without the discipline of such a regular meeting, communication may be difficult. Human nature being what it is, there is a danger that good intentions to consult get put off to the point of never happening. Parents and teachers suffering from shyness or inhibitions may require the more formal setting to draw them into any action at all, and it may increase inter-personal confidence and understanding if handled well. Also, a consultation ensures a degree of dialogue which the reply-slip of a written report will not always elicit, so that teachers may acquire a better understanding of the child in the home setting, just as parents will come to appreciate more fully what the school is striving to do and its difficulties.

For teachers, Bastiani *et al.* (1983, p.63) list no less than 33 objectives of such consultations presented under the three broad headings: Procedural Objectives, Basic Issues, and Broader Purposes. Besides these objectives for the school, there are a further 28 objectives for parents. The latter list includes 'Negotiating a workable deal on behalf of your child(ren)', 'A chance to look around the classroom – and the school', 'A chance to size up the teacher(s)', and 'Putting forward a view/ arguing a case'. While a less competent or less confident teacher may find such parental objectives threatening, their validity cannot be questioned and other, more collaborative aims are not only desirable but essential. There are few arguments, other than those based on expenditure of time and effort, which can be advanced against regular face-to-face discussions.

Arranging a discussion is one thing; making it useful is another. The great majority of parents will accept the structure, comment and pace set by the teacher; indeed, they will expect the teacher to take the initiative. It therefore makes sense for the teacher to plan the meetings so that essentials are covered, uncertainties revealed and home support generated. Like a server in tennis, the teacher has the advantage. Further, he has the expertise and is more familiar with the processes. Not only does the teacher have every reason to have confidence in such meetings, but he/she will be expected to take the lead and has a responsibility to do so. However, time must be allowed for parents to raise points of importance to them also. It is preferable if the setting is private and relaxed and there is not a sense of rush. Goacher and Reid (pp.108–9) report:

The duration of the interviews, which were sometimes as brief as five minutes, also provoked comments and parents were critical too of the lack of privacy, with meetings held *en masse* in school halls.

Nias (1981, p.92) found that 'individual meetings were short . . . and to many parents it seemed as if teachers claimed the right to decide how the allotted five minutes or so would be spent.'

This raises the issue of ensuring that parents really are encouraged to speak and to express their views. In a very practical book on this topic entitled *Listening to Parents*, Atkin *et al* (1988) point out that most work on home–school relations 'is viewed entirely from professional perspectives' and they call for teachers 'to redefine the basis of their professionalism' by taking active steps to listen to parents rather than to see themselves always as the experts who know best (p.174). That poses a challenge indeed.

Consultations are not always easy. Cornelius *et al*. (1983), referring to Danish research, have analysed some of the tensions and inhibitions with which parents may approach such occasions. Sometimes a degree of conflict may be involved. Contrasts of viewpoint can often be valuable and need not always be stressful. In *New Ways of Managing Conflict*, Likert and Likert (1976) argue the importance to our society of having differing human values and that 'Tensions are inevitable and are necessary for creative thinking'. They distinguish between *substantive conflict* which is rooted in the substance of the task, and *affective conflict* which has its origins in emotional aspects of inter-personal behaviour. Obviously a first step is to get rid of affective conflict. A teacher can do this by making the setting for a meeting friendly, relaxed and private. Queues of parents in a crowded, noisy and bleak hall put parents on edge, as does a sense of time pressure. Make sure that the room is pleasant, quiet and private, and that there is adequate time between appointments. If extra time is needed for a particular family, fix a special extra appointment or offer to visit parents in their home at a mutually convenient time. Parents ought not to depart with the problem unresolved or feeling that no steps will be taken to resolve it.

Courtesy also helps. If we had a convention for teachers to refer to parents as 'Sir' and 'Madam', as in airlines, to emphasise that we are providing a service to them, that might help to set the scene. That is unlikely to happen but surely we can convey a sense of respect for parents. 'Thank you for coming', 'I'm grateful to you for your help', 'Please let me know if I can assist in any way': such messages are important.

In regard to substantive conflict, issues must be brought out into the open. Jargon, evasion and padding do not do justice to important or sensitive issues. If there is a problem, it should not be side-stepped; prepare beforehand how you will put it to parents and never be too proud to seek in advance the advice of a more senior colleague or headteacher about how to handle it. If parents raise an anxiety, recognise that, no matter how minor it seems to you, it does matter to them. Treat it with concern.

If a clear difference of view emerges, seek to recognise the valid or defensible elements of the parents' case. It may, for instance, be a wish for extra teaching or facilities which the school does not have the resources to supply, yet their case in principle may be a good one. Recognise that fact openly but explain the practical constraints, or offer to take the matter to a higher level. Alternatively, the disagreement may concern assessments of what the child is capable of achieving. Ask yourself honestly: do you really have 100 per cent certainty that your judgement, based on limited knowledge of the child and, perhaps, the always-uncertain results of standardised tests, is better than theirs based on intimate knowledge of the child since birth? Your training should have told you that environmental factors can influence motivation, attainment and even intelligence; could this be the chance to influence such factors for the better? Likert and Likert point out that the traditional view of conflict is that someone should win and someone should lose, as in a boxing contest. They call this the WIN–LOSE approach. Instead, they argue in favour of the WIN–WIN approach by which participants feel that, after a fair discussion, everyone has emerged not only without loss of status and respect, but with a sense that a constructive solution has been achieved or approached jointly. The aim is not to see the problem as a bone of contention but as a joint challenge. The enemy is the problem, not each other.

Planning for the Child's Future Education

An integral element of private consultations is a discussion of how home-learning and school-learning can be improved in the future for the benefit of the child, and it is in such circumstances that teachers can demonstrate their professional expertise. It is inconvenient, even impossible, for a teacher to outline in private consultation the whole of the coming term's syllabus. In chapter 6 I discuss the class meeting which is the most economical way, in terms of teacher time, of doing this. However, a teacher can pick out special strengths and weaknesses of a child and discuss with parents how they can build upon the former and assist in rectifying the latter. More than anything else this emphasises to parents that education is a cooperative process and that they can take practical action in the home. Availability of books and other equipment on loan from the school gives such discussion an additional tangible effect, but lacking that, specific practical advice is important.

The private consultation may be especially important immediately after the issue to parents of their child's assessment at any of the four national testing ages of seven, 11, 14 and 16. This was discussed more fully on pages 43–5 with regard to written reports, but parents may well require professional help in interpreting the results of these tests. They will certainly need to discuss with teachers future action in school and at home to provide (in the words of the Secretary of State) 'extra help or more demanding tasks.'

At all stages it should be remembered and stressed that parents, not teachers, have prime responsibility for the child's education. This gives them no right to demand special facilities in, or actions by the school, for group provision and its administration are the duties of the education authority, governors and headteachers. However, the final say with regard to the individual child within that framework should lie, as a matter of principle and within constraints of practicability, with the parents. I shall return to this issue in chapter 5.

Parental Access to School Records

Changes of attitudes and procedures are emerging with regard to the right of parents to see records about their child held by the school or by the education authority. At the time of writing this book, both the Department of Education and Science and the Scottish Education Department have issued consultation papers, in some parts quite different in emphasis, in anticipation of passing regulations to give parents greater access to pupil records. In the case of England and Wales the focus is on school-held records, whereas the Scottish proposals include those held elsewhere in the education authority. However, as this book goes to press the regulations have not passed through Parliament and it is not possible to describe the systems definitively.

Plans for England and Wales derive from a section tucked away in the 1980 Act, and not as a result of the Education Reform Act of 1988. The 1988 Act and accompanying debates have put emphasis on information for parents, but most of it has been concerned with *general* information being made available to parents as a body – for instance about the national curriculum, about the nature of schools (to facilitate parental choice), about school finances in governor's annual reports to parents, about proposals to convert a school to Grant Maintained status, and so on. These help to create a climate of openness, but apart from parents' rights to know their child's national test results, most of the 1988 legislation is not concerned with parents' access to information about their individual child. Rather, the changes have their origin in section 27 (1) (d) of the 1980 Act which allowed the Secretaries of State for England and Wales to make regulations about access to records, a facility which was converted into a consultation paper seven years later. The resulting regulations will not apply to independent schools or to the further education sector. The Scottish counterpart consultative paper proposes to take the reforms further. This is discussed separately below.

Before considering the changes in detail, some of the background and logic deserve mention. With all the talk about home–school partnership in education, it would seem obvious that parents, as one element of that partnership, should have access to their child's school record, especially since they are legally responsible for their child's education. In some countries that logic has prevailed. For instance Cornelius (1988, p.5) writes of Denmark, ' . . . the question of whether parents have access to the records of their children can be answered in the affirmative – and furthermore it should be noted that the children involved have the same right.'

In the USA, federal legislation was enacted in 1974 giving parents (and students over the age of 18) the right to inspect 'any and all official records, files and other data directly related to their children'. To prevent schools from holding bland and meaningless official records while sensitive information resides in unofficial files, school boards were required to define what records should be held in schools about each child. 'No one except a school official or a teacher with a legitimate educational interest may see such records without written consent of the parent. Some clarifying amendments to the Act have made certain limited information such as letters of recommendation, confidential information.' (Peterson *et al.*, 1978, p.331.) Thus, not only can American parents see their child's school record, but they have some control over who else can see it and what information is transmitted outside the school. There are also procedures by which parents 'may challenge the inclusion of inaccurate, misleading or inappropriate materials.'

In Britain we are slowly getting to grips with the dangers of unchecked secret records held on citizens. The Data Protection Act of 1984 (which came into effect in 1987) granted right of access by individuals to private data about themselves stored on computers. As Barrell and Partington (1985, p.633) observe, 'use of computers for storing school records of pupils is still in its infancy but it seems likely that it will increase in time, and is subject to the provisions of the Act.' Yet the fact remains that most school records are not on computer and some, such as files and letters about a child, may never be. The need to establish a general right of access by parents, irrespective of the mode of recording, has gradually been recognised.

Some education authorities had taken first steps in this direction before 1988. For instance, Strathclyde Region, the largest education authority in Scotland, instructed its headteachers to allow parents to see official records held on their child, and the London Borough of Brent had the following statement in its *'Parents' Handbook'* (1986):

> Brent Council believes it is quite wrong for matters on your child to be kept from you. Therefore it has ruled that all pupils' records in schools should be open ... but only in the case of a parent's own child. The records of other pupils are of course confidential to them and their parents.

However, Wright (1988, p.17) reported that 'up until June 1987 only 12 of the 104 education authorities in England and Wales had adopted parental access policies.'

New Provisions for Parental Access to their Child's Record

(i) What Records? The DES consultative paper of 1987 and draft regulations do not specify the content or format of records to be kept, except to say that they should cover academic attainment, progress, skills and competences, but would not require schools to record views on behaviour and personality, though schools 'would remain free to keep such records if they wish.' Disclosure would apply to all such records, including those on behaviour and personality if kept. A distinction is made between 'formal records' and 'informal notes which teachers make for their personal use.' Teachers' notes would be excluded from the regulations. The test of whether something is a 'formal record' would be if its purpose was that it should be passed on to other teachers, and that would include passing on their contents orally.

However, media publicity given to problems of reporting on and dealing with child abuse have evidently influenced official thinking with regard to information given by schools to various social departments. The DES Circular No. 4/88, issued in July of 1988 was entitled '*Working Together for the Protection of Children from Abuse: Procedures within the Education Service.*' This recognised that 'school staff are particularly well placed to observe outward signs of abuse, or unexplained changes of behaviour or performance (of a child) which may indicate abuse' (para.5). There would be an understandable reluctance by some teachers to report such cases if they felt that their action would be open to the scrutiny of the parents concerned. Since the consultative document on parental access to school records appeared when the child abuse controversy was building up, it is likely that such issues influenced the inclusion of the following proposed restriction on parental access to school records:

> 8. Special consideration needs to be given to written information provided by schools to outside bodies or persons such as the local education authority, the social services department, medical practitioners, psychologists and education welfare officers. It would clearly be inappropriate for some such information, such as suspicions or evidence of child abuse, to be subject to disclosure. Because of the difficulty of drawing a dividing line between information which can be revealed and that which should be protected, it is proposed that the regulations should not provide any right of access to such information.

Similarly, information received by the school from outside bodies would not be available to parents by right.

Certainly this is a controversial area. However, counter-arguments to make all records, including those to and from outside bodies (perhaps *especially* those to and from outside bodies) available to parents are strong. Not only could an education authority effectively conceal from parents relevant data on their child by requiring it to be held centrally by the authority, but it is often the views, opinions, facts (and perhaps, sometimes, distortions) which go to others outside the school which have special relevance to both child and parents. The same applies to outside data coming into schools. If medical, psychological and welfare information is concealed from those responsible for the health and education of the child, it is a dubious basis for effective partnership. I return to this issue below in a section on reasons for concealing records.

(ii) Available to Whom? Parents of school pupils under 18 years (Scotland 16) would have access if the regulations are confirmed. On reaching 18, the right would pass from parent to pupil. Access would be in response to a written request within a specified number of days of that request (14 days in England), and a parent disagreeing with a comment would have the right to add his or her own observations which would become an integral part of the record. This procedure seems somewhat grudging and complex. There would seem to be a case for being more open and encouraging to parents if they are really to be led to feel that they are partners and that their cooperation is sought and welcomed by the school.

A system which merely *allows* parents access to their child's records held in school or education office presumes that parents must discover their right and then take the initiative to exercise it. The requirement for requests to be in writing, possible delay periods and other bureaucratic devices make the process discouraging. Therefore the parental right, once established, could be publicised, and access not only made easy but actively encouraged by school staff. The simplest way would be to have the school record/file on the child available at the regular private consultation, with the teacher being required to discuss with parents any recent entry made on it or letters included in it since the last meeting. If the school adopts a stance of openness with parents (but confidentially in regard to others) then parents are more likely to reciprocate with similar frankness. Equally a school cannot expect parents to confide private information affecting a child if the school will not adopt the same standard of honesty. Deceit is not a satisfactory foundation for a professional relationship.

There are other grounds for parental access to school records. First, it is parents who are primarily responsible for their child's education, not the school. That places a special onus on the school to share its relevant information. Then there is the question of wrong or misleading information. Once in writing it can continue to do damage so long as the record continues to exist, being passed from teacher to teacher and school to school. One headteacher suggested to me that the test which a teacher should apply to what he records should be: would I stand by this statement under oath in court? Further, a once-off, minor problem can categorise the child long after the problem has vanished. Parents need to be assured that the record is fair and balanced. A passing phase of (say) absenteeism or lateness followed by a steady record of reliability should presumably reflect the latter rather than the former, and a child's passing error should not haunt his post-school life in unfair references.

(iii) Other Aspects of the Systems Both the DES and the SED consultative papers contained a discussion of the arguments for and against disclosure of the contents of references written by schools about pupils for potential employers or further/higher education institutions. The DES seems to be backing away from making regulations on this question and the matter remains unresolved in Scotland.

In England, governing bodies would be responsible for making arrangements for schools to comply with those aspects which appear in regulations. It may be noted that records, held elsewhere in the LEA, other than in schools, are not covered by the English plan, whereas they may be in Scotland. Problems of access in school holidays would have to be allowed for.

(iv) The Scottish Proposals In December 1988 the Scottish Education Department released a consultative paper. The wording of some sections bears a close resemblance to the DES paper, but there are significant differences. The most important are that the Scottish plan envisages access to all records held in the education authority (with specific exceptions relating to child abuse and confidential materials received from outside the education service) and does not place on school boards the responsibilities which the DES envisaged would devolve to governing bodies. The age at which pupils would have rights of access would be 16, compared to 18 in the DES proposal. The same requirement for written requests appears, but instead of a 14 day response period, an astonishing 40 days is proposed. It may be noted that Scottish regulations passed in 1975 had already substantially defined pupil progress records and arrangements for transfer of records between schools.

Common Arguments for Concealing Records from Parents

Such, then, are the proposed systems which, if implemented, must be recognised as a small step forward. We may now consider the grounds which are sometimes advanced for hiding information from the child's parents. The first, and commonest, defence of secrecy is that disclosure of information is a breach of professional confidentiality. Yet surely professional confidentiality is between the professional and the client, while breach would be to a third party. Where parents act on behalf of a minor, then it is to the parents that the professional should confide. It is therefore difficult to see why schools should conceal educational information from parents on grounds of confidentiality. This position ceases to apply after the child reaches the age of 16 and is responsible for his/her own education and so becomes the direct client of the school. I shall deal below with difficult cases such as when a child under 16 confides to a teacher about malpractice in the home, but the general principle seems clear: professional confidentiality must specifically be with parents, not to the exclusion of parents.

The second argument for hiding data from parents suggests that it will be misinterpreted or misused because parents are not trained to understand the material. This is sometimes employed in regard to standardised test results. Schools and education authorities have used various standardised tests, especially at age 11, and the advent of the national system of testing at ages seven, 11 and 14 will put a new focus on the issue. In theory teachers use such test results to supplement, but not to determine, their judgements and the fear is that parents will regard them as being more precise, final and scientific than they are, hence some of the secrecy.

Two worries arise from this. The first is the assumption that parents are incapable of understanding that the tests are only indicative at a moment in time. The second is the absence of checks available to parents that teachers themselves are not allowing test results to influence their judgements of pupils unreasonably. If it is dangerous for parents to know test results, it may also be dangerous for teachers to know them. The only way to cover both points is for the results to be told to parents, as the national system will require, but explained by professional teachers who can clarify the limitations in non-technical language.

Another plea advanced to deny parents the right to inspect their child's school records is that it may inhibit teachers from recording details about home background. Taylor (1983, p.129) has suggested that if they are open to parental scrutiny 'this is likely to mean that teachers will be unwilling to record the most sensitive, and probably the most vital, information, for example that child battering in the house is suspected or, less dramatically, that marital problems are having an effect upon a child's school work and behaviour.'

The first issue to pin here is the unfairness, even danger, of recording mere suspicions or, indeed, making professional judgements about the child, whether recorded or not, on the basis of suspected home circumstances. The very suggestion that teachers' suspicions may be on a child's records provides grounds in itself for those records to be open to parental scrutiny. Similarly rumour and unsubstantiated hearsay have no place in a professional record.

But what if there is good evidence? If there are sound reasons for supposing that personal or family factors are directly affecting a child's educational progress, then before anything is placed on the child's record would it not often be appropriate to verify the matter with the parents (if appropriate, through other welfare agencies)? If the issue is sensitive, it may make sense for the headteacher to deal with it. The essential point is that if home circumstances are affecting a child's educational development, then it is often those involved in the home circumstances – especially the parents – who can rectify or ameliorate those home circumstances. When the matter has been discussed thoroughly, a wording for inclusion on the school record might be negotiated with the parents.

A more difficult case is where a child confides in a teacher (or the teacher suspects) that there are distressing home circumstances and the teacher deduces that they are upsetting the child to the point of being educationally or emotionally damaging. A child, for instance, may claim disruption or malpractice such as sexual abuse or battery in the home. The government's draft guide on inter-agency cooperation for the protection of children (*Child Abuse – Working Together*, HMSO,

1986) states that teachers are 'well placed to notice outward signs of abuse' and should contact social services, the NSPCC or police as appropriate. Education authorities have procedures for such circumstances, but the point which is open to debate is whether, once facts have been established, the entry on the school record should be concealed from parents. It is my view that normally it should not, though particular circumstances may warrant it.

What might those circumstances be? A Scottish Education Department consultative paper of December 1988 suggests the following:

"The Secretary of State proposes that regulations should provide that access to information could be refused by the education authority if –
a. access to the information would be likely to result in serious harm to the physical or mental health or emotional condition of the pupil to whom the information relates or to any other person, or
b. if the information had been given or received in connection with the prevention or detection of crime or the apprehension or prosecution of offenders; or
c. if access to the information concerned would be against the public interest (for example if the information concerned matters which might be the subject of criminal proceedings)."

There is clearly a strong case for reservations of these types in any arrangements made in regard to access to pupil records.

A Code of Practice for School Recording

What, then, might be a proper code of professional practice with regard to school records? Difficulties do arise from the fact that some other professions are not always open with parents about records on their children and this not only sets an unfortunate precedent, but sometimes prevents schools from divulging information provided by those professions. Despite this, I belive that procedures akin to the following could be adopted as a possible approach:

Parents should have the general right to see, at any reasonable time, official records on their child **held either by the school or by the education authority**; and should have a means to challenge and correct inaccuracies or misrepresentations, the governors (in Scotland, the school board) providing a point of appeal at the school level. The child's school record/file should automatically be available at regular or exceptional private consultations and the attention of parents drawn to any new entries of significance. Nobody outside the education service should see the record/file without parents' written consent. Apart from confidential references to employers and institutions of further/higher education, no fact, assessment or opinion about the child should be conveyed in writing or by word of mouth by any member of the education service to anyone outside the education service unless it appears on the official record, and is therefore open to parents to see.

At age 16, when young people become responsible for their own education, the same facilities should be open to them.

Specific reservations may be applicable in abnormal circumstances related to potential serious harm to the pupil or in relation to prevention or detection of crime or when the public interest is at risk.

If education is really to be a process of partnership, then pupil records should be seen as joint parent–teacher property.

4 HOMEWORK AND HOME-LEARNING

It may be helpful to draw a distinction between homework and home-learning. I offer the following preliminary definitions:

Homework   Learning tasks set by teachers to be completed out of class (normally in the home) within a specified time and usually directly related to work currently being done at school.

Home-learning   All learning which happens in the home as a result of family actions. It may or may not be deliberate; it may or may not be beneficial; and it includes knowledge, skills, attitudes and habits acquired by emulation as well as by instruction.

Both are relevant to schools. Of the two, home-learning is, arguably, more important to a child's development, education and schooling than is homework. It is a force which warrants more attention, research and action than has been given to it hitherto. As teachers we are only just beginning to learn how to tap it and influence it. Indeed, the harnessing of this educative source to school endeavours may be one of the more urgent challenges for the profession today. If children from certain kinds of homes tend to do better in school than those from others, then concerns for equality of opportunity, best use of talent and almost any other educational objective would appear to need the reinforcement of home-learning. Although it may be beyond our control, it need not be beyond our influence.

Homework

Homework, by contrast, is a more clear-cut issue and it is to homework that I turn first. Since it is generally set at school, carried out at home and (where appropriate) assessed at school, it is a clear example of collaboration between the two educating centres and an obvious focus for parent–teacher cooperation. I shall deal with it under four headings: the legal position, purposes of homework, homeworking conditions and parent–teacher collaboration over homework.

The Legal Position with regard to Homework
In most European countries homework is a matter for regulation or a

Ministry of Education circular rather than law. Such regulations may prescribe a framework within which it is set, for instance specifying time maxima for different age groups (Luxembourg), limiting it to core subjects and certain ages (Bavaria) or leaving details to the 'school conference' (several German provinces). In the Dutch language sector of Belgium teachers must keep a record of homework set, such records being retained for five years for inspection purposes and 'schools should explain to parents, during parent evenings, the objectives and the nature of homework to be set.' (Le Métais, 1985.) The words 'to be set' imply *advance* explanations to parents.

British law leaves this as a somewhat grey and uncertain area. Statutes (such as the English 1944 Education Act) do not authorise homework but nor do they prohibit it. The Education (School Information) Regulations of 1981, which have the force of law, and similar regulations for Scotland, require that among the information which must be available to parents, a school's arrangements for homework should be included; this therefore seems to accept the valid existence of homework. Barrell and Partington (1985, p.635) comment:

> In sending children to school, parents hand over a portion of their authority to the schoolteacher, and are assumed to assent to all reasonable school rules. It is probable that the courts would decide, at least in the case of pupils of secondary school age, that a requirement that a child should do a moderate amount of home-work is a reasonable requirement and that, where such a rule exists, a parent may not order his child to break it.

Atherton *et al.* (1987, p.123) advise Scottish parents, 'Schools are free to decide on the amount of homework given, but you would be entitled to object to your child not getting enough homework or getting too much in relation to his or her age and ability.'

Taylor (1983, p.121), pointing out that there is even less certainty about the legal grounds for homework at primary level than at secondary, suggests that 'it is particularly important therefore that the [primary] head, teachers and the parent body, if any, try to come to a common view' about arrangements for homework. It would appear to be an appropriate matter for governing bodies to consider.

Purposes of Homework

The European Parents' Association has published the following list of acceptable purposes of homework drawn from the literature (Macbeth, 1987):

1 Consolidation of, or practice of, work already done in class.
2 Preparation for coming class work.
3 Introducing tasks which extend beyond work already done in class, but build upon it.
4 Assisting slower children to catch up with quicker children.

5 Testing pupils' understanding of work covered or competence in skills.
6 Working independently and developing self-discipline.
7 Making use of materials and sources of information (including parents) which are not accessible in the classroom.
8 Enabling class work to concentrate on activities which require the teacher's presence.
9 Strengthening educational partnership between parents and teachers.
10 Providing a means by which teachers can encourage parents to become more actively involved in their child's formal education.
11 Providing a means by which parents can see the sort of work which the child is doing in school, and by which they can assess progress.

The use of homework as a punishment, as an image-maker or to compensate for school deficiencies may be seen as questionable purposes.

There seems to be some international consensus that, at secondary and upper primary level at least, homework is a beneficial and normal element of schooling and the DES Inspectorate has asserted (1987, (a) p.44) that it is 'important for pupils of all ages and abilities'. Rutter *et al.* (1979, p.109) reported that secondary schools which set homework frequently and where there was some kind of check on whether staff did in fact set it, tended to have better outcomes than schools which made little use of homework. The White Paper *Better Schools* (1985, p.25) referred to homework as an important element of independent study and stated that it is not necessarily done at home. The Inspectorate (1987, p.42) has said that homework is 'associated with good education and effective schools' while the Secretary of State has advanced the idea of extra classes for pupils not attaining expected standards.

The Eurydice report (1985) draws special attention to the need for homework to be part of a planned programme if it is to be effective, for it to be checked conscientiously by teachers and for feedback to be given to pupils. It condemns the use of homework as a punishment and a tendency by some teachers to set it in an off-hand way. A study in the Netherlands found that 94 per cent of homework 'is given at the end of the lesson, half of the time AFTER THE BELL HAS RUNG' and 'pupils receive little individual feedback on their errors and misunderstandings.' Clearly homework must be planned as an integral part of the syllabus and be portrayed as such to both pupils and parents. The DES Inspectorate report (1987, p.42) urges that it should 'reflect the objectives of the curriculum', but it recognises the potential for wider experience by stating, 'its function must be to generate a variety of worthwhile learning experiences additional to those provided in school' and it identifies independent study as integral (pp.3 and 25). Advance discussion of homework with parents will be considered in more detail in chapter 5 on class meetings. The sense of seriousness is also enhanced by teachers checking the homework and giving feedback not only to pupils, but to parents also.

Homeworking Conditions

If homework is to be integral to schooling, then the conditions in which it is carried out in the home must be as suitable as it is possible for parents to make them: encouragement, time, space, equipment and lack of distractions being the key elements. Of the five, encouragement may be the most important, but physical circumstances matter as well.

First, the room. A survey in the Netherlands (OPCO, 1985) showed that in a sample of 1089 pupils of all ages, 65 per cent did their homework in their own rooms, 28 per cent in sitting rooms. Wherever it is done, the room should be quiet, relatively free of the more obtrusive distractions, and well-lit. That is not always easy to achieve, but the objective is worth expressing. The DES Inspectorate study (1987) reported some family conditions which were unsuitable but did not consider that to be grounds for not setting homework; rather it urged consideration of alternative places to do it such as the school or public libraries.(p.38). There should also be a flat surface to spread papers and requisite equipment. With regard to timing, everyone with children will know how difficult it is to establish a routine time for homework and perhaps the issue is one of setting priorities rather than fixed times. While the family meal might take priority over homework, the latter might come a close second. If alluring alternative activities are normally made contingent upon the completion of homework, that helps.

That parents have to take active steps to create the right physical and psychological environment for homework suggests that teachers ought to give guidance to parents on the topic through publications, consultations, PTA/PA and class meetings. Many British schools do offer sound advice in their handbooks. First, from a Lothian Region primary school* handbook:

> Homework is set to consolidate work done in class and to encourage independent study. Normally, this would be given only on Monday, Tuesday, Wednesday and Thursday evenings, leaving the weekends free for all to relax. If your son/daughter has given of his/her best and after 30 – 40 minutes at the very most is still struggling with homework, please tell him/her to stop, write a note to this effect on the jotter to let the class teacher know of a difficulty being encountered. Homework will not be given in areas not already covered, taught and discussed in school so your child should normally be able to handle it.
>
> Please take an interest in asking your child to show you his/her work – they really appreciate this – and sign at the foot of each

* Bankton Primary School.

night's work. We request this signing to ensure you are kept aware of your child's progress. Homework repeatedly not signed or repeatedly left at home or not tackled will be investigated. Again, I think most parents will appreciate this concern.

The younger children will probably have little to do at home, other than reading and simple number work but in order to prepare older pupils for the school life ahead of them, we will actively encourage a healthy outlook to the whole question of homework and here parents have a large part to play setting aside at home a regular quiet place and time in an encouraging (but not-over demanding) atmosphere for such.

The handbook goes on to explain the kinds of homework which might be set and the ways in which parents can be involved. There is also a section on the care of books and materials lent to homes by the school and a plea for the parents to ensure that every child has basic equipment. The advice for parents in the handbook is complemented by the following entry in the staff handbook:

Homework – Teachers should set regular homework (excluding weekends) as the routine of this is a valuable exercise for the children and also allows parents some insight into the child's progress. Should a child not work to his/her potential during school hours I would expect you to ask the child to complete the work at home. Please ensure parents sign homework each night. Also please ensure that *all* children are capable of tackling homework set; there is no purpose in giving the class the same piece of homework – it will almost certainly be worthless for the "top" and "bottom" of the class. Regular homework offenders should be referred to the relevant AHT. In event of a pupil being absent for a considerable time due to illness, teachers should consider the possibility of contacting the home regarding allocating some suitable work for the child. Individual class teachers should keep a note of dates when a pupil fails to submit homework. This can prove useful on parents' days etc. and are often an indication of the real parental interest.

The secondary school* handbook which I have selected has a section of general advice on homework and more detailed guidance subject-by-subject. The general section states:

All students have the opportunity of homework and NO PARENT SHOULD BE SATISFIED WITH THEIR YOUNGSTER'S REPORT THAT HE OR SHE HAS NO HOMEWORK.
In many departments written work will be set and this must be done at the time stated and done well. If the student does not conform, we shall tell you. Regular homework not only reinforces and supplements the work of the class but helps the learner to

* Lasswade High School Centre, Lothian Region.

develop independent study habits essential to success in the senior school and tertiary education.

BUT WRITTEN WORK IS ONLY A PART OF HOME-WORK. REVISION AND MORE REVISION IS THE BEST REGULAR FORM OF HOMEWORK AND THE PARENT SHOULD INSIST ON REGULAR WEEKLY REVISION OF THE SCHOOLWORK.

Each pupil is given a school diary to record homework and other matters of importance. Please insist on its use and ask to see it regularly.

The tone of this statement at secondary level contrasts with that at primary; the head is making it clear that homework is unambiguously an integral part of the school process. Within that determined framework, subject teachers are able to give gentler advice and exhortation.

Parent–Teacher Collaboration and Homework

Teachers can recognise the part which parents contribute to homework and can take the initiative. Here is the English Department's contribution to a secondary school handbook for parents:

Parents can help their children by providing a good dictionary for use at home, and by encouraging them to develop the habit of regular and varied reading. Valuable assistance can also be given by parents who ensure that homework time is set aside and that work done at home is sufficient in quantity and quality.

Similarly we find the Art Department encouraging visits to galleries; a request for availability of an atlas, watching certain TV documentaries and assisting with homework in Geography; the historians making various suggestions, including the availability of an encyclopaedia; Mathematicians stressing the importance of homework; the Modern Studies Department urging the use of newspapers and other media (as does the Science Department); while the Technical Department asks parents 'to encourage students to take an interest in the technology of everyday objects.' Having an instrument available in the home is mentioned by the Music Department. And it is the Modern Linguists who provide the fullest range of advice to parents, including the use of dictionaries, watching television programmes in relevant languages, going over checklists with children, encouraging children to speak foreign languages in the home and urging them to get materials (such as the *Astérix* strip cartoons) in foreign languages.

The development of homework as something which parents can be involved in actively helps to make education of the child a process which is recognised by both parents and teachers as being a joint one.

In chapter 5 I return to the issue of homework not only because a class-teacher can explain it to parents in advance but also because having all parents of one class together enables them to seek mutually-supportive arrangements for homework so that there can be local consistency of practice. The anguished cry as a prelude to deferring or evading homework, 'But Dad! Everyone in my class …' (usually in relation to a TV programme) can be evaluated and some common basis of practice established. An essential part of that practice is encouragement and interest by the parents. The extent of parental assistance can also be worked out at such gatherings, and even some social pressure indirectly brought to bear on less supportive parents without, of course, identifying them or causing public embarrassment.

The next easy step is to have a parental signature that homework has been done. Many schools have homework books or school diaries in which pupils record the homework for the day and in which parents not only sign that each day's work has been properly attempted, but may add their own comments. There is sometimes space for a teacher or tutor to add observations for the benefit of the parents.

It is known for schools to have a 'homework' time organised in school for carrying out these studies, though technically, that is not homework. In the French sector of Belgium some schools run an 'École de Devoir' which is a homework class in the school supervised by parents or members of the community. Where there are acute problems of 'latchkey children' a homework class, or simply a club based in the school and run by the parents' association (as in some Swedish schools) does have attractions. However, the essence of homework is that it is done at home and that parents have a degree of responsibility for it.

Some schools, especially but not exclusively at primary level, have designed homework to include family participation, either by asking children to survey family opinions or actions, or by inviting parents to join in the activity. The DES Inspectorate report contains useful examples at different age levels. A Home–School Liaison Teacher can visit homes to encourage parents to help children with homework (Macleod, 1985, p.14).

A variant of parent–teacher cooperation over homework which I have observed in Norway is the joint community project. A project is held each term. Parents and teachers of a given class meet towards the end of the previous term to decide on a broad theme (e.g. money, old age, waste, pollution, etc.) and how pupils can pursue a study of the chosen topic in groups, not only using homes and the community as resources, but utilising the skills of writing, art, mathematics, languages, and so on, within the project. This has a number of benefits. First, it brings together parents and teachers in a working relationship, planning and supervising the project. They get to know each other in a non-stressful situation which creates a relationship of the sort which makes future contacts, perhaps at a time of crisis, easier. It also enables teachers to persuade parents that they can be of practical value to the schooling process and to demonstrate in the setting of a project the sorts of assistance that they can give at other times. Finally, the children enjoy it and gain from it.

One recent development blurs the line between homework and home-learning, perhaps helpfully. This is the growing evidence that parental assistance with reading for young children can be beneficial, and 'paired reading' techniques have gained prominence. Parents are used in schools as classroom aides to reading but that is not the initiative to which I refer. I am talking about parents hearing their own children read at home and I shall return to this development later in the chapter.

In conclusion, homework is probably important and parents should be seen as significant contributors to it. Disturbingly, the DES Inspectorate report (1987) recorded a wide variety of practice in the 243 schools in its survey: cases of schools which had no homework policy and left it for teachers to determine it, examples of teachers who discouraged it, a 'gulf between intention and reality' (p.36) and an overall conclusion that 'its potential is not being exploited' (p.44). In a rather general way it suggested that schools should take full account of the attitudes and views of teachers, governing bodies, parents and pupils', but perhaps a more specific strategy is needed. If it is true that 'successful homework is more likely to occur as a result of a school homework policy ... than when it is left solely to the initiative of individual teachers' (p.43) then the governors might consult the parents' association in the development of such a policy, and they might then implement and monitor it.

Home Learning

We come now to that somewhat neglected, certainly variable and possibly crucial aspect of education, home-learning: all the experiences which a child absorbs and reacts to within the family circle. Discussion of home-learning does not imply that school-learning is unimportant. Schools have substantial impact as studies at secondary level (e.g. Rutter *et al.*, 1979) and at primary level (e.g. Tizard *et al.*, 1988) show. We need to get the balance of emphasis right and to find practical ways to turn exhortation about 'parenting' into reality. If home-learning is as powerful an influence as research indicates and as many of us suppose, it might go some way to explain phenomena which have puzzled us. Consider, for instance, the persistently middle-class nature of university intakes, or the success of independent schools, or findings that traditional teaching methods may be more effective than informal methods (Bennett, 1976). In explaining these, have we perhaps put too much emphasis on what *institutions* can do and too little on the impact of *home*-learning? And if home-learning plays a part in school failure for children from disadvantaged families, how can we influence that home-learning?

Tizard and Hughes (1984) report that relatively little research has been done on learning in the home. We may ask why this should have been so when strong indications have constantly appeared over the past three decades that it could be an important, possibly even a determinant factor, in life chances. Tizard and Hughes (pp.16–17) suggest that there are two reasons. The first is that observation of children in their homes by researchers is difficult and time-consuming. They continue:

> A second reason why so little research has been done on what children learn at home is of a very different kind. The obstacle here is not so much the problem of obtaining information, but the belief in some quarters that there is not much to be gained from attempting to do so. In other words, the reluctance has been due to the general belief that mothers, as educators, have very little to offer.

Their own findings were the reverse. 'It was clear from our observations that the home provides a very powerful learning environment' (p.249). They go on to suggest (pp.250–2) that there are five reasons why the home is an especially effective learning environment for a young child, not only different from but perhaps in some senses superior to, the nursery school. First, the range of activities is greater in the home than in the school. Second, the shared common life enables the mother to help the child 'to make sense of her present experiences by relating them to past experiences, as well as to her existing framework of knowledge.' Third is the small number of children who have to share the adult's time and attention. Fourth, the learning experiences at home are in contexts of great significance to the child. (As Tizard and Hughes say, 'This principle is well understood in primary education, but it is much easier to put into effect in the home than in the school. Because school activities tend to be divorced from the rest of living, teachers often have to devise rather artificial devices.') Fifthly, the relationship between mother and child is close, often intense, and 'she will almost certainly have definite educational expectations, which she is likely to pursue with whatever energy she has available... It's this parental concern that converts the potential advantages of the home into actual advantages.' Their findings applied to working-class homes as much as to middle-class homes, though the emphasis and content of home-learning were sometimes different between the two categories.

Other work seems to give some support to these suggestions. Davie *et al.*, (1984), in their study of 165 pre-school children in their homes, not only found that middle-class children performed better on the Stanford-Binet Intelligence Test, but also that their parents provided more books and educational toys, gave more praise to their children and involved them in more 'real' daily tasks than did working-class parents. The implication was that these learning experiences in the home gave the children educational advantage.

Perhaps it is in part a result of insufficient research and knowledge about the home-learning process that practical guidance and encouragement for parents is not a conspicuous element of the formal school system. In their book *The Needs of Parents* (1984, p.168) Pugh and De'Ath draw attention to the relative lack of information and support available to the parents of school-age children compared to the help and services provided when their children were at the pre-school stage. Books are starting to appear on the market to guide parents, such as *Learning at Home* (Griffiths and Hamilton, 1987) but, useful though such texts are, the problem remains of the attitude of teachers, who have no training or role definition for working with parents. Training, in this context, would include pre-service and in-service training, while role definition is presumably a matter for both contractual arrangements and leadership by governing bodies and headteachers.

To lack of preparation may be added fears by teachers that if parents were encouraged to teach, some of the professional mystique and status of teachers might be lost, and the issue of time is touched on by Hewison (1985, p.42) a little acidly:

> Critics argued that schools had enough to do educating children without trying to educate parents as well; and, as far as can be judged, in the U.K. it was the critics' view which prevailed.

The two difficulties – that there is a dearth of research into home-learning and that little practical assistance is offered to parents to support them in their task of optimising home-learning – are to some extent related. It may be argued that support for parents cannot be provided by teachers if teachers are not trained to give it, and that training is not possible until we know more about the nature of home-learning and how to improve it, which depends on research. Yet such a logic, which implies no action until research has increased, would seem to be only partially valid. Even if there has been a shortage of research which looks directly at home-learning processes, there have been several community-based and school-based interventions which appear to have tapped the forces of home-learning to the benefit of children (for instance those reported in Marjoribanks, 1979; Pourtois, 1980; Berrueta-Clement *et al.*, 1984; Widlake, 1986; Tizard *et al.*, 1982). In chapter 9 I shall consider some initiatives taken in disadvantaged areas and it seems that effective action is possible without precise sociological knowledge of how the home-learning process happens. Further, the correlations between home background and school attainment, so consistently recorded for the past three decades, will not go away. That we cannot yet say exactly why the correlations occur does not mean that we should ignore them, especially when it is clear that adjusting the mechanisms of school structures has had relatively little effect.

The challenge, then, is: what can be done besides mounting intensive research into the home-learning process and the development of practical initiatives (which I discuss in chapter 9)? Perhaps what we need is a clearer model of the ways in which home-learning can be integrated with school-learning, and greater publicity of the effects of home-learning.

Towards a Model of Home–School Integrated Learning

It is not enough merely to recognise home background as a cause of in-school failure, nor simply to exhort teachers to act as partners with parents. A more precise philosophy for relating home-learning to school-learning, upon which practice can be based, is needed. Extreme positions would be to regard teachers on the one hand, or parents on the other, as dominant educators to whose diktats the other partner-group must acquiesce. Assuming these extremes to be unacceptable, we may consider whether *all* learning experiences in the home and in the school are relevant to each other, or whether each has its own sphere of activity with identifiable points of overlap which can become the focus for partnership.

Perhaps it is easier to define areas of responsibility in countries where the formal school curriculum is nationally-prescribed in some detail. The Italian parents' organisation FAES is unusual in that it owns and manages schools, and it is committed to the notions of the family as the central educational force and of parents as the school's clients. It therefore has a special incentive to develop a formula for the division of responsibilities. It refers to the *family–social sphere* of education and the *scholastic sphere* of education, the latter in effect being the school. Each is seen as having '*natural factors*' (essentially human relations) and '*technical factors*' (formal teaching). The division of responsibilities between parents and teachers is related to these spheres and these factors. Thus implementation of the formal school curriculum (prescribed by the state) is the responsibility of teachers, while the human relations element of upbringing in the family (including beliefs) is exclusively a parental responsibility. Between these two 'exclusive' domains are two overlap areas with shared responsibilities: syllabus aspects in the home (including homework) and human relations aspects in the school. Collaboration between parents and teachers (which includes in-service training for *both* partners, some of which is provided by parents for teachers) is focused on these overlap areas.

There are difficulties in transferring such a philosophy to state schools in the UK. However, the advent of a national curriculum for at least the core of school teaching and existence of governing bodies to represent parents and teachers in school governance enable us to consider a tentative model relating home-learning to school-learning on the following lines. (See Figure 4.1 opposite.)

Possible Model for Integration of Home and School Learning

The collaborative elements at the centre of figure 4.1 could be applied at individual, class and school levels through private consultations, class meetings and school-level PA/PTA activities. However, it must be stressed that parents are still responsible for their child's education and that, within restraints of expense and appropriateness as laid down in law, would still have the right to education according to their wishes. Thus, they should still have the right to be consulted over determinant decisions affecting their child in school, as outlined in point 9 of the basic minimum for liaison in chapter 2, and in the case of disagreement might have the final say. Such a model also would not preclude the right of parents to meet at class or school levels to discuss the formal

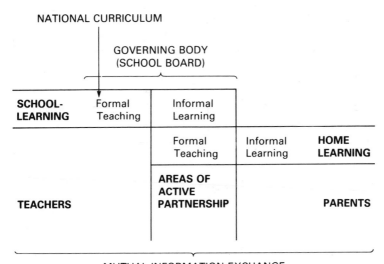

Figure 4.1.

curriculum and to express opinions, though decisions would rest with teaching staff subject to delegation from the governing body.

In his book *Developing Parental Involvement in Primary Schools*, Long (1986) draws special attention to the 'parent–child learning bond', that natural force which is thought to make parents especially effective educationally in their contacts with their children, particularly when very young. He suggests that the traditional role of teachers tended to drive a wedge between parents and their children, thereby failing to capitalise on the positive potential of the learning bond. Instead he advocates what he calls the 'clamp' model by which teachers seek to reinforce the bond and to influence the quality of home-learning. He illustrates the contrast by two simple diagrams (p.4 of his book).

The 'clamp model' has special relevance to the 'formal teaching' element of home-learning and its application is illustrated by the increasing trend by schools to encourage the parents of young children to hear their children read to them. The simple techniques of assisting with reading (Glynn, 1987, esp. p.75) can be acquired by any parent and quite apart from its common-sense application, signs are beginning to emerge that progress can be made in the most disadvantaged communities (Widlake and MacLeod, 1984). The Haringey Project (Tizard, Schofield and Hewison, 1982) showed marked gains by children who had experienced two years of parental involvement contrasted with a control group among whom it was not specifically encouraged. But as Hannon (1987) has pointed out, the Haringey Project included other facets such as home visiting which may have improved techniques in the home and provided personal encouragement, so that this and other resource-related factors (such as generous supply of appropriate books) may also be contributing to progress.

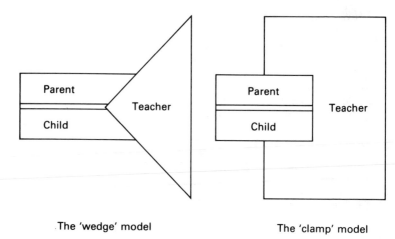

The 'wedge' model   The 'clamp' model

Figure 4.2. (From Long, R., 1986)

Yet the Belfield Reading Project (Hannon and Jackson, 1987) found that the reading scores of more than 70 working-class children in a parent-involvement scheme 'were hardly any better than the reading test scores of comparable children who had passed through the school before parents had been involved' (Hannon, 1987). And the Tizard *et al.* (1988) study of working-class primary children in the ILEA reported that, despite some other home-related gains, there was no statistically significant relationship between primary school progress and the frequency with which parents stated that they read to their child, heard their child read or helped with Maths.

Does this, then, cast doubt on earlier indicators that home-teaching helps? It would seem not. Hannon (1987) argues that we should not draw that conclusion since circumstances and the nature of tests may have influenced results, and we must bear in mind that in the ILEA study the measures of outcomes were school-focused, the home variables were obtained by retrospective interviews with parents and not direct observation and the finding was an absence of a statistical relationship which does not necessarily mean an absence of forces at work. However, the main point made by Tizard *et al.* is that in the Haringey project home-reading was the result of careful organisation and constant contact with parents, whereas home-reading in the ILEA study was parent-initiated, often with little or no support from the school. Thus we seem to have another pointer towards the value of parent–teacher partnership. As Tizard *et al.* report:

> We have already suggested that the apparent ineffectiveness of parental help with reading was due to insufficient home–school liaison about the reading process. We found that children's progress in reading and writing ... was related to the amount of parental knowledge of, and contact with, the school. But we also

found that in most schools it was very much up to the parents to obtain information about teaching methods.

If we remember that the ILEA sample was entirely working class, and if we relate that to findings in other studies (e.g. Davie *et al.*, 1984) that there are social class differences in approach to home-learning, it could be that many middle-class families are successfully acquiring effective techniques to help their children, while other families may require specific teacher-led assistance.

Barbara Tizard (1987) has similarly drawn attention to the multiplicity of forces at work and she speculates 'One possible explanation is that parental help with reading only succeeds if it is part of a carefully planned approach' which 'undoubtedly demands a high level of organisation on the part of the teacher' and 'Parental involvement may only be effective if extra staff are available to support both parent and teacher . . . Without such support, some teachers may devote less time than before to reading, believing that the job can be largely left to parents.' She, too, stresses that 'it would be wrong to conclude from our study that parents cannot help to improve reading.'

Hewison (1985, p.51) refers to evidence arising from her study in Dagenham that

> when the data were analysed, the factor which emerged as most strongly related to the child's reading performance was whether or not the parents reported that they regularly heard the child read. (Not read to the child, but heard the child read.) A strong statistical relationship remained, even after all the other home background factors studied, and the child's tested IQ, had been taken into account.

She summarises a variety of similar studies, including the Haringey Reading Project, the Centre for Urban Educational Studies project entitled 'Family Cooperation in the Development of Literacy' and the PACT project (Parents and Children and Teachers). She concludes cautiously, calling for more evidence and asserting (p.57):

> It is also important, in furthering the cause of parent involvement, to avoid extravagant claims, and the inevitable disappointments to which they lead. Not all parents will wish to take part in plans to involve them; some will always remain hostile to schools and teachers; some may even be actively obstructive.

In my view that highlights the need to put more emphasis upon parental duties rather than to accept that parental responsibility is a voluntary option. However, her caveat must be taken seriously, as must her warning (p.57):

> Another dangerous fallacy is to *assume* that if parent involvement can improve the reading ability of six year olds, then it can also improve the mathematics of ten year olds, or lead to better marks in English essays written by fourteen year olds.

Yet there does seem to be sufficient evidence to enable us to encourage 'paired reading' and other techniques in the home for all children. And here there is an irony. While some Ministries of Education (and many schools) have consistently discouraged homework for children under ten years old, the indicators emerging appear to give us confidence that guided home-learning (which might be called homework, but with a touch of fun injected) could be precisely what is needed for that group.

In this as yet unresolved area of investigation four conclusions do seem to be gaining a consensus of agreement. The first is that parental involvement in reading, number and other taught elements is unlikely to be harmful. The second is that, given some circumstances, the nature of which have to be defined more exactly through research, working-class children probably can be helped to read, write and learn better through the involvement of parents. The third is that much parental help with reading, writing and number happens in many homes of all social classes anyway and schools can encourage this to increase. The fourth is that even if the *reasons* why parental involvement is effective are complex, and even if the *circumstances* must include parental confidence and motivation which are not always easy to generate, the *effects* of parents helping with learning seem to be positive, given the right support and encouragement.

Most of these examples have been taken from the primary sector. This is partly because research into early learning has turned the spotlight onto the early years, partly because most action has happened at that level, and partly because parents feel most comfortable and confident at being involved when their children are small. As I explained in chapter 1, this book does not consider the pre-school period but that is not to suggest that it is unimportant; quite the reverse. It is easy to concur with Osborn and Milbank (1987) when they pointed to the value of parental involvement (pp.196–9) and especially argued for pre-school provision.

Johnson and Ransom (1983) found a reluctance on the part of parents to be overtly involved at secondary level and a rationalising for not being so. Although many community schools are secondary schools, their emphasis is as much on involving parents in the school's facilities for community reasons as to assist their children at home, and the technicalities of secondary school curricula often make much participation difficult. That, however, should not rule out parental interest and encouragement of children, nor their involvement in consultations about the child's progress.

Home-learning, then, is an under-researched and probably under-estimated facet of the child's educational experience. We know enough about it, however, and its correlation with school attainment to suspect that it could be one of the essential keys to improving children's capacity to benefit from other educational settings such as schools. We may agree with Glynn (1987, p.69):

Few would dispute that home and school play complementary roles in children's learning. Since parents and teachers share overlapping areas of interest and responsibility for the same children, with whom they interact in different settings, two things might reasonably be expected. First, a co-operative partnership between parent and teacher in helping children to learn should be both feasible and effective. Secondly, the study of children's acquisition of academic skills in one setting and the utilisation of these skills in the other setting should be a major focus for applied behavioural research. Surprisingly, progress in *either* of these directions has been somewhat limited. It is interesting just how much the home and the school settings remain isolated one from the other.

5 PARENTAL CHOICE

The Secretary of State, speaking in the House of Commons on 1st December 1987 about his proposed education reforms, stated

> I would sum up the Bill's 169 pages in three words – standards, freedom and choice.

The Conservative Party has publicised its commitment to parental freedom and choice, but these also appear to accord with the ideologies of other political parties. Indeed, the last Labour Government had a parental choice Bill before Parliament which probably would have become law if Labour had not lost the 1979 general election. Egalitarians in other countries, such as Christopher Jencks *et al.* (1972, p.258) in the USA, have argued for choice of school as a means of 'equalising people's claims on a public resource'. Far from being 'ghetto-creating', choice can represent the reverse by preventing children from being trapped educationally by their zone of habitation. Legalised choice provides for all families a privilege otherwise limited to those who are able to purchase houses in favoured areas. Where the parties appear to differ is in their objectives. The Conservatives want to simulate and stimulate market forces, as well as providing opportunities for less favoured families. Other parties, while supporting the second, seem less sure about the first.

There is some evidence that headteachers tend to favour the concept of parental choice, even if there may be reservations about aspects of its administration. The majority of headteachers in a study of 153 Scottish schools (Glasgow University, 1986) expressed support in principle for parental choice between schools, while in England the General Secretary of the National Association of Head Teachers wrote before the 1988 Act had been passed:

> Parental choice, like some other aspects of the Bill, such as a national core curriculum and financial delegation, is a sensible concept. But the detailed application of the idea has not been thought through clearly. (Hart, 1988, p.169.)

Yet it is still quite common to encounter teachers who reject parental choice. The first part of this chapter therefore considers the arguments about choice in education. Then choice is discussed in two categories: choice *between* schools, which is what most of the public debate has been about, and parental (and pupil) choice *within* schools.

Two aspects of parental choice are *not* discussed in detail here. These are the choice not to send the child to school at all, and the choice to use the independent sector. Schooling is not compulsory. Parents may educate their child at home if they wish. Organisations such as the *World-wide Education Service* and *Education Otherwise* offer assistance to families embarking on home teaching. A sensible compromise arrangement is just beginning to appear. This is an arrangement by which parents educating their child at home can utilise specific classes on an opt-in basis when they do not have adequate facilities or expertise themselves, or where group-work is necessary. Science lessons requiring laboratories or expensive equipment and team sports provide obvious examples, though specialist teachers may be more important still.

There is a long tradition of parents utilising independent schools in Britain, but since there is minimal state subsidy of such schools (or subsidy of parents wishing to use them) the system is often seen as socially divisive. In countries such as Denmark and the Netherlands where most of the costs of independent schools are state-financed, access by all becomes a reality. In such countries independence is more in the running of the schools, not in their funding, thereby greatly increasing parental choice for all. The present chapter is written on the assumption that such an approach will not appear in Britain in the near future.

Arguments about Choice in Education

Choice for the Client

Parents are legally responsible for their child's education, including schooling. This makes parents the legal clients of the school, until the child is 16 even if other groups (pupils, the education authority, employers) may have different and subsidiary claims to client status. In our society it is normal for clients to have choice both with regard to the professionals whom they patronise and with regard to objectives. Thus patients (or the parents in the case of a child) choose which doctor's panel they wish to be on and define when to use his services and for what purposes. Comparisons between professions have inherent difficulties, but the general point is clear enough. If someone is legally responsible for something, it is reasonable that he or she should have some discretion in fulfilling that obligation.

Freedom and Choice

Choice is associated with the freedom of the citizen. Some who have written about choice of school have accepted it as a largely self-evident virtue (see, for instance, Kemble's '*How to Choose a School*', 1981, or Taylor's *Choosing a School*, 1981) while Peters (1966, p.307) argues that a democrat 'would also demand, as a rational being committed to liberty, as well as to fairness and the consideration of interest, that as much freedom of choice should be given to parents and to children as is consistent with the pursuit of objectives falling under the other two fundamental principles', those two principles being education available to all and being fairly distributed. Occasionally those who advocate choice in the name of freedom also defend the retention of barriers of access to education on other grounds. For instance, in their *Education and Freedom*, Cox and Marks (1980) support parental choice of school (p.9 and p.29) but state that 'some selection in terms of ability might be necessary' (p.31).

Economic Arguments about Choice

Economic arguments have mostly favoured choice in order to replicate market forces within a government monopoly or near-monopoly. It is argued that competition enhances both effectiveness (getting the job done) and efficiency (getting it done at the best price). Counter-arguments concern the thwarting of professional judgements to meet the demands of an ill-informed public, and disadvantage to pupils whose parents make no choice, as well as reduced facility for area planning and economies of scale.

An associated argument is that schools become more accountable if they are obliged to respond to market forces. Accountability of schools may be interpreted as a rendering of account (explaining) or as institutional responsiveness. It is accountability in the second sense that is associated with parental choice. However, evidence of schools in fact changing their professional practice to meet parental preferences is scant and the topic deserves research.

Weak and Strong Choice

Tickell (1980, p.16) has distinguished between 'weak' choice which is between options prescribed by others (as between TV channels, or items on a menu) and 'strong' choice involving the chooser in formulating the options so as 'to produce the best possible matching between what is wanted/needed and what is provided.'

In Denmark a group of parents can get 85 per cent state subsidy to set up and run their own school in the way they want, and the resulting 'little school' movement has blossomed. This is strong choice. It may be argued that the Grant Maintained or 'opting-out' system introduced by the 1988 Act is a move in that direction since it allows parents to take their school out of LEA control and to receive a central government grant to enable its governors (among whom are parents) substantially to run it. However, the character of the school cannot be changed immediately and once one generation of parents has opted out, the next generation is largely bound by that decision. It is a long way from the Danish scheme. If parents were a voting majority among the governors, as they are on Danish state school boards, the claim to 'strong choice' might be more convincing, but it seems that professionals rather than parents may continue to determine the objectives of British schools, with a few exceptions in the fee-charging sector.

Thus, ours is a system of 'weak' parental choice – choice between options prescribed by others. As such it is largely non-threatening to the 'educational establishment', though its implementation involves more administration than if bureaucrats were to allocate children to schools or learning groups. It also introduces some uncertainties and limitations on advance planning by LEAs, as will be discussed later.

The Group Nature of Schooling

Parental choice is especially relevant with regard to attaching a child to a learning group. Of necessity schooling is organised in groups. Schools, classes, sets, streams, bands, blocks, subject options, pastoral care units, and so on, are all aggregations of pupils. The *modes* by which grouping is implemented may be open to debate, but the *need* for grouping is unquestioned. Even if one-to-one personal tuition for all children were desirable, it is an economic impossibility. We tend to make virtue out of necessity by pointing to social and, in some cases, educational advantages in having children working together, but there is no practicable alternative. The day may come, we are told by futurologists, when each child may stay at home to learn from individualised computer programmes, thereby making redundant schools and their sub-groups; but I feel safe in predicting that for several generations children will continue to attend specialist school-like institutions and will continue to be organised in groups. Certainly if we consider present-day schools, nobody can deny that children are grouped and that buildings, classrooms, timetables and educational processes are structured for groups.

The decisions by which a child is attached to groups can be important, sometimes determinant, with regard to the quality and effectiveness of his/her schooling. Even the most 'comprehensive' school system is full of diversity. Every school, class, course, remedial or pastoral group has its own characteristics which influence the nature of educational experience within it. The effect of the 1988 Act will be to decrease diversity in the curriculum but to increase it in other ways. If the nature of a group does indeed matter, then the decision which attaches a child to a group also matters. The central question here is the extent to which parental choice should play a part in such decisions.

Selection, Allocation and Choice

Some words to denote the attachment of a child to a group are neutral, not indicating who makes the decision. ('Attachment' and 'placement' are examples.) Others are associated with specific processes. 'Selection' implies that there are qualities in the child which can be identified by professionals and used as the grounds for attaching that child to a particular kind of group – for instance, selection for remedial help. The word 'allocation' is sometimes used to indicate random attachment by bureaucratic methods (e.g. catchment area, alphabetical order) unrelated to the characteristics of the child, while 'choice' has come to imply that the decision rests with the parent or the pupil. For convenience I shall use these words on that basis:

Selection Attachment of children to groups by professionals (including teachers) based on the supposed qualities of the children related to the specialist nature of groups.

Allocation Attachment of children to groups by bureaucrats (including teachers) on a random basis without reference to the qualities of either the children or the groups.

Choice Attachment of children to groups through decisions by parents or pupils.

Since the comprehensive movement is often viewed as anti-selective, it is worth noting that all three processes can be found in a typical comprehensive system. The child may attend a school through parental choice, may be allocated to a class because of the first letter of his surname, and may be selected for remedial help or a Mathematics set. The essential question at each stage is: who decides? The comprehensive movement was, in part, a reaction against the perceived unfairnesses in selection to different kinds of schools. Now we are beginning to recognise that blind allocation can also involve unfairness. It could be that there is a place for all three modes, supplemented by consultation; but in each instance someone must have the final say. The debate about selection, allocation or choice is about who should make that final decision, but it is also about administrative convenience set against citizens' rights.

Diversity and Choice

The phrase 'diversity and choice' appeared in Jencks' book *Inequality* (1972, p.257) as part of an egalitarian argument, and it has been used to describe a movement in Australian education (Brown, 1980; Pettit, 1982).

Choice is meaningless without diversity. A menu with only one dish precludes choices, apart from the option of walking out of the restaurant; and most families cannot afford to walk out of schooling. One of the ideals of the comprehensive movement was to remove diversity of provision, but it is unlikely that anyone seriously regards that as a practical proposition today. We are bound to accept that there are dissimilarities in the personalities of headteachers, the aims and ethos of schools, the composition of pupil intakes and areas from which they come, the competences of teachers, the content of syllabuses, teaching methods, the age and structure of buildings, the extent of facilities, the size (and therefore provision) of schools, and many other features which result in disparate provision.

The 1988 Inspectorate report on English secondary schools catalogues differences in formal curricula, organisation, management, resources, staffing and standards. It contains statements such as:

> Nearly three-quarters of the schools inspected were performing satisfactorily in general and half had some notably good features. Fewer than one in 10 was judged poor or very poor overall, but a further fifth had some major areas of weakness. (para. 10)

> ... the continued shortage of properly qualified teachers of physical science, mathematics and design technology affected the work of some schools. (para. 18)

> There was a considerable amount and variety of assessment undertaken but, because of a general absence of over-arching school policies to determine practice, there was undue variation in the ways in which it took place. (para. 26)

With regard to subjects offered in years 1 – 3 'a fairly standard pattern' was recorded, but Appendix 4 shows a huge variation of subjects on offer after that.

Lest anyone imagine that the Scottish system lacks such diversity, the Scottish Inspectorate (1984) includes statements such as 'generally authorities leave headteachers to run their schools with a large measure of freedom.' (para. 2.7.2) and refer to 'variety in teaching styles' (para. 3.3.2), 'the variable quality of professional competence in almost all departments' (para. 3.9.4) and that 'The subject departments are virtually free to decide what to teach (within the national syllabuses), when things should be taught, and how they should be presented.' Researchers repeatedly report the same. Syllabuses, assessment procedures, modes of contacting parents (or not), and examinations taken can be markedly different. An analysis of 188 Scottish secondary schools' handbooks showed that the number of subjects taken in the Scottish Certificate of Education (Higher level) could vary from as few as eight subjects in one school to as many as 28 in another, with 18 being the commonest number.

I have devoted space to emphasising the degree to which we have a patchwork of approaches in our schools since a myth appears to persist that 'comprehensiveness' means sameness of provision; that a child is as well off in one school as in another. The falsity of this belief is important in the issue of choice. If schools can differ so much, then those responsible for the child's education deserve some facility to choose.

Although the national curriculum slightly reduces *curricular* diversity (i.e. makes schools marginally more 'comprehensive'), other aspects of the 1988 Act increase the degree of variation between schools and therefore the case for choice. Not only does that case apply as much to primary as to secondary schools, but it is relevant to choice *within* a school, as are all the general points made above.

Equality and Choice

Reference was made earlier to Christopher Jencks' influential book

Inequality and his argument that parental choice is a means for equalising people's claim on a public resource. In particular, choice of school in the past has been the privilege of those able to buy houses in favoured areas, whereas open enrolment extends this privilege to all families, though with administrative restrictions, which will be discussed later.

The counter-arguments are these. First, even if open enrolment gives equal opportunities to *parents*, it does not necessarily do so for all *pupils* since the benefits of choice depend upon the parents exercising the privilege. In particular, it has been suggested that the facility will largely be used by middle-class families, not working-class parents. Preliminary evidence does not support the class-biased argument. In Scotland, where open enrolment was introduced in 1981, the Glasgow University national study (1986) of 153 schools found that slightly more placing requests were made by manual worker families than by non-manual worker families, and that the proportions of social class groups making placing requests generally reflected the proportions of those groups in the study areas. In brief, choice was not a middle-class phenomenon.

The second argument that choice may be inegalitarian is that if families in disadvantaged areas use the facility, they would damage neighbourhood schools by deserting them, perhaps to the point of forcing their closure. The Glasgow University study found some limited evidence of this, but also found that falling birth rates, migration patterns and housing policies had greater effect.

Finally there is the suggestion that choice creates 'ghettos' as choice 'may come to be exercised on grounds of social and racial prejudice.' (Tomlinson, 1988, p.11). Any family may make a choice, irrespective of social and racial origins. Surely it is only if the people of an area are *denied* choice that they or their children are trapped in a ghetto? Open enrolment may cut across LEA schemes by which catchment area boundaries are drawn to create as wide a social mix as possible in schools, and there is some evidence that parents use the facility of choice to seek or to avoid schools where certain languages or cultures predominate, but if the Scottish rate of requests resulting from open enrolment (just over 2 per cent of the pupil population a year) typifies the effects of open enrolment, then generally the impact will be relatively low. Having said that, the ethnic density of some schools is likely to increase with parental choice and that has to be set against the benefits of the scheme.

Are Parents Competent to Choose?

It has been suggested that most parents do not have the technical competence to choose either a school or a work-group for their child. Yet if all schools and all classes are staffed by professionals and inspected, how is it possible for parents to make a 'wrong' choice – or a worse one than allocation would produce? Much allocation is done without knowledge of either the school or the child, either by catchment area or by some 'blind' system such as alphabetical order of surname.

The parental incompetence argument would seem to be an irrelevancy except where there are specialist (e.g. remedial) classes.

Parental Choice and Pupil Attainment

I would like to advance a hypothesis, not an assertion: that pupils' improved in-school attainment may be related to successful parental choice. We know that there is a correlation between home background and in-school attainment and at least some of the home effect seems to involve parental encouragement of the child's learning process. If attitudes affect motivation, then we might expect better performance from pupils whose parents have confidence in the school. Conversely we might expect less high achievement from those whose parents convey to them constant lack of confidence in the school. A useful study might therefore be carried out to see if *improved* attainment correlates with parental choice.

Open Enrolment to Schools

The general points made above apply to both choice *between* schools and to choice *within* a school. The special circumstances of each will now be considered, though the question of 'opting out' (which may be seen as a mode of group choice) will be discussed separately in chapter 8 on governing bodies.

The 1988 legislation on open enrolment will influence the actions of education authorities more than those of schools, but since this books is written for teachers it will concentrate on aspects over which schools, rather the LEAs, can take initiatives. It will make only brief reference to administrative problems facing education authorities. Also, detailed procedures will differ from LEA to LEA.

The essence of the law, however, is easy enough to describe. There has been controversy for a long time about whether the legal obligation, established in the 1944 Act (and counterpart Acts in Scotland), that pupils should be educated in accordance with their parents' wishes gave the right to parents to choose a school, and various test cases began to clarify the limitations. However, laws of 1980 for England and Wales and 1981 for Scotland confirmed parents' rights to request a preferred school and they required education authorities (and governors) to agree to the request unless certain conditions applied, in which case the parents' request could be turned down. Also each education authority had to have an appeal procedure and provide information to assist parents.

The Scottish law of 1981 was more detailed than its English 1980 counterpart and, crucially, amendment to the Bill removed a loophole. The Bill's original wording would have allowed education authorities to proclaim intake maxima by which authorities so-minded might virtually deny parental choice. That was removed in the Act. A Scottish school is deemed to be full on the basis of two main measures: the physical capacity of the school and the fact that class size maxima are laid down in Scottish teachers' contracts. While this formula does not overcome all problems, the national study of the system carried out shortly after its implementation (University of Glasgow, 1986) generally reports it working well, with difficulties in only a minority of mainly urban secondary schools, little effect on most schools and satisfactory uptake by working-class families. Another Scottish advantage is the fact that an education authority can transfer a teacher to another school at will. Thus adaptation of staff numbers to suit pupil numbers is a relatively simple and inexpensive matter.

The English 1980 Act, however, while clarifying broad principles, was sufficiently vague in its wording to enable authorities to apply it variously, in some cases seemingly evading the spirit of parental choice.

Stillman and Maychell (1986) picked out the two main weaknesses of the Act:

> First, the Act places clear limitations on the requirement of an LEA to comply with parents' wishes, thus sowing the inevitable seeds of dispute as to what constitutes efficient use of education and resources. Secondly, the Act consistently uses the term 'preference' as opposed to 'choice', thus again giving scope for misinterpretation. (p.3)

Two broad approaches emerged, one using catchment areas and one not. Some authorities operating catchment areas expected children to go to their designated (local) school unless the parents expressed a wish for an alternative school. Systems differed as to whether the parents automatically received a form on which to apply for a school outside 'their' catchment area, whether they had to apply for such a form or whether they had to write a letter. The ease and helpfulness of the scheme obviously affects the rate of uptake of choice. It was even known for a few English authorities to have indicated that a parent, having expressed a preference for an out-of-catchment area school and failing to get a place there, might forfeit any preferential right to a place at the local school (Maychell, 1986, p.15). In other words, encouragement or, by contrast, disincentive to state a preference could be built in to the local system.

Other authorities used the second approach by which parents are given a list of schools and are invited to select from it. In some cases only one choice was permitted, in others more. Where parents could nominate several schools their choices might all be treated as equally strong or the system might ask parents to list them in order of preference.

There was a problem in deciding the point at which a school is oversubscribed and families could be turned away. Authorities in England and Wales were permitted to determine (and had to publicise) the admission limit for each school each year. Authorities had a high level of discretion in deciding the grounds upon which the maximum intake might be determined. Describing it as 'this arbitrary figure', Maychell (1986, p.16) stated that in England or Wales 'an LEA which operates a linked primary/secondary system and which sets each secondary school's intended intake figure to correspond exactly with the number of pupils in the final year of the contributary schools leaves no scope for parents outside of that linked system to opt in, unless parents of children already within that system opt out. Even in Authorities without catchment areas or linked systems, intended intakes can be set very tightly . . . in order to leave very few vacant places . . .'

The most important change with regard to choice of school introduced by the 1988 Act was to remove artificial barriers to schools which still had spare places. Although the effect is similar to the Scottish 1981 system, the mechanism is different. Schools (starting with secondary schools from the school year 1989–90 followed by primary schools), must admit pupils at least up to their 'standard number'. The 'standard number' in essence is the number admitted in 1979. However, an authority may admit more than the 'standard number' if there is space in the school and a higher figure than the 'standard number' would apply if the 1988 admissions were higher. The governors of a school or the LEA can request the Secretary of State to allow a figure lower than the 'standard number' to apply, for instance if it has reduced space, and since some schools have converted rooms to specialist use (e.g. laboratories which hold smaller class numbers) this is an important safeguard. Voluntary schools can retain pre-existing rights to reserve some places for pupils of particular religions.

Some Administrative Difficulties

Most of the reservations about open enrolment have cited administrative difficulties rather than objections in principle. To keep these problems in perspective, it may be helpful to note the greater difficulties – and costs – which have been faced in countries where choice is carried further than in the UK. Belgium provides an extreme example since on top of the usual categories of denominational/non-denominational schools, comprehensive and 'traditional' approaches, geographic factors and local reputation, it also has the massive problem of three languages, and in Brussels allowance is made for these in a system of choice. In the Netherlands where independent schools are state-subsidised choice has additional relevance. Open enrolment in the various British systems does pose some, but comparatively less extensive, administrative difficulties. Some of the more prominent are listed below.

1 *Open enrolment will accelerate school closures.* Hart (1988, p.168) has predicted the 'severely undersubscribed schools will have to close because surplus places will have to be taken out of use' and he guessed 'that the economics of the situation will force LEAs to close them rather than to keep them open with additional financial support.' If so, he argues, 'this will lead to fewer schools and a further reduction in parental choice.' This may turn out to be true, though it is a matter for debate whether the right to choose an unwanted school is really choice at all, and the scale of the problem *directly*

resulting from enrolment preferences may be small. Birth rate, migration patterns and housing policies generally have more impact on closures than do choice patterns.

2 *The 'rump' left in an unpopular school will still have to be given education.* This is true. However, since most choice happens in urban areas where schools are relatively close to each other, transport to another school is a feasible solution, though disruptive to a community, to families and to teachers.

3 *Denial of travel expenses to disadvantaged families wanting to make choices means that choice is income-related.* Again, this is a valid objection and it may be noted that there has been little discussion of means-tested travel vouchers.

4 *Old buildings, huts and temporary accommodation may have to be reopened if the 1979 'standard number' is to be met.* Some schools have thankfully closed unsatisfactory buildings since 1979. Since the 'standard number' for enrolment is based on the 1979–80 roll, popular demand for places could force the reopening of such accommodation.

5 *Accommodation which has been transferred for community use since 1979 may have to be reclaimed to meet the 'standard number'.*

6 *Choice patterns may be based upon social and racial (rather than educational) opinions and may result in schools which are more culturally skewed than would otherwise be the case.* This is likely to happen. It may be noted that when it does, the receiving schools may in some instances achieve a 'better' social mix as a result, especially where schools in middle-class or other favoured areas are required to take in pupils of social and ethnic types less common in their areas. Usually, however, the effect is the reverse.

7 *The facility for politicians and administrators to plan ahead in terms of pupil rolls and catchment boundaries is reduced.* This is true, though the low take-up rate in rural areas makes it mainly an urban problem. However, the problems arising are not insuperable and the facility, for instance, to adjust catchment zone boundaries to increase the balance of social or ethnic groups remains, even if choice patterns sometimes work against it.

We are therefore concerned with what is, seemingly by general agreement, a desirable objective – increased, though not unfettered, parental choice – accompanied by practical difficulties which have to be faced by administrators at LEA and school levels when and if they arise. The Scottish experience of open enrolment suggests that these problems are likely to affect a minority of English schools, but that most will encounter few or no difficulties. It is also likely that those wanting, for whatever reasons, to discredit the system will give publicity to the problems in the pockets where they happen and that the press will willingly highlight them.

We summarised one of the findings of the Scottish national study (Glasgow University, 1986, p.334) with the following words:

Administrators in education offices have borne the brunt of extra work, especially in initiating systems and where full schools result in large numbers of refusals. Preparing for appeals also creates work.

Yet, we also found that schools generally found the system straightforward to operate: that the impact on school closures was small; that staff morale (reported as low for other reasons) tended to be unaffected by parental choice, with a few clear exceptions; that choices rarely resulted in curricular changes; that parents found the system easy to use and found information prepared to be helpful. Despite dire warnings of widespread chaos which preceded open enrolment in Scotland, the system generally operates smoothly – largely thanks to the work of administrators in education offices.

Relations with Parents: Information

Moving from the problems of administrators to positive action to involve parents, which is the theme of this book, the question of information for parents is crucial if parents are to make well-informed choices. Authorities and school staffs can either make facts readily available, conceal them or distort them. They can either give advice or refrain from giving advice. There can be little doubt that from the client's viewpoint the most open, honest and helpful approach is preferable. However, a long tradition in Britain of regarding not only the curriculum but all aspects of the school as a 'secret garden' reserved for teachers does not disappear easily, though, like the Cheshire cat, this attitude does seem to be passing through a phase of coming and going.

Open enrolment has financial implications for schools, and these are linked to information. If funds are allocated to schools on the basis of age-weighted pupil numbers, then parental choice can have direct impact upon a school's income. Pupils are equivalent to money, like a voucher scheme without the voucher. Schools must therefore assess their communications with parents not only for reasons of professional/client relations and good education, but for income reasons also. Expressed bluntly, schools may want to attract customers by improving their methods of communication.

For parents there are three main sources of information: education authorities, schools themselves and other agencies. 'Other agencies' includes national organisations such as NCPTA, SPTC, PTAW, ACE, CASE, NAPE, CEDC, the Consumer Councils and others, which are discussed more fully in chapter 7. Magazines and newspapers carry articles of advice to parents. Even estate agents, aware that a good school in the neighbourhood can affect house prices, have been known to advise potential buyers about schools. Then, of course, there are other parents.

Guides to parental choice of school are also on the market. One of the most controversial is a booklet (Anderson, 1982) which adopts a somewhat negative approach by advising parents on how to detect a bad school. The advocated process includes standing by the school gates to see how many staff and pupils arrive late in the morning, analysing political stickers on cars in the staff car-park, making an informal and unannounced visit to the school to supplement the formal visit, making a point of viewing pupils' lavatories as well as classrooms, and a series of probing questions for the headteacher. The indignation which this prompted among some teachers was understandable; but is such indignation justified? Surely the essential point is that covert detective work by parents should not be necessary. Few could seriously question the right of parents to have the information which they need to make judgements in choosing a school, so the first step, presumably, must be to make it easily accessible. Allow parents to see the toilets and the car-parks. Encourage them to do so. Even though the booklet is amusingly extreme and sometimes deals in sweeping generalities, it does challenge us as teachers to stand back and to ask just how open to scrutiny our public service (and its use and misuse by pupils) is and how helpful our provision of information is in practice.

Education (School Information) Regulations, 1981, require education authorities in England to send certain 'general information', free of charge, to parents whose children are progressing to secondary or middle schools. Others may obtain it on request, and it must be available in schools, education offices and public libraries. It includes the names, addresses and telephone numbers of maintained schools, their sizes and age ranges, particular features (e.g. whether denominational, coeducational, comprehensive), arrangements for transport and other practical matters. Besides this general overview material, each school must publish, must up-date annually and must make available free of charge certain detailed additional information. This includes descriptive facts about the kind of school it is, arrangements for parents to visit it and the names of the headteacher and chairperson of the governing body. With regard to the syllabus, the subjects provided at different levels and special provisions must appear, as must arrangements for sex education and religious education. Secondary schools must also give details of public examinations for which pupils are prepared, and recent public examination results for the school. Details of streaming, setting and homework must be included, as must the organisation of school discipline, school uniform policy and (in secondary schools) arrangements for careers guidance.

There are similar rules in Wales, and there are special requirements for information about teaching of Welsh and the use of the Welsh language as a medium of instruction. The Scottish regulations (published in 1982) are comparable but not identical to those of England. (For details see SED regulations, regional leaflets, and Atherton *et al.*, 1986.) Thus, apart from general guidance leaflets published by the Government, the first level of information must be the education authority. Some education authorities provide the basic, required information in a dry bureaucratic form, and only the minimum points required. Others set out to make the information widely known and to present it in a readable and helpful format including, in some cases, maps showing how to get to each school, photographs of schools, and lists of people who can be contacted for further information. The booklets of the London Borough of Brent have been especially lively, not only drawing attention to the fact that it is the parent '– not the teachers – who is ultimately responsible' for education of the child, that schools do differ from each other, that they have 'their own jargon and all too often in the past have seen parents as an interference' and that 'it has become harder for parents to understand what schools are doing and why.' Having urged parents to visit schools, the booklets discuss key issues so that parents will have confidence to ask the right questions. Checklists are even provided of questions which parents might ask themselves and of questions which they can pose to each school before making their choice.

The handbook published by the school itself is also an important document. There is a fuller discussion of school brochures and hand-books in chapter 10. Here the obvious may be recorded: that hand-books should provide as much information as simply and as clearly as possible, making sure that parents are involved in compiling such publications, either through the parents' association or by some other mechanism. Obviously those responsible must review the document(s) annually. Besides the main formal handbook, it can be helpful if topic guides are produced either on particular aspects of learning or for specific levels of the school. The parents' association might also have a leaflet with contact addresses and telephone numbers of parents who are willing to discuss the qualities of the school as seen by families using it.

In the University of Glasgow study of parental choice in Scotland (1986), we found that handbooks, usually written by teachers, were often formal and impersonal in tone and sometimes contained unex-plained jargon; some seemed more concerned with laying down the school's requirements than with providing information which parents might need. Most of the parents in our study stated that they had visited the school before sending their child there, but that does not provide good grounds for neglecting the preparation of handbooks.

However, it would seem reasonable to expect teachers themselves to be sources of both information and advice. Curiously, there are signs that they sometimes prefer not to be so. While factual information is usually provided by headteachers or teachers on request, advice is less easy to come by. In our study some interesting indicators about the nature of advice from teachers emerged. Where teachers did give considered opinions about schools to assist parents in choosing, it tended to be influential, but that advice *was usually given unofficially*, especially by friends or relatives who happened also to be teachers. Headteachers interviewed were unhappy about either themselves or their staff making value judgements which could affect parents' choices. Even if they knew the children and local schools well they felt uneasy about judging fellow-teachers, and there was strong resistance to developing competition between schools. Further, teachers were often surprisingly ignorant about the nature of neighbouring schools.

Yet at the same time there was a tendency to condemn parents for making choices on the basis of 'rumour', 'gossip' and 'the jungle drums'. If the profession itself cannot or will not provide sufficient information and advice, surely it cannot reasonably complain if parents turn to the other obvious source: parents with children having inside knowledge. The closing of ranks by teachers poses an important professional problem. Concealing information and views about colleagues is as old as the professions. Yet even a doctor may recommend specialist A, thereby *not* recommending specialist B, without actually saying that B is not much good. It seems to me that teachers, especially headteachers, at one level of the system ought to make themselves conversant with the differences between local schools at the next level and feel able, at least, to recommend a school, even if they stop short of condemning another. They should also be able to describe special features of schools. The question of providing accurate information and reference-points for advice with regard to choice of school could be an issue which every governing body might discuss with its parents' association, if necessary setting about the systematic gathering of relevant information from neighbouring schools, perhaps with the assistance of their governing bodies and parents' associations.

Another technique is for parents' associations to provide members who can act as guides for the school. Not only does this mean that enquiring families can feel that they are getting a parents' eye view and are able to ask questions which they would hesitate to ask teachers, but it saves staff time. A brief session on technical questions can be held with a teacher or headteacher after the guided tour. I was once shown round a school in Denmark by a mother who paused occasionally to suckle her baby; what a sensible arrangement. The use of pupils to show visiting parents around the school has the advantage of providing an insider's view, but it is unfair if it distracts them from their studies too often.

While information is essential for well-based choice, it has an even more important place in the continuing liaison between home and school after the child has entered the school. We should not make the mistake of assuming that handbooks and other sources of information exist only for purposes of choice.

Clause 14 of the 1988 Act gives the Secretary of State the power to make regulations about what additional information the LEA, governors and headteachers are to make available in relation to both the National Curriculum and the testing associated with it at the ages of seven, 11, 14 and 16. The particular question of publishing aggregated test and examination results is discussed separately in the next section. However, it is clearly important to parental choice that syllabuses, teaching methods and the ways by which each school implements the national curriculum be made readily available to parents before they choose a school. The notion of charging parents for such information, raised in section 14(3), is not unreasonable as long as the charges are not so high as to deter parents from obtaining the information. This requires some nice judgements on the part of the governors and headteacher.

The attraction of collaborating with the school's parents' association with regard to both content and costs is obvious. However, the parents' association may prefer to prepare its own information material more geared to what parents need to know than what governors want them to believe. Much will depend on the quality of the school's professionalism and the extent to which local parents are convinced of it.

Publication of National Test and Public Examination Results

Chapter 3 discussed national testing at the end of the four 'key stages' of education identified in the 1988 Act: at seven, 11, 14 and 16. It quoted the Secretary of State's three purposes for such testing: first, informing parents and teachers about a child's progress; secondly, identifying problems and diagnosing needs of the child; and thirdly, assessing the achievements of schools and education authorities. This third purpose, is quite different from the first two which are concerned with the individual child. Assessing institutional performance has high relevance to choice of school, but the extent to which tests of pupils and examination results can be used validly to assess the quality of a school has been a matter for debate.

There are those who point to examination results as being important indicators of a school's quality. Anderson (1982) maintains that examination results not only indicate the academic standards of a school but also provide a clue of the extent to which it is a caring school. For schools to be 'warm' and 'happy' places, he argues, is not enough; to help children to have examination success is also a sign of caring. Yet much material on this topic argues that there are dangers in publishing each school's results. Smith (1985, p.153) provides a typical example:

> The criteria through which parents exercise that choice and the decisions which they make can cause serious problems of distortion for the secondary head. All schools' public examination results are now public property in the local library. It may only be a matter of time before the first 'Good learning guide' compiled by a parent pressure group along the lines of a 'Good eating guide' appears on the local newsagents' shelves. Value judgements are arrived at without taking account of staff movement, quality of entry, local authority policy or any of the other multifarious factors which skew results in a particular subject in a particular year.

This raises the bigger and more complex issue of how the effectiveness of a school can be measured, and some research has been done on the issue. It is rather sad that, in the words of Gray *et al.*, (1983, p.275) 'our general view is that the question of school effectiveness in contemporary Britain is unresolved.' However, that does not mean that we should ignore the indicators which do exist and, of course, examination results not only exist but also can be tabulated, and the same will apply to national test results. The difficulty is that the forces leading to good or bad examination results are not solely the efforts of the school. There is evidence that home background and home learning affect them as well, so that a school's results are not entirely to the credit or discredit of its teachers. As Gray *et al.*, state (p.294):

> As a mere description of how pupils from a school perform in examinations, the publication of results cannot be faulted, always provided that the results are based on all pupils in the age–group and not just on those who are entered for the examination. More-over, examination results are a very good measure of at least two characteristics of a school: the social composition and the intellec-tual composition of its intake.

Gray *et al.*, (pp.296–7) go on to question the claims that the policy of publishing examination results identifies effective schools, enables parents to choose the best school or encourages good practice. They state (p.296):

> The evidence, both from our own study and from others, is suffi-cient to show clearly that, if the unadjusted examination results of a school were to be used as a measure of a school's effectiveness, this would be seriously misleading and unfair to schools, parents and pupils alike.

The report of the Task Group on Assessment and Testing (Black Report, 1987, para. 12) made the following seemingly discouraging statement about experience in other countries:

> Publication of test results for use outside the school is virtually non-existent, except in some States in the USA. These results have been published with adjustments for socio-economic background effects: but while this can give a fairer reflection of the achieve-ments of a school, it has made the information too complicated for the general public to understand.

However the Black Report switches to a more optimistic note, pointing out (para. 18) that 'these factors do not of themselves affect the validity of a criterion-referenced attainment target', and that results can be aggregated in different ways – by class, by groups of classes, by subjects, by schools, by groups of schools (para. 24). Having argued that 'the use of such results to compare schools' performance would be liable to lead to complacency if results were adjusted, and to miscon-ception if they were not' (para. 133), they offer a solution (para. 134) that:

> Reports to the public of national assessment results should there-fore always be by means of a report produced by the school, authenticated by the local education authority ... Results should not be adjusted for socio-economic background but the report

should include a general statement, prepared by the Local Authority for the area, of the nature and possible size of socio-economic and other influences which could affect schools in the area.

Yet it is possible that rather more can be done with regard to examination results than a (perhaps somewhat defensive) statement in a school report. First, instead of casting doubt on the value of publishing results, we should question the propriety of concealing them. Since results do exist, surely there would have to be very good reasons indeed (such as national security) to deny their ready access to citizens, so let us start by assuming that they will be available and that they *should* be available and that parents will make reference to them. The next point is that, although the emphasis of public debate has been upon the unfairness of comparing schools and teachers on the basis of something which is profoundly influenced by factors outside the school, we must presume that the quality of teaching does have *some* effect on them. Indeed, the evidence of Gray *et al.*, and annual analyses by the ILEA, as well as those of Rutter and his team (1979) and others do provide evidence of differential effects from schools. Teachers do influence examination results to some extent and few teachers would want to deny that.

The next point is that if results reflect out-of-school learning as well as in-school learning, to what extent have the schools attempted to influence the former, and especially home-learning? At primary school level it is becoming accepted that teachers can and should encourage parents to assist with reading, number and such like; but rather less has been done at the secondary level. Would a sign of a 'good' or an 'effective' school be the extent to which it recognised education as a partnership? Could it encourage for all children what middle-class parents already provide for theirs? Could test and examination results come to reflect, among other things, the level of a school's initiatives in home–school liaison as well as its preparation of pupils for examinations? It is possible, but we do not yet know.

However, even if examination results do not provide a fair or accurate picture of *teachers' efforts*, they may provide a useful guide for *parental choice*. If parents want to choose not only good teacher performance but also good home support, a setting where fellow-pupils' backgrounds tend to encourage them to aspire rather than to give up, an ethos which takes school and its work seriously, then examination results, since they reflect a mixture of these things, may be indicators of the learning environment and therefore grounds for choice. There are broad social objections to this argument, of course, but the individual parent is not concerned with those.

One approach is to compare a school's test or exam results with those of three or four other schools having similar catchment areas or intakes, as measured by incidence of free meals, clothing grants and truancy which can be amalgamated into a common index of intake for each school. If comparison is with schools of similar intake, then differences in examination results are more likely to reflect in-school processes. An education authority, a governing body or a PTA could carry out such an exercise for a locality and make results known.

Finally, there is the technique of comparing a school's results with several previous years for the same school. Since the broad nature of its intake will remain relatively constant, a steady increase or decrease in good test or examination grades could reflect in-school forces. Again, the importance of viewing this subject-by-subject deserves attention as does the need to relate results to the total numbers of pupils in the exam-taking age group for each year. Perhaps every governing body (school board in Scotland) should prepare such information and make it public.

The purpose of this section has not been to provide an easy answer to a complex problem, but rather to suggest that on balance it is better to publish test and examination results (perhaps accompanied by caveats and comparisons) than to conceal them; that their publicity does more good than harm; but that they should be considered in terms of what they reflect. Hopefully more work will be done to help parents make better informed use of them. That parents do make use of examination results in choosing secondary schools is certain. According to question-naire responses in the Glasgow University study (1986), half the parents who made placing requests at secondary level were influenced by examination results either 'quite a lot' or else they regarded them as 'most important'. The system cannot now retreat from publishing examination and test results; it might therefore assist parents to inter-pret them more precisely, especially by providing them in more mean-ingful comparative forms.

Parental Choice Within a School

Broadly speaking it would seem that the arguments which favour parental choice *between* schools also apply, within obvious administra-tive limits, to parental choice *within* a school, and the issue deserves consideration by headteachers and teachers. At the same time it is worth recalling that even if the school claimed to itself the right to have the final say with regard to any particular decision affecting a child's education, that does not prevent teachers from *consulting* with parents before decisions are made.

When discussing item 9 of the suggested 'basic professional mini-mum' in chapter 2, reference was made to 'main determinant decisions' affecting a child's educational future. I suggested that such categories of decisions should be the subject of discussion with parents when the pupil is below age 16, and that in the event of disagreement, the wishes of the parent(s) should prevail. What sorts of decision warrant parental consultation or choice? Those by which a child is attached to a learning group are potentially important, but the reasons which lead to groups being different to each other can be of several sorts. Most obviously and least controversially, there is the question of subject options. It is not difficult to consult with both parents and pupil before allocating the latter to a particular group of subjects, but timetable considerations do enter the picture. We may find administrative convenience competing with, and perhaps squashing what is educationally appropriate or preferred. When this happens, appeal can be made to timetablers or other staff to be as accommodating as possible, or to parents to be understanding; but the prelude to that must be consultation.

More difficult is the question of sets and streams. It is not appropriate to discuss here the benefits and disadvantages of mixed-ability classes, nor those of setting and streaming, though it is interesting to note that the 1988 Inspectorate report on secondary schools states (para. 21):

> There was no evidence that any particular way of organising teaching groups, such as streaming, banding or setting by ability, or mixed-ability grouping, improved teaching and learning in themselves.

However, the point is that allocation to a set or a stream can be a crucial decision for the pupil affected and to do it without parental involvement is, in my assessment, unprofessional; yet it happens. I like the Danish approach by which it is considered so important that it is built into the law (Folkeskole Act 1975, section 11.3). At the age of 14 pupils are split into fast and slow streams (or 'courses') and prior to that the teacher(s), parent(s) and pupil must have a three-sided consultation to decide the question. Not surprisingly there is usually agreement, and of course the professional assessment by teachers, supported by relevant data (which must be available at the meeting), often determines the issue. However, the law makes it clear whose view is decisive if there is disagreement; being responsible for their child's education, parents have the final say.

When the child is coming up to the public examinations, taken at about 16 years of age, a similar meeting must occur to decide which subjects he/she will take in the examination. At this stage, when the young person has reached (or is about to reach) the stage when parents are no longer responsible for his/her education, it is the pupil who decides in the event of disagreement. Such an arrangement seems to me to be logical. It means that established principles rather than the convenience of teachers determine the issues.

It may be noted that these events happen at two important decision-making ages: 14 and 16. It may be that in the English system, if significant decisions are to be made about the child in light of assessment at seven, 11, 14 and 16, something akin to the Danish approach might be applied at all four stages. At the least it seems reasonable that each school should have a clear and well-publicised appeal system by which parents or guardians can refer upwards for reconsideration any decision affecting their child with which they are not happy.

Moving further along the scale of controversy, what about parental choice of teaching methods? For some this would appear to be impossible since teaching methods are generally common within one school.

But not always; let me give an example. I know of two schools which were amalgamated, and their primary level philosophies were quite different. One was committed to integrated day teaching, the other to providing increased subject-based teaching from the age of ten onwards. To solve the problem the school took an imaginative step: it allowed the parents of ten-year olds to choose which method they wanted for their child. The upshot was the creation of two integrated-day classes and one subject-based class at that level.

One source of difference between learning groups which is repeatedly identified by pupils and parents but generally only acknowledged informally by teachers, is the difference in quality of teachers. How often does one hear the comment at primary level, 'He's lucky. He's in Mrs X's class this year,' or at secondary level a complaint such as 'She's hardly done more than mark time in Maths this year. She's got that incompetent Mr. Y.' Undoubtedly such personalising can be exaggerated, but it is a factor and, being seen as a factor, it influences both attitudes and motivation. What would be the effect if parents (and/or pupils) could choose their teachers? It is likely that some subject opting in secondary schools already reflects judgements about staff as well as the intrinsic contents of subjects. However, I know of no system by which parents can make choices of staff for their children within a school, and the administrative problems and tensions likely to arise from such a proposition would almost certainly deter head-teachers from initiating it. Of course, for those anxious to increase accountability of individual teachers and to create market forces within a school, such an approach would have attractions, but in reality it is unlikely to gain much support.

Choice and consultation are closely allied. A school which constantly consults with parents about their child's learning processes and progress and is sensitive to the views expressed by parents, will probably find that the more definitive issue of choice need not arise. It is where teachers make unexplained and sometimes arbitrary-seeming decisions without any reference to parents that their professionalism is cast into doubt and grounds for parental choice can most easily be advanced.

6 CLASS-LEVEL LIAISON

Reasons for Class-level Liaison

The class is a unit. As teachers we regard its unity in terms of children plus associated teacher(s) committed to a structured learning process. Generally we do not see parents as part of this unit, and we tend to ignore the potential of the class as a focus for liaison with parents who have (or should have) a common interest in the educational experiences of one class.

The class unit may be one of the most promising levels for development of home–school relations in education. In primary schools and in the lower layers of many secondary schools pupils remain in one group throughout most of the school day and the school year. Even though activities in detail may be individualised, pupils are sharing a common educational experience, a common curricular approach and usually a common cadre of teachers. If that common experience for pupils is the legal, moral and educational concern of parents, then it would seem reasonable to build upon that centre of interest in order to seek parental cooperation and a sense of joint commitment; what Winkley (1985, p. 82) has called creating a 'classbond'. Class-level liaison also offers hope for overcoming some of the school's most frequently bemoaned problems in the effort to establish active rapport with parents. These are:

1 **Not all parents respond to the school's initiatives to involve them**. This is often expressed in the staff-room as: 'The ones we really want to see are the ones who don't come.'
2 **Some parents find schools to be uncomfortable, even intimidating, places.**
3 **Many parents find meetings designed for all levels of the school to be boring, over-formal and not the sort of setting in which they would express their views**. They are usually boring because the topics are of general rather than specific interest. The formalism is often because of the size of gatherings and, it has to be said, because some teachers feel more in control in a formal setting. Size and formalism also often deter parents from expressing views since most are unaccustomed to speaking in public meetings.

4 **Many school events for parents appear to be irrelevant to the immediate education of their particular child.**

5 **Some school events for parents are designed to get money from them**. There would seem to be an urgent need to dissociate parent–teacher liaison from fund raising, especially if high priority is being given to involving more disadvantaged parents.

As was noted in an earlier chapter, the myth of parental apathy has now been exposed. The great majority of parents do come to private consultations about their child's personal progress (unless the school has organised and publicised these meetings badly) and this concern by parents to know about their children's work is a source of motivation which can be tapped. Class-level communication, either written or face-to-face, can build upon this personal interest and may help to meet the problems listed above. A class meeting can be relatively small, informal and friendly and therefore can avoid the intimidating atmosphere of large school events; yet it is also enough of a group to enable the timid to remain quite anonymous without embarrassment. Discussion, if it is about the specific learning experience of the children of **all** present and how these can be assisted in the home, can be seen as personally relevant. And it should be proclaimed widely and repeatedly that class meetings will never be used to prise money out of parents. Making such meetings both educationally relevant to their children's education and non-threatening to parents would be essential to maintain parental support, and some in-service training in these skills could be appropriate.

There is another advantage of such gatherings. Invitations to them can be personalised. I shall describe later the ways by which two or three parents, working in close partnership with the class teacher(s), can contact all parents relevant to the class in a friendly, encouraging and above all individualised way, thereby using gentle neighbourhood pressure to attend which teachers cannot apply unaided. This is possible because the number of parents *for each class* is small.

Class-level liaison is also cheap, both financially and in terms of teachers' time. If explaining to parents the coming curriculum and enlisting their help are desirable objectives, then a monthly or termly informal meeting and perhaps the occasional newsletter require relatively little effort. Of course this makes the assumptions that teachers are sufficiently organised to have planned their teaching in advance and are sufficiently professional to be able to explain it. A disorganised teacher who is simply muddling through might find the prospect of explaining his/her work to parents to be worrying; yet, conversely, it might be argued that a requirement to explain the work of the class to parents might provide precisely the necessary incentive to become organised. For most teachers, however, class liaison is a simple and economic approach, especially when aided by two or three competent and supportive parents.

The value of the class as a level for home–school collaboration is receiving international recognition. In 1986 the European Commission sponsored a seminar of specialists from several countries, to discuss appropriate mechanisms. The following nine **objectives of class-level liaison** were advanced.

1 **To sensitise** parents to their duties, rights and educational importance.
2 **To inform parents** about the curriculum (including teaching methods) in their children's class.
3 **To encourage parents** to support that curriculum by providing appropriate in-home education and interest.
4 **To train** parents how best to provide in-home education for their children.
5 **To involve** parents in discussions and joint activities between home and school.
6 **To inform teachers** about parents' views on schooling and education for that class.
7 **To influence decisions** for that class.
8 **To elect parental delegates** to:
(a) assist in the coordination of educational partnership between parents and teachers of that class, and
(b) represent the parents of that class at school and class councils.
9 **To negotiate** so that the wishes of both parents and teachers can influence the nature of educational activities.

The concepts of parental delegates, influence on class decisions and negotiation reflect traditions of involvement which are commoner in some Continental countries than in Britain. These involve an assumption that the school curriculum is a matter for public concern and not the private property of teachers. However, negotiation is not an inevitable part of class-level liaison, in my view. Also the above list fails to reflect the attractiveness of class meetings as enjoyable, friendly, social events.

There is a danger that the term 'parental delegates' will conjure up visions of shop stewards bargaining with the teacher. Yet different models are possible. I shall use the term 'class parents' to refer to those parents in a class who help to act as intermediaries between the class teacher(s) and the parents with children in that class. Although class parents can be elected by the other parents, this is not the only possible approach. Another is for the class teacher(s) to have the right to invite two or three parents to assist the process of coordination. This could establish a bond of mutual confidence between those parents and staff. Class parents can help to plan class meetings or class newsletters in collaboration with the teacher. In particular they can make personal contact with the other parents.

In Sweden it is common for each class to have a 'class mum' and a 'class dad'. Since no class can exceed 30 pupils in number, this means that if the task of contacting parents is divided between them, each would have to make only 15 calls by telephone or in person as well as by circular. Alternatively, 'telephone chains' can be used to supplement notes. Such friendly, personal invitations to meetings, with emphasis upon the relevance of those meetings to each child's learning, increases the likelihood of turnout. The informal nature of the meetings themselves also encourages involvement since they need not be awe-inspiring or stuffy. A particular technique can be used to get commitment from those who are timid or reluctant: such parents can be asked to play a specific but low-profile part in the arrangements, such as being asked to provide biscuits to go with the coffee or to help assist with arranging chairs in advance.

Further, class parents can help to 'protect' the teacher against improper, unfair or difficult situations. They can set the tone of meetings as amiable and they can ensure that ground-rules are followed, for instance that discussion about the performance or problems of **individuals** is inappropriate. This can apply to teachers and parents as individuals as much as to pupils as individuals. This does not mean that discussion would be individually irrelevant. On the contrary, relevance is the object of the exercise. But nobody would be embarrassed by public consideration of individual problems and discussion can concentrate upon the content and methods of learning rather than the idiosyncrasies of people. If enforcement of such guidelines comes from the class parents rather than from the teacher, that will help to protect the teacher's status.

Since schools which run regular class meetings are still in the minority in Britain, brief further discussion of typical fears by teachers may be appropriate. I have found that resistance by teachers unaccustomed to class meetings can be strong. Lack of confidence in facing the unknown is probably the predominent emotion, though few teachers would admit it. Instead they dwell upon the possibilities of challenge to their professional autonomy, distortion of the curriculum, exposure to attack by an articulate minority and undue commitment of time without extra pay. These points deserve consideration.

With regard to the challenge to professional autonomy and possibilities of distortion of the curriculum, it can be made clear to everyone attending a class meeting that curricular policy is a matter for government (national and local) initiative and coordination, but that much is delegated in turn to the governing body and headteacher and then to individual teachers. The system is not designed for parents of one class to make decisions about what shall be taught or how. Yet, citizens do have rights of assembly and speech and teachers should respect the views of their clients and welcome the chance to explain what the class is doing and why. This last is especially important with regard to modern teaching methods. If the child experiences one mode of learning in the school but that mode is subjected to critical comment in the home, it could undermine faith in the school and motivation. Thus, the sooner that parents understand the methods used by the schools and the reasons for them, the better. Similarly, we must accept that the debate which has been labelled, rather simplistically, 'the traditional versus the progressive' is far from dead among the ranks of teachers and most of us would accept that there is no single, agreed, 'right' way to teach. In such a circumstance, the informed views of parents may be relevant. If suggestions arising out of such discussion are, in the professional view of the teacher, positive ideas which might augment what is taught (either at home or in school), then the teacher might give encouragement or make adaptations.

I have already explained how the establishment of ground-rules, the refusal to discuss individuals (either adult or minor) and the protective use of class parents can minimise the possibility that class meetings would be used inappropriately. Teachers experienced in class meetings confirm that most parents are cooperative and non-aggressive and that such awkward situations as haunt the imaginings of those who have not experienced class gatherings may be exaggerated. Five points are worth bearing in mind by teachers who are hesitant to put their toes into the water.

1 One way of dealing with an unreasonable parent is to leave that task to the influence of the great majority of entirely reasonable parents.
2 Presumably the educational benefits from class meetings are not worth sacrificing because of personal uncertainties.
3 When a majority of parents expresses concern about something, it probably means that the issue does deserve careful consideration by the teacher.
4 Class meetings can be thoroughly enjoyable gatherings, generating a sense of positive achievement.
5 **Most important**: class meetings ought to assist children's education by stimulating and guiding the home-learning element of it to reinforce school-learning.

Finally, there is the question of teachers committing time to class meetings without extra pay. I do not propose to comment on whether such activities should result in additional pay; that is a matter for negotiation and education authority policy, though I return to the issue in chapter 10. If we assume that contact with parents is a normal part of a professional teacher's duties, then one needs to add only that the amount of time involved in class contact is not great relative to other modes of liaison, and if it is potentially beneficial to children then surely it must be professionally appropriate. Besides this there remains the perfectly proper argument that salary should reflect effort, commitment and professionalism.

The Practice of Class-level Liaison

In the EEC survey of nine countries (Macbeth et al., 1984), the 1744 headteachers approached were asked the question 'How often does each class have a general meeting for parents of children in that class to discuss educational matters?' It will be noted that the question referred to **each** class and to **educational** matters; separate questions about school-level meetings helped to ensure that there was no confusion between levels nor with meetings for non-educational reasons. The primary school average for those countries was two meetings per class per year; the secondary school average was 1.7 meetings per class per year. Differences between countries were quite marked as the following national averages, aggregating primary and secondary responses, show:

BELGIUM	1.90	meetings/class/year
DENMARK	2.08	meetings/class/year
FRANCE	1.61	meetings/class/year
W. GERMANY	2.76	meetings/class/year
ITALY	4.13	meetings/class/year
LUXEMBOURG	1.15	meetings/class/year
NETHERLANDS	2.24	meetings/class/year
REP. IRELAND	0.73	meetings/class/year
UNITED KINGDOM	0.89	meetings/class/year

It is immediately obvious that the UK and Ireland use the mechanism of the class meeting less than other countries. Further, nearly one-quarter of headteachers from the UK and Ireland did not answer this question at all and we may guess that this was simply because they were puzzled by a phenomenon which was unfamiliar to them.

Distinctions may be made between different types of class meeting. Earlier in this chapter I described a type of meeting which was open to all parents with children in the class, involved the teacher and presumed that the school would take the initiative to call such meetings. However, other approaches may be found in Europe. We may

(i) distinguish between **open class meetings** (for all parents with children in a class) and **representative class councils** (consisting of elected class delegates);

(ii) distinguish class meetings/councils which are **required by law** from those which are **initiated by the school** or which are **initiated by the PTA/PA**;

(iii) distinguish between class meetings/councils which are **for parents only** and those which are **for parents and teachers** jointly.

The class meeting which is open to all parents and involves teachers is probably the commonest, though there is some variation in the degree of formalism. In chapters 7 and 8 I shall return to the question of elected parents on representative class councils and the present discussion concerns open meetings only.

Opinions differ about whether such meetings should be required by law. Most German provinces have representative class councils by statute, but some also require open meetings. One of the tasks of the Class Care Committee in North-Rhine Westphalia (*Schulmitwirkungsgesetz*, 1977), for instance, is to organise at least two parents' evenings a year for the class. In Baden-Würtenberg (*Schulgesetz*, 1976) the chairman of such a committee must be a parent and it is he/she who must call the open meetings, rather than the class teacher, though that teacher would be present at such meetings. In Hamburg (*Schulgesetz*, 1977) elected parents for each class must keep other parents for that class informed about developments, and they call and lead class meetings.

Legal requirement is not necessary to create class meetings as normal practice. Although Danish law places much stress upon parental involvement in the school system, class meetings are voluntary. Yet they are common, and where they happen, teachers are under a contractual obligation to cooperate. In Sweden it is the national parents' organisation *Hem och Skola* (Home and School) which has especially adopted the class as its basic 'cell' and the class meeting as an important mode of liaison. This will be discussed more fully in chapter 7 on voluntary organisations, but the following extract from a report from the European Parents' Association (EPA, 1988, pp.16–17) may illustrate this approach:

> A class may hold two or three meetings a year and may organise outings or other activities, as well as getting parents to assist in teaching activities for the class. The aim is to make everyone feel that they have a part to play. The 'class delegates' do not organise individual events, but through a coordinating process get **other** parents to volunteer for planning sub-committees concerned with various class activities. Thus the aim is to get everyone involved or feeling that they are involved. Although the school (and its teachers) take responsibility for the first meeting of each school year, the class members (parents, pupils and teachers) take over subsequent events. 'Telephone chains', by which messages are passed systematically between parents by 'phone, are used between meetings.

Class meetings in Sweden are held between 7 and 9 pm and topics are chosen by parents and teachers jointly. These may be curricular or other. Participation is part of every teacher's duty and is written into the teacher's contract, though hours are not specified. This does not involve extra payments (Andersson, 1986) and it may reflect different assumptions about the professionalism of teachers held by both the employing authorities and the teachers than are usual in Britain.

The question remains about whether the parents of a class should be encouraged to meet separately from the teachers before a joint parent–teacher meeting. One view is that this creates suspicion and a them-and-us atmosphere. The opposite argument points out that teachers meet separately from parents and that parents should do so too, especially as a prelude to representative school or class council meetings for which a parental viewpoint about policy is sought. There would appear to be no clear answer to the problem of whether parents should meet separately and it may be a question of circumstances determining appropriate action. Certainly parents should not be led to think that it is improper to meet as a group, and facilities and information can be made available by schools to assist them if they wish to do so. Those British education authorities which currently make financial charges for parents to hold meetings in schools might review, and hopefully, reverse such a policy. At the EEC-sponsored seminar on class meetings some of those present felt that meetings of parents only, to the exclusion of teachers, were an important first stage to make education a genuinely collaborative, constructive activity by providing parents with a base comparable to that already enjoyed by teachers, thereby enabling the development of a parental dimension to education.

At the same seminar constraints upon the effectiveness of class meetings were recorded as '... the perceptions and attitudes of both parents and teachers, problems of availability of time and finance, and the quality of coordination by class delegates.' An obvious additional reservation is that class meetings become less relevant the more that pupils of one class split up for options or into sets. This is especially so at the middle and upper levels of secondary schools. Here there is a case for age-group meetings or, if the age-group is too big, then any other arrangement which brings together parents whose children have a similar curricular experience – for instance, if there is a 'house' (vertical) system of pastoral care, to have age-group meetings within each 'house'.

The National Curriculum as a Focus for Class Meetings

If the better education of children is the purpose of parent–teacher collaboration then what is taught and how it is taught must surely be central to class-level liaison. In several countries where class meetings are common (e.g. Sweden, Denmark, Italy) the curriculum is centrally (i.e. nationally) determined to a high degree. Perhaps this makes it easier for teachers to countenance discussing the curriculum with parents because the curriculum is already public property and teachers would not feel that dissatisfaction about it reflected on them. The advent of the National Curriculum in Britain may serve the same purpose, and explanation of it and how it is being implemented in a particular class could become the focus of its class meetings.

Yet the National Curriculum still allows much scope for discretion for LEAs, schools, governing bodies and headteachers to adapt teaching content and methods to local needs or simply to the preferences of individual teachers. Thus local interpretation and initiatives are valid topics for class meeting discussions. Indeed, the ways in which home-learning can be shaped, encouraged and directed to support the nature of school-learning could be a significant part of that local adaptation. The curricular potential for parent–teacher class meetings could be enhanced by the arrival of the National Curriculum.

Return to Homework and Home-learning

A particular reason for class-level liaison is that class teachers expect parents to cooperate in the home by providing the support and facilities (and sometimes involvement) necessary for the completion of homework. It is an issue which may be discussed in either formal or informal class councils or meetings, and in the EEC report we stated (Macbeth *et al.*, 1984, p. 64):

> The sorts of issues which parents and teachers can usefully agree upon (perhaps in class meetings) are the conditions in which homework is carried out, the time of day, the appropriate amount of time to be devoted to it, the extent to which parents should or should not give advice and help, and the methods by which the school follows up the homework carried out.

Homework and home-learning were discussed in chapter 4, but aspects relating to class-level liaison warrant emphasis. The first point is that if parents are to give support and encouragement to the school's curriculum, they are more likely to do so if they understand it. Class meetings are an appropriate mechanism for explanation and encouragement.

Next, there are elements of the curriculum which are more clearly than others the joint responsibility of both home and school: what might be called the 'overlap curriculum'. Health education, sex education, religious education and social studies provide obvious examples. The European Parents' Association's public statement about teaching young people of the facts about AIDS (1987), for instance, gave focus to class meetings. It drew attention to parents' prime responsibility for their children's education and therefore their duty to forewarn them about the nature of AIDS, and it called on governments and schools to make information available rapidly. It also said that parents should be involved in decisions about what should be taught in schools about it. It then called on governments 'to make sure that every class with children aged from 13 to 18 throughout the whole of Europe should have parents–teachers meetings devoted to the question of AIDS' (item 4).

Finally, if it is true that teachers are professionally competent to provide guidance to parents on how to improve the quality of home-learning – and paired reading for young children and other advice outlined above in chapter 4 provide examples – then the class meeting is a means by which that can be put into operation, especially if guidance booklets are made available in support. There is a practical limit to the number of class meetings which can be held and to the amount of time which parents and teachers can devote to them. That being so, class meeting time should not be wasted on minor and peripheral items or class entertainments. Arguably the best rule-of-thumb would be to concentrate on the curriculum which the children of that class will be covering in the coming term and how parents can reinforce it. Exceptional meetings can be held on exceptional issues such as AIDS.

'Class Parents' and Class Delegates

The two roles of class parent (assisting the class teacher in coordinating liaison with parents) and class delegate (representing parents, perhaps at the school level as well as the class level) are different, but as a matter of convenience the two functions can be combined. Discussing class delegates, Isaacs (1986) has suggested that the main qualities which they should possess are:

1 Understanding of and acceptance of the goals of the school.
2 A sense of responsibility.
3 Competence and preparedness to accept training.
4 Concern for other parents.

While this list may dismay activists because of its hints of subservience to the school, it has value in that such parents are likely to gain the confidence of teachers and thereby provide the enabling mechanisms (such as constructive class meetings) from which mutual confidence may grow. Although this list emerged from Spain, it accords well with the Swedish practice already described. The emphasis is more on collaboration than on representation, more on enabling action than on the demanding of rights. Perhaps at the class level this is appropriate. I have already argued that educational partnership for the benefit of children should be the focus of home–school liaison at individual and class levels, while negotiation (involving representation of the parental dimension) is the proper mode of functioning at school, regional and national levels. Thus, a parental class delegate who is charged with representing parents of that class at *school* level should have sufficient flexibility to shift from an enabling, cooperative mode to a representative mode when he/she is a class delegate rather than a class parent. The distinction is a difficult one to operate in practice and it may be valuable to specify the difference in a school handbook. The essential point with regard to class-level liaison is that the class parent should be a facilitator who strives to reconcile the interests of parents and teachers while encouraging, for the sake of the children, a constructive dialogue leading to a sense of mutual support between home-learning and school-learning.

The possibilities for developing class meetings as an integral part of PTA/PA organisations is discussed in the next chapter.

7 PTAs, PAs and EAs

The Parental Movement

In Britain voluntary bodies such as parent–teacher associations and parents' associations have often been seen as peripheral to the schooling process, but their image may be changing and their potential for genuine educational liaison might be considerable if they were to adapt. Yet, they pose a problem for those writing seriously about home–school relations. On the one hand, PTAs represent a substantial and established network of goodwill in a tangible form; on the other, they usually fail to be educationally central, often do not involve the majority of parents in a school and, by their very existence, may impede the introduction of structures which do. This chapter reviews the strengths and weaknesses of current PTA and PA practice, examines purposes and expectations for PTAs, considers some alternative models, and finally argues that voluntary organisations *could* be educationally valuable if they discarded their traditional PTA assumptions.

The Size of the Movement

It is difficult to estimate how many PTAs and similar bodies exist in Britain at any given moment. Not only do they parade under different names (Friends of the School, School Committee, etc.) but they wax and wane, come and go, and there may be variation from area to area (Sharrock, 1970, p. 123). The signs are that the number is increasing. The Plowden Committee (1967, p. 39) reported that 17 per cent of primary schools in the National Sample had PTAs in England and Wales. More than a decade later Cyster, Clift and Battle (1979, p. 31) recorded that of 1401 headteacher questionnaires returned, 35 per cent reported PTAs and 26 per cent other less formal associations. A survey in Scotland suggested that in 1978 one-third of Scottish schools had a PTA or PA, almost three-quarters of which had been formed since 1970 (reported in Atherton 1974, p.14). In a follow-up survey in 1984 the Scottish Parent Teacher Council recorded that 62 per cent of the 1409 Scottish schools responding to a questionnaire had a PTA or PA, with a further 8 per cent having other sorts of organisation.

It may be reasonable to assume that a majority of British schools now have some kind of voluntary organisation involving parents, and that the number is growing. This suggests a wish for parental involvement, and it is too big a feature of our educational system to be dismissed with a sideways glance; yet that is what usually happens in our educational literature.

Bad Press for PTAs

Books on school management, where one might expect discussion of such a phenomenon, scarcely touch on voluntary organisations for parents. Three valuable and well-compiled English compendia on school management, two of about 500 pages (Bush *et al.*, 1980; Hughes, *et al.*, 1985) and the other of nearly 400 pages (Glatter *et al.*, 1988) contain between them merely seven indexed references to PTAs, much of the discussion being devoted to fund-raising. The official DES booklet describing the educational system acknowledges the movement and states that it is growing (DES, 1985, p. 26), but the SED counterpart makes no reference to PTAs.

We might expect the literature on home–school relations to give PTAs greater prominence. Yet this is only marginally the case. I took from my shelf 34 British books on home and school, accountability, participation and parent education, all published in the past two decades. Only one of these had a complete chapter devoted to organisations for parents (a thoughtful discussion by Jennifer Nias in Elliott *et al.*, 1981, pp. 109–22) and two had sub-sections (Stone and Taylor, 1976, pp. 162–7, and Atherton, 1987, pp. 149–51). Eighteen of these books had no indexed reference of any kind to PTAs or PAs or comparable bodies, and some indexed references, when pursued, turned out to be minimal such as 'Organise a Parent–Teachers Association to arrange social events,' (McConkey, 1985, p. 54).

An admittedly less representative selection of publications from other countries conveyed a mixed impression. German books give them prominence because parental organisations are integral to the system and are even required by law in most provinces. The EEC report on school–family relations contains a full chapter on parents' organisations (Macbeth *et al.*, 1984, pp. 147–80). However, others were less interested. In one American source entitled *Parents as Partners in Education* (Berger, 1981), out of more than 400 pages, the PTA earns less than one page; its activities being described as 'fun outings for families' which 'usually increase the treasury' (p. 109).

When we then look at what little *is* written, we find that much of it casts doubt on the usefulness of organisations for parents. Observations abound, such as 'Parent associations are a mixed blessing for parents and teachers' and official reports have damned PTAs with faint praise. The Taylor Report (1977, p. 42), suggested that some had 'failed to win the support of the generality of parents.' But it is the Plowden Report's (1967, pp. 39–40) cautious nod of recognition followed by reservations which most often appears in British writing:

Yet we do not think that PTAs are necessarily the best means of fostering close relationships between home and school. They can be of greatest value where good leadership is given by the head. They may do harm if they get into the hands of a small group.

The commonest complaints about PTAs are easily listed. Each deserves consideration, and it is on giving that consideration that the possibility starts to emerge that some of the criticisms may say as much about teachers' wish to protect a privileged level of autonomy as about the shortcomings of PTAs.

1 PTAs interfere in school matters

The Plowden Report helped to explode this myth: 'Some who have given evidence to us expressed the fear that PTAs might interfere in the school, and referred expressly to American experience.' But the Committee went on to say that it found little evidence of this on either side of the Atlantic, even though they sought examples in the USA. Yet the word 'interfere' often passes the lips of headteachers, and it is worth asking what constitutes 'interference'. Parents or members of an organisation who (say) physically disrupt a class, prevent someone else's child from attending school or ring the school fire alarm without permission, would be interfering. But is it also 'interference' for them to ask for information or to make suggestions about the school's management or curriculum? Could these not be seen as merely utilising freedom of speech upon matters of both parental and joint concern? The truth would seem to be that '. . . school systems have traditionally restricted their capacity to accommodate dissent by insisting upon cooperative modes of interaction with citizens' (Lucas and Lusthaus, 1981, p. 57) so that the fault may lie with teachers rather than with alert and active parents' organisations.

2 PTAs avoid controversy

This complaint is the reverse of the first. It sees PTAs as spineless and ineffective in tackling school matters of concern and perhaps controversy. 'Because the aims of PTAs are to encourage consensus and agreement between homes and schools, they rarely incorporate mechanisms for dealing with conflict. Thus, when the interests of parents and schools do not coincide, PTAs may be of little value.' (Tomlinson, 1984, p. 87.) Johnson and Ransom (1983, p. 63) similarly noted that while associations adopt an official ethic of service and loyalty to the school, many parents did not share that view.

3 PTAs are placebos and impediments to real parental involvement

The argument here is that some headteachers seem to have used PTAs not only to give a false appearance of parental involvement in the school, but as a diversionary tactic to syphon off the energies of concerned parents into fund-raising and side-issues. The very existence of such a body makes it difficult (though not impossible) for a more educationally-relevant one to be established.

4 PTAs are composed of an unrepresentative minority of parents

It is probably true that many, if not most, PTAs as currently consti-tuted in Britain obtain active involvement of only a minority of members. This criticism appears in many guises.* A particular version is to castigate the PTA movement as middle class. Not only does that beg the question of what the term 'middle class' means, but it may be that the *leadership* rather than the *membership* has such a bias. With regard to leadership, much depends on how terms are defined, but it may be middle-class parents, accustomed to paperwork and com-mittees, who are best equipped to coordinate PTAs. Little and Wiley recorded that ethnic minority parents were less likely to attend PTAs than were 'white British' parents (see Tomlinson, 1984, p. 20), thus adding a different social element.

5 Parents are deterred by the nature of a PTA's work

Repeatedly *fund-raising* is recorded as a (the) prime PTA function and parents are often expected to attend meetings with their mouths shut and their wallets open. If so, then it is scarcely surprising that some parents are deterred. Nias (1981, p. 122) found that *social events* 'receive the least support from parents and teachers'. The formality, dullness and large size of whole-school PTA meetings may also put off many parents. However, the biggest deterrent for parents, arguably, is that the activities of the PTA are generally not seen by parents as being relevant to the *particular school experience of the family's own child*. It is clear that parents are interested in their own child's educational environ-ment and advance, and the literature is full of examples of parents attending, for instance, private consultations about their son or daughter. They tend to be less interested in the broader management and curricular problems of the school and are probably happy to leave those issues to professionals and to the parental representatives on the governing body and the executive committee of any voluntary organis-ation. To get widespread personal involvement of parents in voluntary organisations probably requires changes in both structure and functions.

6 Parents are intimidated by the presence of teachers

'Intimidated' may be too strong a word for the reluctance of some parents to express opinions or even to speak at all when gatherings are dominated by the confident voices of teachers. Perhaps there are good grounds for arguing that parents ought to meet separately from teachers to develop a distinctive interest group viewpoint on issues in order to present a parental dimension on the schooling process; this will be discussed later in the chapter.

7 Research evidence does not relate PTAs to good education

There has been little research carried out to examine whether the PTA can enhance the quality of education, though the absence of evidence

* Apart from the Plowden and Taylor reports, see Johnson and Ransom (1983, p. 23), Benn and Simon (1970, p. 382), Nias (1981, pp. 109–110) and Stone and Taylor (1976, p. 163).

does not mean that parental bodies may not enhance children's learning. It may be that PTAs in their common form do not, while reformed parental associations might. However, Mortimore *et al.* (1988) reported in their analysis of factors associated with educational outcomes in the ILEA that parental involvement generally was 'a positive influence upon pupils' progress and development', but:

> One aspect of parental involvement was, however, not successful. Somewhat curiously, formal Parent–Teacher Associations (PTAs) were not found to be related to effective schooling. It could be that some parents found the formal structure of such a body to be intimidating. (p. 122)

8 The PTA is resented by teachers as irrelevant unpaid overtime

The Plowden Report (1967, p. 40) suggested that a PTA could absorb too much of a headteacher's attention, thereby implying its relative unimportance in the Committee's eyes, and Nias (1981, p. 114) records teachers objecting to PTAs as a drain on their time. This sense of wasted time must, in turn, reflect a feeling that the functions are not valid, or at least are not sufficiently central to education to warrant teachers' commitment.

Purposes of Voluntary Parental Associations

Part of the problem of PTAs is what Johnson and Ransom (1983, p. 22) refer to as 'uncertainties of aim and scope'. In the words of a Scottish Parent–Teacher Council booklet, 'Sometimes a PTA is established on a wave of enthusiasm, but once it is in existence the members are not sure what to do and fall back on fund-raising and social events.' We can identify six main areas of potential purposes for parental associations which may or may not be adopted by a given organisation:

1 To provide support for teachers.
2 To represent parents' interests.
3 To provide a forum for educational discussion and a means of communication.
4 To foster educational partnership between home and school for the benefit of children.
5 To assist members who have difficulties.
6 To advance an ideology (e.g. religious, educational, etc.)

Some of these potential purposes may conflict. For instance, representing parental interests may necessitate being critical of teachers or resisting the school's adoption of one ideology to the exclusion of others. However, in most instances the objectives are compatible and since an important function could be the provision of a forum for debate, differences of viewpoint might be welcomed rather than shunned.

It may also be noted that the PTA is parent-centred. Representation of the interests of parents is included in the above list of purposes but representation of those of teachers is not since they have their own unions, staff meetings and other mechanisms for jointly influencing school policy. The parent-centred role of a PTA is often implicit, but is usually not made explicit in the constitution. It would therefore seem essential for any association to identify its broad purposes and to state them clearly in its terms of reference or constitution so that those who do not subscribe to those ends may either withdraw membership or seek to change the constitution or set up their own body. (Here we may note that there is nothing to stop one school having several parental groups and that the headteacher has no authority to sanction or prevent their establishment.) We may now consider each of these purposes in turn.

1 Support for teachers

This objective is often expressed as 'support for the school', but a school's functioning is one of human interaction based on decisions made by people. Teachers have gained such control over decision-making in schools that they are able to represent their actions as those of 'the school'. Yet in different ways parents, pupils and non-teaching staff are part of 'the school' and when a PTA gives support for teachers, we must be clear that it is *parental* support which is thereby being given, and usually it is given for the ultimate good of children. Such support may be divided into four elements:

(i)   Backing the decisions and actions of teachers.
(ii) Providing finance and equipment for teachers to use.
(iii) Relieving teachers of chores, or carrying out work of a lower order which, if not done by parents voluntarily, might not get done at all.
(iv) Assisting in the educational processes.

Not surprisingly, support for teachers is the objective most often espoused by teachers and headteachers. For instance, one headteacher has written:

> But above all, school associations must be supportive organiz-ations, and it is only within that context that they can perform effectively in a way which will benefit children. (Harris, 1980, p. 175.)

An adaptation of the 'support' philosophy is the view that cooperation ought to debar dissent. This view urges that even if partnership with parents is publicly espoused, the ideal is that parents and teachers should not conflict. 'Cooperation', meaning agreement with teachers, is the watchword. But, as Cleveland has written, 'You can always get cooperation, after all, by eliminating the real issues that divide people from each other'. If parents cannot raise points of disagreement with teachers in a PTA then it ceases to be a partnership and probably ceases to be creative.

Several commentators on PTAs have noted the weakness of PTAs which espouse subservience in the name of cooperation:

Where issues demand opposition to established school policies, however, the responsiveness of these associations has been fundamentally limited by a primarily supportive and cooperative orientation towards the school. (Lucas and Lusthaus, 1981, p. 57.)

And Nias (1981, p. 118), having reported cases where teachers had asserted that the PTA was not an appropriate forum to discuss school problems, states:

Parents in all schools were left wondering where they could voice legitimate criticisms.

2 Representation of Parents' Interests

It seems odd that teachers, who are employed to be of service to parents, should expect subservience from parents. There is a growing trend towards regarding the PTA/PA as an interest group for parents and discarding (or carefully limiting) the 'support' function discussed above. To regard the PTA/PA as a parental interest group to some extent does reflect current assumptions. For instance, Denys John (1980, p. 129), a secondary headteacher, writes of consulting 'the parents of the PTA'; and the Taylor Report, in its only recommendation about PTAs, asserted 'that parents themselves should be free to choose what type of organisation, if any, is best suited to their needs.' (1977, p. 42, para. 5.22.) The Taylor Report's consequent recommendation is worth quoting in full:

We therefore confine ourselves to the RECOMMENDATION that the parents should have the opportunity to set up an organisation based upon the school, developing its aims and methods of working in consultation with the headteacher and the governing body.

This is akin to the tradition common in Continental Europe. Although there are exceptions (such as Sweden's *Hem och Skola* movement), most European countries favour **parental** organisations rather than **parent–teacher** associations. In Britain it is often assumed that the creation of a PA is a sign either that the headteacher has refused to accept a PTA, or that the PTA is unsatisfactory. However, industrial action by teachers and reluctance to give 'voluntary time' to PTAs has led some headteachers to encourage the establishment of a PA simply because staff will not collaborate.

The Continental pattern recognises that parents' interests do need to be crystallised and represented, especially if parents bear 'The first and fundamental responsibility ... in the education of their children' (CNAP, Belgium, 1977). One pattern is for such parents' organisations to elect representatives who meet those of the teachers and of the administration in a formal, statutory body (comparable to school governors); but that does not prevent parents from inviting teachers to the parental meetings. The existence of a PA does not necessarily mean conflict.

We may note the distinction between an interest group and a pressure group. According to the *Dictionary of Modern Thought* (Bullock and Stallybrass 1977, p. 316):

> *An interest group* defends a particular interest; a *pressure group* . . . may promote an interest or cause and make propaganda for it, the 'pressure' lying in the application or threatened application of a SANCTION should the claim or demand advanced by the group be denied.

Thus, a teachers' union which argues a case could be acting as an interest group, but when it uses or threatens strike action it would be a pressure group; a PTA or PA would be an interest group unless its members threatened sanctions, such as withdrawing their children from a school *en bloc* for a specified period of time, an action which may be legal, arguably, as long as parents make some educational provision during that period. As an interest group then, a PA can go some way to counterbalancing the generally close-knit teachers' interests which are readily articulated through unions, staff meetings and less formal communication. Some Continental associations even discourage or debar teachers who happen also to be parents from holding office in their parental organisations.

To some teachers the idea of a PTA/PA being an overt interest group for parents (and even occasionally a pressure group) may be abhorrent and seem threatening. However, interest and pressure groups are part of the modern way of life and it may be unreasonable for us as teachers to resist in others a trend which has increased in our own ranks. Further, if PTAs do not adapt in that direction it is possible that other parental interest groups will develop in parallel as has happened in Canada. (Lucas and Lusthaus, 1981, pp. 57–64.)

An interest group can praise as well as criticise and advise. I know of one PTA which had its own association headed notepaper printed specifically so that it could send letters of thanks and appreciation to teachers and parents whose contributions had been special. The PTA as an interest group is also able to provide to teachers feedback which might otherwise fester as garden-gate gossip, and to represent a client perspective. Perhaps most important, the interest group function does not preclude the support function or any of the purposes listed below.

The need for parental interest groups increases as governing bodies acquire more responsibilities and as parental representation on them becomes more important. I shall return to this issue later in the chapter.

3 Provision of a Forum for Educational Discussion and a Means of Communication

Communication may be seen as the essence of a PTA or PA. Teaching staff already have mechanisms for one-way communication with families, but these concentrate upon teachers' preoccupations, tend not to deal with educationally-central issues, and are often exhortations or instructions to parents to collaborate with teacher-determined procedures. The PTA/PA can provide the means to both widen the scope of information to parents and to bring parental views to bear in the school. Some detailed methods are discussed in the section 'Purposes into practice' later in this chapter.

4 The Fostering of Educational Partnership between Parents and Teachers for the Benefit of Children

There has been much rhetoric about educational partnership, less practice. It would not be appropriate to portray limited, support group PTAs as if they were partnership organisations. Further, if the organisation's concern is the education of children, and if that education is an amalgam of home and school learning, then the association is properly concerned with the nature of *home* learning as well as the nature of *school* provision. It should be able to discuss (but not to determine) homework conditions as much as school syllabuses, bed-times as much as timetables, the impact of TV in the home as much as computers in the curriculum, home support for the school as much as school support for the child.

In one circumstance only can a PA/PTA make decisions binding upon the school. This is if the body or person with responsibility for a school function (e.g. governors, headteacher) exercises the right to delegate authority to the PTA/PA, for instance to design a school report form or handbook.

The concept of educational partnership as a central purpose for a PTA is summed up in the definition of a PTA adopted by the Scottish Parent Teacher council:

A PTA is a group of people who recognise that the education of a child is a process of partnership between parents and teachers, and who wish to take joint action to improve the quality of that partnership.

5 Assisting Members who have Difficulties

This function is self-explanatory and requires no comment.

6 Advancing an Ideology

Some of the best-organised parents' associations in Europe are Roman Catholic. The notion of parents as prime educators is integral to Roman Catholic thinking. In his visit to Britain in 1982 the Pope stated:

It is only right that parents should be more involved in educational structures. For are not parents, in the sight of God, the primary educators of their children?

Christian values, then, have become an additional objective for associations in certain schools. Yet ideologies need not be church-based. In Denmark the government provides 85 per cent of the running costs of any school established by a group of parents, and the 'little schools' movement has thrown up some with left-wing or communist tenets as the foundation of their curricula. Parents and teachers run one school as an educational commune, perhaps the most extreme form of a PTA.

Finally, an ideology may be espoused by a school, or considered to be influencing its provision, which is not to the liking of parents. Governors, if they lack the means of access to local opinion, need facilities, such as a PTA can offer, for the expression of parental views in such a circumstance.

Other Advantages of Voluntary Associations

Apart from basic purposes, other advantages have been identified in having a voluntary home–school association for every school. The Taylor Report asserted that many associations 'have increased parents' commitment to their schools' (1977, p. 42). Sharrock (1970, p. 111) suggests that they could be involved in parent education; Pugh and De'ath (1984, p. 176) cite New Zealand as an example of where this happens, and in Belgium the government contributes to national parent organisations' funding on the grounds that they are centres for adult education. Stone and Taylor (1976, p. 162) argue that

> ... there are definite advantages in having some kind of formal structure. In the first place, its survival does not depend on the enthusiasm and goodwill of individuals alone and so it is more difficult for a head quietly to dispense with parents altogether. A second advantage is that communications from a committee are more formal and less personal. One emotional parent putting up a fight on behalf of his own child may provoke an aggressive reaction from the head. A formal request from a committee who have reached a consensus calls for a rational reply.

Harris (1980, p. 175) asserts that parents are more likely to be actively involved if they have a specific role to play and that the PTA can provide this; he suggests that it is useful for teachers to be able to approach parents via other parents; and he values the relaxed social setting of a PTA which makes contact with parents easier.

Finally, Nias (1981, p. 122) concludes that, despite their drawbacks,

> Parent associations are the only formally-constituted body, other than the governors, through which parents can criticise the school, help and support it, and take educational initiatives on its behalf. Unlike the governors, association officers are not politically appointed and have no legal responsibility for the school. This generally gives the association a freedom of action which, in some instances, the former lack.

The Need for a New Image

Titles can help or hinder. It is my view that the *term* 'PTA' now does more harm than good. It is associated with educationally peripheral activities, such as fund-raising and social events. It implies partnership but usually purveys petty subservience to teachers. The existence of a traditional PTA may be used by isolationist heads not only to prevent the introduction of a more effective body concerned with education, but even to claim that the school has good relationships with parents because of the existence of the PTA.

Yet, as was argued at the start of this chapter, a large network of PTAs exists nationally. The question would seem to be one of adaptation. What steps could a school take locally to convert a traditional PTA into one which concentrates on the parental dimension of schooling and on educational partnership combined with effective communication? What policies might regional and national organisations representing parents and the parent–teacher movement espouse and advocate to their members? It seems to me that the abolition of the term 'PTA' would be a first step. After that, there would appear to be two different possible routes: what I shall call the PA approach and the EA approach.

The PA Approach

In essence this would be the pattern common in some Continental countries, making the parental interest group purpose predominant. A parents' association network would unambiguously represent the parental dimension of schooling, would provide a reference point and a structured base from which parents and parent governors can operate, and would give emphasis to the family element of children's education. Such a PA movement would release associations from undue teacher influence and would help to remove the ambiguities of objective sometimes experienced by regional and national parent–teacher groups to which school associations often belong as members. An individual PA would still be able to espouse educational partnership as its goal and it could still invite teachers to join in discussions and collaborate on projects. However, the leadership and perspectives would remain parental.

The EA Approach

The EA approach would put emphasis not upon the parental interest group purpose, but upon *educational* partnership. The term 'Education Association' (EA) has two main advantages:

(i) It would concentrate upon educational partnership between parents and teachers, the central function which many PTAs currently ignore.

(ii) It does not prescribe and limit membership in the title (as 'PA' and 'PTA' do), but gives emphasis in its title to what could, arguably, be its main function.

There are also disadvantages. The distinctive parental perspective would be blurred and the term, being new and unfamiliar, might be adopted only slowly and cautiously.

An Education Association would recognise that home is as important as school in the education of the child and would concentrate upon
ways by which the influence of parents and teachers would coincide, to
optimum effect, not only in attitudes, but also in practical teaching
functions.

Purposes into Practice

Returning to the recommendation of the Taylor Committee quoted
earlier, we may now consider whether we have a basis to fulfil it. That
recommendation contained the following elements:

(i)   *parents* should have the opportunity to set up an organisation;
(ii) it should be based upon the school;
(iii) there should be consultation with the headteacher and the
      governing body about its aims and methods of working.

In the text preceding the recommendation, the Taylor Report (para.
5.22) had emphasised the parent-centred nature of such a body by
stating 'that parents themselves should be free to choose what type of
organisation, if any, is best suited to their needs.' The reference to
consultation with headteachers and governors in the recommendation
may be noted; headteachers and governors would have neither control
nor the power of veto. Also implicit is a recognition that different types
of organisation are possible. If we discard the traditional PTA as one of
them, I offer three possible models:

(i)   The PA, as described above.
(ii) The EA, as described above.
(iii) A combination of PA at school level and EA at class/age-group
      level.

It is the third model which seems to me to be the most promising, and it
is the model which is often adopted in Scandinavia.

If the *class* at primary and lower secondary levels (and the age-group
at upper secondary levels) is the grouping which predominantly determines each child's detailed educational experience (see chapter 6),
then that is the point at which grouped educational partnership is
presumably most appropriate. It is also the focus of common interest of
all parents with children in the same class/age group. In terms of the
most efficient use of teachers' time it makes sense to have group
consultations about the curriculum if educational partnership is the
objective, *though such meetings should never be replacements for the individual
consultations.*

Yet there is also a place for a parents' interest group at the school
level. This can act as a coordinating centre, an open forum, a means of
representation for parents on policy matters and a point of contact for
parent governors to enable them to have links with their constituents.
An ideal parental association might be organised:

(i)   to reach out to and appeal to all parents;

(ii)   to tackle issues seen as central to parents as an interest group;
(iii) to focus on education and associated decisions at school and class levels;
(iv)   to be relevant to teachers professionally;
(v)   to be seen by parents as relevant to their own child's educational experience;
(vi)   to include consideration of home-learning as well as schooling;
(vii) to provide a forum for discussion, a means for grassroots consultation and a mechanism for informing and advising parent–governors.

Conventional PTAs do not answer to such a description; the school PA, linked to a network of class-level EAs, would seem to. I shall refer to the latter as *mini-associations*.

The Mini-Association

Many of the traditional PTA's problems stem from what seems to me to be a false assumption: that the school is the prime unit of educational organisation. It is not. The class is. Schooling is provided in groups. The class may be constant throughout the week (in many primary schools) or may split into sets or options and re-assemble. It is provision for the class/option/set which determines the nature of each child's schooling experience, and it is that experience which interests, or ought to interest, the child's parents.

Having small 'cells' of a PA involves many more parents in active organisation and reduces the danger of control by an isolated clique. The work of contacting parents is spread out more evenly, and since the units are small it can be done personally, thereby encouraging participation by those who have traditionally not been involved. Also, lower level meetings can be cosier, easier to organise, less formal and more friendly, as well as being directly related in the educational experience of the children of all assembled. These factors do much to encourage participation and to give a real sense of purpose to the mini-association. They have been discussed more fully in chapter 6 on class level liaison.

The Swedish *Hem och Skola* voluntary movement has based its structure on the class. Holberg (1976), having referred to the old-style school-based fund-raising organisations, states that as society changed so did such associations. Work became concentrated upon what has been translated into English as 'class conferences':

> These class conferences have become the parent–teacher movement's most important working form. They involve the parents and pupils meeting with the class teacher (form-master or home-room teacher) to discuss in a small group school matters considered to be crucial 'right now'. It is here, in this little group, that the major decisions in reality are taken. . . . Within the small group of parents, who often know one another from the start or come to know one another during the years their children attend the same class, those who normally have difficulty expressing themselves in

public dare to speak out. Barriers and inhibitions tend to disappear in a small group where you 'talk normally' and where you are not under pressure to prepare your arguments in advance, as in larger gatherings. Usually the questions raised at class conferences are those which are palpably concrete for the participants.

A distinction might be drawn between primary and secondary schools at this point. It is easy to see how the notion of a class meeting can apply to primary schools and those classes of a secondary school where pupils remain in one group for all subjects. However, where there are setting and subject options it may be that the mini-PA should be the age group.

The mini-association is economical with the teacher's time since many families are contacted simultaneously (perhaps once a month or once a term) and it is directly relevant to his/her professional practice since its emphasis would be upon the syllabus of the coming month/term and how parents can best reinforce it through home-learning.

We may now move to the nuts and bolts of running a mini-association. What follows is, of course, open to modification and represents one approach only.*

(i)   **Getting it started**   The 'class teacher' and 'class parents' (perhaps two) could be the coordinators. Introducing teachers to friendly class units may require overcoming some initial apprehension in the teacher's mind until he or she gains self-confidence. The class teacher could therefore have a predominant say in choosing the interim 'class Dad' and 'class Mum'. (After that, it might be up to the class unit to develop its own procedures for appointing these officers, say annually.)

(ii) **Approaching the interim class Dad and class Mum**   Once names of likely interim class Mums and class Dads have been put forward, someone on the PA executive committee can then contact the chosen parents in question, explain what is expected of them and ask if they will serve. A personal visit or a telephone call make this process more informal.

(iii) **Briefing teachers**   This might best be done by the headteacher, with members of the school PA executive committee present to add to this discussion. Educational reasons should be stressed. The purpose of class meetings is to explain what curriculum is being taught in the school, why it is being taught and how parents can reinforce the learning at home. Much will be looking into the future, and discussion in the class units might modify or improve upon the curricular plan. Text-books can be shown and new techniques discussed.

(iv) **Briefing class Dads and Mums**   These essential link-peo-

* This section on mini-associations is an adaptation of text which I wrote for the Scottish Parent–Teacher Council booklet *Ideas for an Active PTA* (pp. 18–19) and I am grateful to the SPTC for allowing me to re-use that material.

ple for the scheme can be briefed by the PA executive committee with the headteacher present to give support.

(v) **Frequency of class meetings**   Once a term might be appropriate. If the coming term's work is to be the main topic, the meeting could be held early in the term. Alternatively, twice a term, or monthly in term time.

(vi) **Time and place**   Evening. The children's classroom or the staff common room are obvious sites, but village halls, private homes or even pubs are worth considering.

(vii) **Facilities**   Arrange seats informally if possible; not rows of parents facing teacher(s). Avoid a 'them and us' impression. Class Dad or Mum might persuade two other parents in the group to lay on coffee and biscuits. Expenses should be reimbursed from association funds.

(viii) **Agenda**   An informal, approximate agenda can be discussed by the class teacher(s) and the class Dad and Mum beforehand. It could include explanation of the coming term's/month's teaching plan and special features or problems and discussion of how the parents can help at home.

(ix) **Particular issues**   These can be discussed 'cold', but it may be better for one or more members to consider them in advance. It is possible for a PA executive committee to arrange for a teacher or a parent to become a specialist on a given topic and to move from class to class providing introductions to that topic when it arises in a class unit. The number of topics is almost limitless, but the following provides some examples:

The National Curriculum   What the children ought to be covering in the coming term/year, how the particular class will approach that learning at school and how parents can reinforce it at home.

Homework   Nature, amount, circumstances, extent of parental encouragement, extent of parental help.

Project work

How children are assessed

Health education, sex education, moral education.   What, when and how. Home reinforcement.

Reading   Home encouragement. Use of libraries. Paired reading methods.

Mathematics   Home reinforcement. Simple steps at younger ages; use of calculators, etc. at older ages. Access to computers etc.

Choosing new text-books   Teachers may value the opinions of parents if a new set of text-books is to be introduced and there is choice available.

(x) **Class projects**   Projects jointly organised by teachers and parents, carried out both in class time and out of school, are discussed under main PA activities but it is worth noting that a particular class can organise such a scheme.

(xi) **Airing of anxieties**   There should always be a chance for either teachers or parents to raise anxieties concerning the class, but the problems of individual children should *not* be discussed.

(xii) **Representation to the school PA executive committee and/ or the governing body**   It makes sense for the class Dads and Mums to meet periodically to compare notes and to suggest ways to improve class meetings. The school PA should therefore call such a meeting towards the middle of the school year. These class representatives can also be a means for the PA to communicate downwards to classes from the central PA committee and upwards from grass roots to the governors. Indeed, it is neat and convenient for the PA executive committee itself to be composed of the parental representations of each class; this provides a cohesive system of two-way communication.

Secondary Schools

Class units are easy to organise for primary schools. This might work well in lower levels of secondary schools where one class stays in the same group for all lessons, though specialist staff cannot attend all meetings and may have to rotate. Some secondary schools (especially at older levels) find it more profitable to have age-group meetings rather than class meetings.

One very practical question may occasionally arise: what should parents do about mini-associations if teachers decline to cooperate? The answer must surely be: go ahead, regretfully, without them. Clearly, if a class-level EA is to fulfil its objective of *partnership* in education, the presence of teachers is important, and hopefully most teachers would want to be involved on grounds of professionalism, both in terms of concern for parents as clients and in terms of what will benefit the children. But much of value can still be attained if parents of one class meet regularly to compare educational and parenting experiences. First they can exchange views and, to some extent seek common standards with regard to home practices such as time allocated to homework, the conditions in which it is carried out and the extent to which parents assist and in what ways, as well as bed-times, use and abuse of TV, pocket money, moral education, health and sex education, drug-watch syndicates, and a range of other home-based learning/teaching activities. They can combine in weekend and holiday projects.

Further, they can compare notes on what they understand (from their children's work and books and from discussions with their children) to be the curriculum. They can assess text-books and teaching methods used by the school and they can frame questions for the class teacher(s), to be posed by post or in 'working hours', express views and pass opinions to the teacher(s). If they feel that the occasion is appropriate, they can similarly communicate with the headteacher, the governors or the executive committee of the PA. None of this is as satisfactory as it would be if the professionals were present, but arguably it is better than nothing.

In such a situation, much more depends upon the quality of leadership from the class Mum and the class Dad – and the executive committee of the school PA – than if the teachers are professionally involved. They must constantly remind the groups of the foundation principles, lest parents feel that in some way their action is improper. They should emphasise that they, the parents, are responsible for their children's education, that they all have a common stake in what is provided for the class, that it is their right to meet and express views as with any voluntary organisation, that their active support is likely to enhance their children's school performance and that some sort of consistency of action between them is likely to provide mutual confidence.

If there is no PA (or PTA) to coordinate the mini-associations, then teachers can take the initiative, as described in chapter 6.

The PA, when the Focus is on the Class-level EA

If the focus of the association were to shift to the class level, that leaves the school-level PA with four main functions:

1 To ensure the smooth running of class unit EAs.
2 To provide a forum for parental consideration of school-level issues, especially in conjunction with parent governors.
3 To provide mechanisms for dissemination of information to parents. These may include conventional meetings (directly concerned with the school and its educational provision, of course), PA newspaper, questionnaires and referenda, etc.
4 To collaborate with regional or national parental organisations.

The 1988 Act

The Education Reform Act for England and Wales is not specifically concerned with PAs and PTAs.* However, its provisions could lead to an enhanced role for them and for class-level mini-associations. I shall take each of the main provisions in turn and suggest some related actions which are possible.

National Curriculum and Testing

Parents ought surely to be aware of the aspects of the National Curriculum which their children will be experiencing at each stage, the methods by which they will be taught and the ways by which they can assist that process at home. If so, then logically this should happen in advance of the teaching. Since such information and guidance is either class-specific or age-group-specific, the most obvious ways of achieving this are through class meetings (see chapter 6) supported by duplicated

---

* The Scottish 1988 Act, which is entirely different from that for England and Wales, does require the new school boards to 'encourage the formation of parent–teacher or parents' associations' in section 12(1).

materials. The potential for a mini-association for each class (or each age group in the upper parts of secondary schools) is obvious. It can provide a support mechanism for the class teacher(s), organise the meetings and circulate any duplicated information. Similarly, at those stages where there are tests, the class-level mini-association could explain in advance how the testing is carried out and then analyse the aggregated class results afterwards. (See chapter 5 for a discussion of such analysis.)

A well-led school PA (or PTA) can organise meetings to brief parents in a general way about the National Curriculum and testing, but much more importantly it can ensure that there is an effective system of class (or age-group) meetings and information as described above, and it can make and disseminate analysis of the school's test results. (See chapter 5.)

Open Enrolment

A school's PA can assist those parents who are wondering about choosing that school. First it can ensure that the school's handbook not only contains the sort of information which parents would want to know, but that it is accurate and expressed in jargon-free language. If the PA is not automatically involved in the preparation of the handbook and associated brochures, the head and/or governors can introduce such an arrangement or the PA can ask to have it.

At the same time, the PA can publish, either in the school handbook or in a leaflet of its own, a list of parents (with addresses and telephone numbers) with children already at the school who are willing to discuss it with parents contemplating making a choice. The head and/or governors might similarly seek a list of parents who are prepared to give guided tours of the school to other parents. The PA might even provide open meetings, advertised in the local press, for parents contemplating choosing that school and might hold greeting-and-briefing gatherings for 'new parents' when their children start. A leaflet about the PA might be a standard enclosure with the school handbook for parents contemplating that school.

Opting Out

Collaboration between the PA/PTA and the governing body is discussed in greater detail in Chapter 8, but it would be an obvious step for the governors – especially parent-governors – to use the PA/PTA as a preliminary sounding-board if governors are contemplating seeking Grant Maintained status. The PA/PTA could also be used to assist in the various mechanisms of informing, debating, and holding public meetings and administering the ballot in the process of opting out.

Local Financial Management

The PA/PTA can provide a mechanism for informing parents and a forum for discussion. The question of charging for school activities could attract particular attention. However, the PA/PTA should not be seen as a provider of school finance.

Regional, National and International PAs

The issues at regional, national and international levels are political. By 'political' I mean concerned with the resolution of differences of view rather than party-political. Party-politics does enter the scene, of course, but most school issues are not tied to the ideologies of left, right and centre; indeed there is a high level of consensus between parties over most educational matters, even if the system and the media tend to highlight the differences. Teachers have been well organised for many decades to influence policy decisions to suit professional perspectives, but parents have not. One reason for the somewhat muted parental voice in regional and national affairs has been the fact that it is more difficult for parents to coordinate compared with teachers who are relatively homogeneous, who have the work-place in which to meet and who have financial and other incentives to contribute to the funds of self-interest organisations such as unions. Another reason why the parental dimension has been less fully represented in policy decisions has been the British tradition by which PTAs rather than PAs exist at school level and teachers continue to influence the joint parent–teacher organisations at regional and national levels. In brief, Britain lacks a 'pure' parent movement.

How proper is it for parental interest groups to be influenced or even dominated by teachers and their organisations in policy matters? I would suggest that parental organisations benefit from the information and advice which teachers and educationists can provide, but that policy-making should be overtly and unambiguously parental. This has been normal on the Continent and it reduces the likelihood of confusion. It protects the policies of such bodies from getting adapted to teacher union preferences and it ensures that education authorities, ministries and governments know that they are dealing with a genuine parental movement. Some teachers will plead that they are also parents, but it is difficult for them to discard their teacher perspectives and it is arguably better that they remain in an advisory capacity and decline to hold executive office.

There are various national bodies in Britain which, in one way or another, seek to represent parents in the education system at national level. Their objectives differ. Most are not 'pure' parental organisations. Cooperation between them does happen but it is limited. However, each is genuinely concerned with the welfare of children and it may be hoped that some consensus of perspective, especially in advancing the parental dimension, may in time develop.

The largest British organisation offering to represent parents is the National Confederation of Parent–Teacher Associations (NCPTA). Membership is mostly by school rather than by individual or family and its General Secretary in 1987 reported that it had 6000 school committees in 40 area federations (Jones, 1987, p. 5). It is difficult to estimate how many individuals – parents and teachers – that represents. Although several of NCPTA's chairpersons have been teachers and it has had headteachers in the General Secretary post, it has taken recent steps to reduce teacher influence. For instance, the number of teachers on its executive committee must now not exceed one-third of the total. It has an extensive organisation throughout England and it produces a variety of useful publications as well as services such as a preferential insurance system for its members.

Both Wales and Scotland have comparable bodies: the Parent Teacher Associations of Wales and the Scottish Parent Teacher Council. Each has about 500 member schools and although the word 'Teacher' appears in the titles of both, they appear to have veered rather more than NCPTA to being parental groups. PTA Wales, however, is affiliated to NCPTA and its notepaper carries the statement 'Part of NCPTA'. In some respects, therefore, it may be seen as a quasi-autonomous regional federation of NCPTA.

The Scottish body, by contrast, is independent and, having been founded in 1948, is long-established. Although it has some teachers on its executive committee, its chairmen have always been non-teacher parents, and a study of its history (Furnish, 1985) notes an increasing parental interest-group stance over time. Determinedly non-party-political, its public statements in recent years have been guided by parental interests. It has never had formal links with Scottish teachers' unions and its support for some of the government's initiatives (for instance over parental choice and school boards) have, if anything, served to increase that separateness. This does not mean that SPTC lacks teacher support and there is a growing, if belated, recognition among teachers in Scotland of the importance of parents, a phenomenon for which the SPTC can take some credit.

Apart from the PTA movement's national bodies, other organisations with national status exist, especially in England. The self-description of CASE (Campaign for the Advancement of State Education) reads:

> CASE is a national organisation which campaigns for a first-class state education service throughout life, with equal educational opportunity for all, regardless of where they live, their home circumstances, their ability, sex, race or religion ... Now some 35 local groups are affiliated to CASE, all working in their own ways to improve local state education. Within broad lines of policy these groups are independent, deciding their own priorities, but through CASE they can support and learn from each other.
>
> CASE is non-party and non-sectarian. Its members include parents, teachers, local councillors of all parties, and interested citizens.

As its name suggests, the National Association for Primary Education (NAPE) concentrates on the primary sector. Founded in 1981, it seeks to bring together parents, teachers, governors, taxpayers and politicians to promote a better understanding of primary education and to 'build bridges between homes, committees and schools.'

Other national bodies take an interest in parents and parent–teacher relations in specialist ways. For instance ACE (The Advisory Centre for Education) provides advice and information, and it has produced a wide range of valuable publications for parents. The National Children's Bureau has carried out research and published reports on parent–teacher partnership. NAGM (National Association of Governors and Managers) 'Campaigns for effective school government, so that schools are accountable to the community they serve', and is concerned to provide training and information for governors, especially parent–governors, and 'to create a national network which will enable parents to have real influence on the education system.' The three consumer councils take an active interest in children and have taken valuable initiatives, especially the Scottish Consumer Council which has been highly effective in educational (and especially parental) matters without creating any sense of rivalry with SPTC. A variety of smaller groups, sometimes local, sometimes responses to particular but temporary events, have also emerged.

Turning to the international scene, the European Parents' Association is an aggregation of national and provincial parents' organisations. Its origins lay in a conference sponsored by the European Commission in Luxembourg in 1983. EPA came into formal existence in Milan in 1985, supported financially by the European Commission, and its internal working arrangements were ratified at a General Assembly in Brussels in 1987. Several of the UK organisations are members, and the UK has two representatives on the Administrative Council of EPA.

EPA's functions are to represent parents (*not* the parent–teacher movement, it will be noted) at the European level, to encourage partnership between parents and teachers with regard to education and to disseminate information. In most European countries the philosophy is now well-established that, while cooperation between parents and teachers is an essential objective at the individual and class levels, one contribution towards achieving it is to represent a strictly parental viewpoint at policy levels, i.e. the school, the region, the nation and internationally.

8 GOVERNING BODIES AND SCHOOL BOARDS

Setting the Scene

The present chapter is not intended as a general guide to the practice of school governance. Rather it considers governing bodies (in Scotland, school boards) in terms of parent–teacher relations, a more modest objective.

It is sometimes assumed that the presence of parents on a governing body or school board itself constitutes liaison between the school and the families it serves. Certainly the governing body offers the potential for developing such liaison. Yet, despite the appropriateness of parental representation, an elected parent on a governing body may have little contact with his/her constituents, may have few channels for ascertaining their concerns, may be 'socialised' into approaching the school's aims and problems from the viewpoint of the education authority or of the staff, may be diverted from central educational issues of the school, and may do little to encourage or enhance a sense of partnership between parents and teachers at different levels within the school. In such circumstances, the governing body may be representative, but it is not necessarily a mechanism for home–school liaison. The purpose of this chapter is to explore ways by which it might be such a mechanism. To do so, the concepts of governance, representation and accountability are considered with their implications for governors. Potential obligations for governors to enhance parent–teacher partnership, including the implications of the 1988 Act, are then discussed.

The 1970s and 1980s witnessed a growth of local democratic influence on school governance throughout Europe. The system of governing bodies in England and Wales has undergone recent changes initially through the 1980 Act which, in effect, ensured that each school had its own governing body and took the first steps to standardise membership (including parents and teachers); then more importantly through the 1986 Act which spelt out in detail both the structure and the functions of governing bodies. These reforms were overdue. The Taylor Committee which reported in 1977, influenced both by a general unease about the ineffectiveness of such bodies at a time of educational tensions and by specific evidence (e.g. Baron and Howell, 1974), concluded: 'in short, the extent to which managing and governing bodies carried out the functions assigned to them in rules and articles was slight. In many areas they did not, in any real sense, exist at all.' (p. 8, para. 2.11.)

Even after the 1980 Act there were signs that governing bodies were low-status affairs. Kogan *et al.* (1984), reporting on their research into the practice of governing bodies, could state, 'If in both structure and behaviour the governing bodies are weak, so are the expectations of local authorities and of governors themselves of the governing body role.' But the researchers were optimistic that 'Governors can develop corporately and individually if they are given the right information, argued with as equals, and expected to occupy roles well beyond those of symbolic representation ... They can be empowered to view the school's self-evaluation critically and fully ...' Then the importance of governing bodies was increased by the combination of the 1986 Act, which restructured governing bodies and specified their basic functions (especially with regard to the curriculum in sections 17 and 18), and the 1988 Act, which increased their powers (especially with regard to local financial management and the right to opt out of LEA control). These are significant changes with important implications for involving parents. I shall return to them later in this chapter.

Meanwhile Scotland had been dragging behind not only England but most of the rest of Europe. Largely ineffective bodies concerned with groups of schools called school councils had been analysed and found wanting by the Glasgow University Report published by the Scottish Office (Macbeth, MacKenzie and Breckenridge, 1980). It was not until 1988 that legislation was introduced to create a school board for each school. While Scottish school boards may be likened to English governing bodies, their composition and powers are different. Of special note is the voting majority of elected parents. Such an arrangement is not unique. New Zealand Secondary schools (Barrington, 1981) have a parental majority, while in Denmark parents are the only school board members permitted to vote (Cornelius, 1986). A voting majority of parents is new for Britain. Scottish school boards were not empowered by the 1988 legislation to have the degree of control over curriculum and finance which English governors enjoy, though 'opting-out' will appear in Scotland, and the legislation already includes mechanisms by which a school board can request extra powers for itself.

What is School Governance?

It may be helpful to define school governance. Official publications have concentrated on the membership, structure and functions of governing bodies without making entirely clear why they exist, and a definition of the process – that is, governance – should encapsulate *purpose*. We may recognise in passing that participatory schemes may be misused for unsatisfactory purposes, for instance as a dumping-ground for unpalatable tasks (such as interviewing the parents of truants), as a shock absorber (acting as a buffer for criticisms), as a means to acquire the appearance of local support where in reality it is lacking and as a diversionary mechanism (diverting the 'interfering public' into peripheral matters). Baron (1981, p. 8) adds reservations about incompetence and ignorance of participants. Lucas (1976, pp. 153–4), having described arguments for participation as 'eloquent rather than exact', considers that such arguments have been exaggerated, doubts whether we can consult everyone about everything and even asserts, 'Too much information is almost as bad as too little. It clogs the system and submerges the important messages with irrelevant noise.' To those may be added fears of extreme activist take-over, waste of money, the 'pooling of ignorance' and inefficiency. In brief, there are practical objections to something which is conceptually desirable.

The answer to these charges must surely be provided through clarity of purpose. Some have criticised as confusing the 1986 Act's assertion that curricular responsibilities are shared between central government, education authorities, governing bodies and the headteacher, but this compromise, messy though it may appear, does provide a system of checks and balances which reduces the potential for extreme activist take-over *at any level*. To make such a system of checks and balances effective at the level of the school requires some definition in the minds of governors about what governance ought to be.

Towards that end, I offer the following provisional definition of school governance: **stakeholders' influence on major (especially curricular) school-level decisions about the school and about its relations with others having educational responsibilities**. Elements of this definition deserve consideration in terms of practice.

Stakeholders

Stakeholder theory is integral to notions of local democracy (Abrahamsson, 1977), especially that those affected by a decision should be able, through representatives, to influence – though not necessarily to make – that decision. Various categories of people have a stake in a school, but the nature and extent of their stake in it can differ.

Parents, being legally responsible for their individual children's education, clients of the school and co-educators of their children, must clearly take pride of place among those adults with a stake in the school. It is not surprising that some countries have given them a voting majority on boards or, as in many German provinces, the French primary sector and some Australian states, half the voting power.

Teachers have a stake in the school as their place of employment and (rather different) as the organisation through which they practise their professional craft. Since non-teaching staff provide support for, but do not practise, that craft, their stake in school policy is less than that of teachers.

Pupils might appear to have a claim to representation because their school contributes, often importantly, towards their education. But we must remember that before the age of 16 they are not responsible for their own education. Their parents are. Since parents have that serious duty it is they who are the stakeholders not only in their own right as affected individuals, but on behalf of their children as well. Young people over the age of 16 are stakeholders to an enhanced degree.

Members of the community have an interest in school matters as local residents, as tax-payers and rate-payers, as local politicians, as potential employers, as those involved in linked services, or simply as citizens. Yet it would be difficult to claim that these groups had a stake in the school comparable to that of parents, staff and senior pupils. It is not surprising that in most European systems the main members of school councils are the headteacher and representatives of parents, teachers and senior pupils. In cases of church schools, religious representatives are commonly found as well. There would appear to be only limited logic for the inclusion of LEA-appointed governors. Just as Members of Parliament do not expect to have reserved places on education authorities, so it would seem inappropriate for local councillors to control places on governing bodies. However, the law requires it for England, along with co-opted members from 'the local community' but not in Scotland where the local councillors may attend as non-voting advisers.

Representation

The next problem concerns the representativeness of elected parent governors. While it is easy to devise a system whereby teachers can choose colleagues to represent them on a governing body and means by which they can report back, since teachers are relatively small in number and regularly meet in the same building, it is less easy to achieve the same for parents. The elected parent can find reporting back to his constituents awkward unless there is an effective PA. Further, one frequently hears the accusation that a parent-governor is not 'representative' because he/she does not *typify* all parents. 'She's middle class, so she's not representative' or 'He was only elected by five per cent of parents'. However, are not these arguments missing some essential points? Of course electoral procedures should be made as appropriate as possible, but a low turn-out does not prevent an individual from representing the parental dimension in governors' meetings. Still less does a representative have to be typical. As Likert and Likert (1976) point out 'effective participation requires ... skills that a sizeable proportion of the population lack. If effective participation is to occur, an interaction-influence network is required that is more complex than most people have experienced or have the skills to function in.' In other words, a good representative is *un*typical rather than typical. It is his capacity to be well-informed, articulate, confident at committee work, skilful at handling people and conscientious in contacting the parents whom he represents that matter more than how 'typical' he is or how many votes made him a governor.

The next problem is whether the representative operates as a *trustee* or as a *delegate*. A trustee functions as an individual, according to his own assessment of events and conscience, without feeling an obligation to refer back to those who elected him on any given issue. A delegate, by contrast, would constantly seek the views of the parents whom he represents. Eulau and Prewitt (1973, p. 24) have argued that 'the degree to which the governors are responsive to the governed is the *sine qua non* of whether democracy in fact exists'. If responsiveness is thereby the essential element, then some mechanism of reference back to the body of parents would seem to be appropriate and the parental representative therefore needs a PA, PTA or EA, or some other group through which he can make such contact. However, this does not necessarily mean that he should seek a parental vote before contributing to any decision. An intermediate mode, sometimes called 'the theory of electoral accountability', can be operated whereby a representative can sound out opinions through an organisation such as PA, but ultimately contribute towards governors' decisions as a trustee having weighed the evidence given to him.

Feedback and contact mechanisms are obviously important and the need for governors to establish regular lines of communication with both voluntary parental organisations and class-meeting groups is difficult to contest. In practical terms, therefore, there are strong arguments for governors to encourage the creation and active involvement of such parental groups as have been discussed in chapter 7.

Influence on Major Decisions in the School

Important policy decisions are made at the level of the school. These can include aspects of what is taught, how it is taught, the allocation of internal resources (especially staff time and finance), decisions affecting the ethos and philosophy of the school and the extent to which the education of children is seen as a shared function between teachers and parents. Because of the highly decentralised nature of our school system, quite marked variations exist between schools. These are not just the structural differences of selective/comprehensive, church/secular, single-sex/co-educational, large/small and so on which are readily reflected in handbooks, but they can be differences in *process* which are less easily expressed as simple alternatives and are usually questions of degree.

School-based decisions which create these differences could be open to neighbourhood, especially parental, democratic influence. Perhaps herein lies the main justification for governing bodies. Those affected by a decision should have a mechanism by which they can influence (but not necessarily make) those local decisions through their representatives. It is a matter of opinion whether governing bodies ought to stand in direct line of authority between the LEA and headteacher, but the need for a forum in which differing views can be expressed about essential decisions is a proper part of a democratic society. This is not to deny to the headteacher the ultimate right to make certain decisions (for instance with regard to the organisation and application of the curriculum) but it should ensure that he does so in a framework of local policy-making and in a way by which he is accountable for his actions.

There is a tendency to over-simplify the functions of a governing body as being either 'advisory' or 'executive'. It may be more appropriate to think in terms of four types of action, each of which has two subsidiary modes:

Informing (i) Making information accessible on request.
  (ii) Publicising information.
Advising (i) Unrestricted (petitioning).
  (ii) On request (consultation).
Ensuring (i) Calling to account (requesting explanations).
  (ii) Rendering of account (explaining).
Deciding (i) Policy decisions (rule-making).
  (ii) Executive decisions (rule-applying).

The ways in which a governing body operates may give more or less emphasis to any of these elements. For instance, the potential for a governing body to provide **information** about the school to parents could be considerable if it combined a policy of openness with the use of the PA/PTA as a means of dissemination. It can also open channels so that parents seeking information can get it.

In other instances it may wish to give **advice**. Section 18(4) of the 1986 Act makes the headteacher responsible for the 'determination and organisation of the secular curriculum' within policy guidelines from the LEA and governors. However, this does not debar governors from proferring their views on detailed aspects of that curriculum nor does it prevent the headteacher from seeking their views. Indeed, the governors must take account of petitions from parents and from the community and, as representatives, they would have a duty to both seek and pass on such views. This is especially important for the representatives of parents. Quite apart from the Annual Report from the governors and the Annual Meeting of parents (both required by the 1986 Act) there is a practical need for a constant flow of information throughout the year. The danger with an Annual Report and Annual Meeting is that both will tend to look *backwards* to past events and decisions, while governance concerns *future* decisions about which the advice of governors can be helpful.

In some instances governors themselves will **make decisions** rather than just give advice. The 1986 Act envisages some specific decisions to be made by the governors, for instance with regard to the school's curricular policy (related to the LEA's statement), sex education, the availability of information to parents, the appointment (along with others) of staff, and use of premises.

However, between advising and decision-making there is the function which, arguably, could be the most important element of governors' work. Yet it has received insufficient attention with regard to governance, in my view. I have called it **ensuring**, though the term **accountability** has been much used.

Adults have responsibilities for children and for their education, either as parents or as professionals. The state has a responsibility to ensure that those adults are carrying out satisfactorily the duties required of them. Being local and being representative of the interested groups, the governing body is the most appropriate centre for such an ensuring function. There has been much debate about the nature of accountability in education and a valuable range of books has emerged* but there is insufficient space here to discuss the issues. For simplicity, and to provide a rule-of-thumb for practitioners, we may regard accountability as a rendering of account, or **explaining**. The adult with duties (parent or teacher) may be called upon to render an account to the governors about those aspects for which he/she is responsible. The prime active function of governors may therefore be one of constantly **ensuring** that people are fulfilling their duties. Indeed, governors cannot properly compile their Annual Report, required by the 1986 Act, without such checking. The Government consultation paper on the National Curriculum of 1987, for instance, referred to the governing body being involved in 'the essential process of regular evaluation' of the curriculum of a school against local and national standards.

The process need not be inquisitorial, and a good teacher will welcome the chance to explain processes and to seek the backing of governors with regard to initiatives. Official inspections by the inspectorate are infrequent, while education authorities are generally too remote to know what is happening in detail in every school. The task of regular, rotational calling to account of those with responsibilities can and in my view should fall to the governors who can build a systematic plan for reviewing the school's and the parents' contributions into the schedules of their work. (If pressure of other activities makes this difficult, governors might analyse the nature of those other activities and consider which of them are in reality peripheral and can be delegated to sub-committees or to staff or abandoned.)

In their book of advice to governors (written before the 1986 Act, but still valuable) Burgess and Sofer (1986, p. 15) urge governors to read carefully their local Articles of Government and be clear about their responsibilities, which vary from authority to authority. They add the important point that 'even the most vague or limiting articles can be used for the benefit of the school if governors are prepared to think about them and use them.'

The School and its Relations with Others having Educational Responsibilities

In my provisional definition of school governance above I drew attention to stakeholders' influence upon in-school decisions. However,

---

* Becher and Maclure, 1978; Sockett *et al.*, 1980; Elliott *et al.*, 1981; Becher *et al.*, 1981; McCormick (Ed.), 1982; Lacey and Lawton, 1981.

education is more than just schooling. A governing body is formally concerned with a particular school, but since a school cannot function in isolation from its setting or its educational partners, nor can a governing body.

Parents, of course, are especially relevant. By one viewpoint parents are not 'outside' the school at all, but are part of it and its community. In that case 'the school' cannot have a relationship with parents, but rather the staff and parents of a school have a partnership with each other within the school community. The alternative viewpoint is to see school-learning (teacher initiated) and home-learning (parent-initiated) as being separate, but in need of coordination, in which case parents are 'outside' the school. This latter approach is the more generally accepted one and I shall adopt it here.

Official reports and legislation under governments of different colours have put increasing emphasis upon parents with relation to schooling. The Taylor and Astin Reports (1977 and 1979), the Warnock Report (1978), the White Paper *Better Schools* (1985), the Scottish Main Report (1986) and separate English and Scottish laws of 1988, have devoted space to the role of parents both in the education of individual pupils and in the governance of schools. It seems that governing bodies would be remiss if they did not regard the creation and monitoring of parent–teacher relationships as a matter of central educational concern.

If so, how can they implement such a policy with regard to involving parents? One simple device is to pose, as a matter of normal routine, the following question with regard to all policy matters or decisions to which they are giving consideration: **'What is the parental dimension of this issue?'** To the usual pupil-centred and teacher-centred approaches could be added a parent-centred perspective. For most school issues do have a parental dimension.

The next step is to build into the governing body's schedule for the year an annual review of the school's mechanisms for educational partnership with parents and their effectiveness. To give focus to that review, an idea might be taken from the Republic of Ireland's Curriculum and Examination Board. To ensure that the parental dimension was not neglected in its report compiled to overhaul the national curriculum, the Irish Curriculum and Examinations Board (1986) set up a sub-committee called the Parents in Education Committee, and all the working papers were analysed by it to ensure that parental facets had not been neglected. A governing body could do the same thing. Its parental sub-committee could have an additional duty to write a parental section to the governors' annual report. The elected parent-governors would, of course, be members of that sub-committee and one should chair it.

Next, the Governors could establish recognised links with the PA, PTA or EA of the school. This may be considered in two parts: first there are the links between the governing body as a whole and the parental organisation; and secondly the relationship between parent governors and the parental organisation.

The Taylor Report (1977, pp. 113–4) made the following recommendations about relations between governors and parents:

> 29. Parents' organisations should be encouraged and facilities for their work should be made available within the school.

> 30. Parents should have the opportunity to set up an organisation based upon the school, developing its aims and methods of working in consultation with the headteacher and the governing body.

> 31. As a basic minimum the governing body should ensure that parents have access to the school for a weekday evening meeting once a term and the means of publicising their activities.

> 32. The governing body should satisfy itself that adequate arrangements are made to inform parents, to involve them in their children's progress and welfare, to enlist their support, and to ensure their access to the school and a teacher by reasonable arrangement.

> 33. The nature of the relation between the school and the individual parent should be set down in a letter sent by the governors to every parent at the time of their formal acceptance of a place at the school.

It will be noted that the Taylor Committee referred to *parents'* organisations rather than PTAs, and a fuller discussion of this issue was presented in chapter 7. The Taylor Committee's recommendations seem entirely sensible and I shall accept them as a starting-point. What else might be done?

First, rather more emphasis than the Taylor Report suggested might be put on establishing a regular two-way flow of information and views between the governing body and the PA. As a minimum, the minutes of non-confidential elements of the governing body's meetings could go to the PA's committee, and those of the PA to the governing body. Also, on any selected longer-term issue of policy, the governing body could ask the PA to gather the views of members and to report them back with comments, on the clear understanding that parental views will not alone determine outcomes. As a matter of annual routine the governors could ask the PA to review and to comment upon the content and layout of the school handbook and all other documents designed for parents, and perhaps every two or three years to assess the school rules.

Next, the governing body could use the PA/PTA as a publicising mechanism. If the PA/PTA has a regular newspaper, that can have a governors' section, while class meetings and other gatherings can be used by governors to make known their work and decisions (proposed and taken) and to obtain reactions. If the governing body is to be a channel of communication between the education authority and parents, then the publicity function of the PA can be especially relevant to governors.

It is unusual for either a headteacher or a governing body to consider delegating decision-making powers to a PTA or PA, yet over some issues this would seem to be a logical action. Authority can be delegated, not responsibility. When a head delegates to his staff (for the running of a department, for instance) he does not thereby divest himself of responsibility; he is still answerable for the results. A head (or governing body) could delegate to the PA the task of designing a handbook for parents, for instance, or of writing the parental section of the Annual Report or of reporting to governors on issues of homework or, theoretically, anything for which the head (or governing body) had the original authority to do. Guidelines or conditions might accompany such delegation, but the possibility of using the PA more directly for liaison rather than fund-raising purposes deserves increased consideration. Of course, it would be up to the members of the PA/PTA to decide whether they wanted to carry out the functions requested of them and they could reasonably decline if the actions were beyond their abilities or inappropriate. A request to raise money for the school, for instance, might reasonably be rejected by the PA/PTA.

The Confidentiality Committee

There is one difficulty which perhaps deserves the joint attention of a PA and a governing body. This is that parents may be reluctant to express an anxiety about or make a complaint against a school for fear that the school might discriminate against their child if the identity of the parents were known. As teachers, of course, we tend to reject the possibility that a child would be unfairly treated by the school because the parents had complained. However, I do know of parents who consider that this has happened, and others who have desisted from expressing their views for fear that it might. To demonstrate that they do not subscribe to such implicit blackmail, it would be relatively easy for governors and staff to introduce a confidentiality committee.

A confidentiality committee can consist of two citizens in whom both school and PA/PTA have trust. These might be, perhaps, retired people whose previous occupations made them accustomed to handling confidential information, or else they might simply be two of the parent-governors. The governors or PA/PTA can circulate the addresses of those confidants. Members with problems which they wish to raise confidentially write, giving name and address, but with the knowledge that these will not be passed on to the school, and express their anxiety. The committee may take one of three steps:

(i)   Decline to take further action, other than acknowledging receipt of the complaint.
(ii) Seek further evidence.
(iii) Tell the school's headteacher or chairman of the governors without identifying the complainant.

Otherwise nobody would know the details of issues raised. However, each year the confidentiality committee could tell the governors:

(i) How many letters or verbal complaints it received.
(ii) How many were referred to the headteacher, or chairman of the governors.
(iii) With regard to how many action was taken.

Expenses of the confidentiality committee should be reimbursed.

Either, as suggested above, the governors can be the originators of such a scheme or, if the governors decline to do so, the PA could be the initiator.

Parent-governor Initiatives

Parent-governors, on appointment and subsequently, may find themselves under pressure to conform to patterns of behaviour which are supportive of the bureaucracy. *Notes of Guidance for Governors* or other training media are likely to stress pre-established procedures. Of course, such procedures must be adhered to. However, there may be less clarity about whom a governor represents and how he/she responds to that trust. The Open University training pack for governors (1981, p. 3) cautiously referred to the two-fold responsibility of all governors 'to ensure that the school is run in a way which expresses the community's wishes, and ... to support, and possibly protect, the interests of the school.' Yet we may ask if such a prescription is not open to modification in the case of governors who *represent a specific group*, such as parents.

Some might argue that parent-governors are elected, not to represent a particular group, but merely to be of that group, with a duty to conform to the needs and wishes of the bureaucracy – that is, administrators and teachers. In the past such an argument might have been sustained, and texts published before the 1986 Act sometimes reflect that assumption. For instance, Burgess and Sofer (1986), in a book first published in 1978, could advise governors 'You are appointed by and are responsible to the local education authority.' Yet it seems clear that this was not the intention of the Taylor Committee whose report describes them as representatives and specifically refers to them 'speaking for the general body of parents' (p. 28) and functioning 'in keeping with the normal democratic processes.' If so, then **the first duty of parent-governors must be to represent the parental dimension of governance;** the functions of reflecting the wider community's wishes or 'protecting' the school must presumably be subsidiary.

The Astin Report for Northern Ireland (1979) saw the Board of Governors as 'a local focus and forum for all groups which have a major and direct interest in the life, character and well-being of the individual school, as a channel of influence for such interests' (p. 3), and the parents' representatives as 'members who feel a special responsibility to speak from a parental point of view and to draw attention to considerations which might be of special concern to parents.' That would seem to be the proper philosophy for parent-governors.

Kogan *et al.* (1984) report that many parent-governors 'found they had to operate as trustees, putting forward their own views in the hope that these would be in the best interests of all parents' (p. 136) because of the embarrassments they experienced not only from having been elected by a very small proportion of their constituents but also because of difficulties in establishing lines of communication with fellow parents. But in their research Kogan *et al.* recognised that the PA/PTA might assist the parent-governors:

> In certain cases the existence of a PTA means that parent governors can use it as a representative forum to collect views and report back on governing body activities. It also provides an alternative channel for pressure upon the school. But it is more likely that the PTA has no links with the parent governors and acts solely as a support mechanism for the school. (p. 65)

Although this research finding is not encouraging, the moral may still be that links between parent-governors and the PA/PTA are of special importance. The potential is considerable, even if present practice neglects those links. A parent-governor should, of course, attend open meetings of the PA and encourage it to use the parent-governors as two-way channels of communication with the governing body. The PA may invite the parent-governors to attend meetings of its executive committee and class meetings of parents. In brief, the PA (especially one with class units, or mini-associations) may be the only way that a parent-governor can genuinely carry out a representative function with any real sense of electoral accountability.

Yet even a parent-governor who has no PA through which to contact those whom he represent can still approach all governors' work by seeing it 'through a parental eye', and other governors should encourage him to do so. It may also be helpful for parent-governors of several local schools to meet together periodically to compare notes and to reinforce their identity.

Governing Bodies as Initiators of Parent–Teacher Partnership

Governors – all governors, irrespective of whom they represent – might see the stimulation of active parent–teacher partnership as one of their central educational tasks. While parent-governors may reasonably give emphasis to the wishes and rights of parents, the governing body may find it appropriate to concentrate more upon the *duties* of parents and teachers. Many of the difficulties encountered in establishing an active working relationship between parents and teachers for the benefit of children have arisen from the greater convenience to both parents and teachers *not* to operate in partnership. Governors could well start any consideration of parent–teacher liaison on the assumptions that neither set of adults wants to do it, that it is easier for each group to leave the other alone but that liaison is still needed for the good education of children. The justifications of home–school cooperation do not rest on what people want: they rest on legal duties, moral obligations and some indicators from research that such liaison might increase equality of opportunity for children.

The problem for governors, then, is not just one of making facilities for cooperation available, but of getting the two groups of responsible adults to use those facilities. Since most parents are interested in their own individual child's educational experience, then it would seem sensible to start with the individual and class levels where that motivation predominates. This can be backed by high quality and constant publicity of the issues, the duties and the actions at those levels. Such publicity can be circulated through the PA and, hopefully, the class parents if there are mini-associations.

The 1986 and 1988 Education Acts (England and Wales)

Provisions of the 1986 and 1988 Education Acts place on governors responsibilities which put them in a position to influence school policy to a high degree. This chapter is not about policy making but about governors' relations with parents, parents' access to governors and ways by which reconstituted governing bodies may enhance home–school relations. For the sake of simplicity the following comments relate to the law for county, controlled and maintained schools, but the principles of liaison with parents apply to aided and special agreement schools; indeed, I see no reason why they should not apply to independent schools also.

Curriculum

Sections 17 and 18 of the 1986 Act lay down the duties and powers of the LEA, governors and headteachers with regard to the secular curriculum. The 1988 Act then introduces the broader framework of the National Curriculum. At all levels communication beyond the school gate is envisaged, and there are opportunities for informing, consulting, petitioning and influencing if relevant people – especially governors, headteachers and parents – determine to use them.

The education authority is required to keep the secular curriculum under review, including a written statement of their policy which shall be available and published 'in such other manner as the authority consider appropriate' and the headteacher 'shall make it available, at all reasonable times, to persons wishing to inspect it.' The governing body must make a statement about whether they consider that the LEA's policy should be modified, having regard to 'any representations which are made to them'. The headteacher is responsible for 'the determination and organisation of the secular curriculum' and in carrying out this function must have regard to 'any representations which are made to him . . . by any persons connected with the community served by the school.' The 1988 Act envisages that the Secretary of State would make regulations about the provision of information to interested parties. Thus the opportunities for dialogue between parents and teachers with regard to the curriculum are considerable.

How might these opportunities be used? Hopefully, the governing body as a whole and the headteacher would make arrangements for regular communication with parents about the curriculum. Many schools already circulate booklets explaining what the school is teaching and how parents can complement it in the home. The PA/PTA can assist in such a process. Class (or age-group) meetings, outlined in chapter 6, can be especially relevant for explaining details of the National Curriculum to the parents whose children are about to be involved in a particular stage. If the school does not have such meetings, then mini-associations of the class/age-group can do so under the general guidance of the PA/PTA as explained in chapter 7. Aware of the educational importance of parents, the headteacher would be the most likely person to take initiatives of this sort, but if not, then a special onus falls on parent-governors to stimulate such arrangements. It may be hoped that any training for governors will put particular emphasis upon these communicating and advising functions.

The 1986 Act makes an exception of one aspect of the curriculum: sex education. This is one of the clearest examples of what I call 'the overlap curriculum'. Along with such issues as moral and religious education and health education, sex education is probably as much (if not more) a parental responsibility as a school one. Under the Act, the governing body of a school must consider whether or not sex education should be part of the school curriculum. They have a duty to maintain a written statement of how sex education should be taught. Surely this ought to be an issue of fullest consultation with parents, to be repeated regularly to ensure not only that consensus is reinforced by each new group of parents, but that parents are fully briefed on how the school intends to handle different aspects, exactly when for every level of the school and with the opportunity for parents to see texts, films or other audio-visual materials to be used.

To be anecdotal, I recall returning from work one evening and asking my then nine-year-old daughter what she had done at school that day. 'We saw a film.' I asked her what it was about. 'It was called *Don't Go With Strangers*. [pause] Dad, why mustn't I go with strangers?' Parents should never be confronted with serious issues of this sort without thorough advance notification from the school, preferably having seen the film/text/materials and discussed them in a class meeting for parents. Parents will then be able to adapt their home teaching to fit in with the school curriculum, and they will be able to follow up questions or misunderstandings.

National Testing and Public Examination Results

National testing is also discussed in chapter 3 on communication about the individual child, chapter 5 on parental choice and chapter 6 on class level liaison.

Test results of an individual child are to be confidential to the school and to the child's parents. The governing body may want to ensure that a thorough system of reporting and explaining these results to parents operates, followed by private consultations to determine appropriate subsequent action. Test results will appear when the child is aged seven, 11, 14 and 16. Some of the communication should be in advance of tests results, some consequent to them.

A first step might be to ensure that every parent has a leaflet explaining test results *in relation to individual children*. (Explanation of the more complex issue of aggregated results to judge professional performance should be presented separately to avoid confusion.) A separate leaflet might be available for each of the four stages. Such material may well be available from other sources 'off the shelf', either from the LEA or from national bodies. If so, care should be taken to ensure that ready-made leaflets are appropriate. Do they seek to grind a partisan axe? Do they take each age-level in turn? Do they lump the question of aggregated results in with that of individual results?

If governors decide to create their own school's explanatory leaflets, it makes sense for staff to join forces with representatives of the PA/PTA to ensure that materials appear in a form that parents can understand. There must be explanation that assessment is a combination of standardised test results and teachers' own judgements. The ten levels of assessment and the profile components reflecting the attainment targets might be made clearer by examples of the methods used and how GCSE fits into the picture. The formative, diagnostic, summative and evaluative purposes should be explained, and the ways by which assessment is to be criterion-referenced and progressive. My last few sentences have been full of the sorts of semi-technical terms which may quickly be dismissed as jargon devised by teachers to confuse parents. So simple explanations, perhaps based on the excellent definitions provided at the start of the 1987 report of the Task Group on Assessment and Testing, might be devised.

Class or age-group meetings of parents (see chapter 6) or mini-associations (see chapter 7) can be held to explain the nature of the tests, the ways in which teacher assessment plays a part and how the school will utilise the results in consultation with parents. Such meetings, of course, should be held before the results appear, and it will be for governors to take the initiative. Governors will also have to give thought to problems of children (such as immigrants) with language difficulties and should regularly review assessment procedures for gender, ethnic or other biases as suggested in sections 51–53 of the Task Group's 1987 report.

After consolidation of the test results there should be private consultations with the child's parents to consider any future action.

However, national tests are also intended as a means by which governors, parents, education administrators and the public can judge the performance of classes, schools and education authorities. This has been the more contentious element of national testing because test and public examination results reflect more than the school's performance; they are influenced by out-of-school factors, especially home background (see chapter 5). This poses a delicate task for governors with regard to communication with parents. Clearly aggregated test results must not be concealed. However, they must be made public in a way that is both fair to teaching staff and meaningful to parents.

The 1987 Task Group's report concluded that the complex formulae used by some American states to express test results with allowances for home background factors were confusing. They therefore advocated that results, unadjusted, should be issued within an explanatory statement about the nature of the school and its intake. That is certainly one approach. However it may be possible for governors to make comparisons (and publish them) as long as like is being compared with like. Figures indicating the socio-economic background of a school's intake are often available in the form of numbers of free school meals and clothing grants, or the occupation of fathers. If a school's results are compared with three or four local schools with similar intakes, that might be helpful. Another approach is to analyse one school's results over time, comparing one year with previous years on the assumption that the nature of the intake is relatively constant. Another method at primary level is to compare the socio-economic composition of classes within a school and then cross-relate classes; or, at secondary level, to compare results of similar subjects.

Governors can then discuss the results and comparisons with the committee of the PA/PTA and decide by what methods they should inform the parent body as a whole, incorporate results into handbooks for parents contemplating choice of that school and inform the local press.

Open Enrolment

Chapter 5 is devoted to parental choice and it contains discussion of ways by which a school can assist in the choice process. Chapter 7 draws attention to the ways by which parents with children already in the school and their PA/PTA can provide an advisory service for parents contemplating placing their child in that school.

Local Financial Management

The 1988 Act delegates to all secondary schools and to all primary schools with more than 200 pupils the responsibility for managing their own budgets. Governing bodies are responsible for expenditure on most items and services other than home–school–home transport, advisory and other specialist services, and pay, tax and superannuation. Although LEAs continue to be teachers' employers, governors have powers with regard to promotions, selection of staff and taking on extra teachers if they can meet the cost. These are substantial powers and it will not be surprising if governors take decisions as trustees – that is, without debating the issues with the parent body or others in the community.

However, issues of a general nature leading to staffing and expenditure decisions might well be topics of consultation and discussion in the forum of the PA/PTA. For instance, a decision to put new emphasis upon computer studies involving not only changes to the timetable, but also staff recruitment and expenditure on equipment – all of which mean resources not going to other activities – could well be discussed in advance with those having an immediate stake in the school, especially parents. The governors could emphasise that the final decision rests with them, but that they would like to sound out local views. Such a procedure could also help parents who might want to purchase home computers compatible with the school's equipment, but it would be the broader curricular implications upon which parents ought to be consulted also. Such an approach could apply to any major shift of school policy and it would give additional legitimacy to decisions taken.

'Opting-out'

'Opting-out' from local authority control, more properly that of obtaining grant-maintained status and therefore funding from central government, is available initially to maintained secondary schools and to primary schools with at least 300 pupils. It remains to be seen whether the facility will be extended later to smaller primary schools. The procedures are quite complex, but essential to this book is the involvement of parents.

The process can be initiated *either* by the governors *or* by parents. For parents to originate such a move, a request must be signed by 'a number of parents of registered pupils at the school equal to at least 20 per cent of the number of registered pupils at the school.' In either case, the next stage is a secret postal ballot among parents. If 50 per cent or more of the parents eligible to vote do so, then the result of that ballot (by a simple majority) is conclusive. If fewer than 50 per cent of the parents vote, then a second ballot is held within 14 days and the result is conclusive regardless of the proportion of parents voting.

The remaining formalities on the road to grant-maintained status in which governors, LEA and Secretary of State play parts, need not concern us here. It is the initial stage, outlined above, which involves parents. It sets in train a process which, once completed, would be difficult to reverse. Thus there are good grounds to make the local debates as full and as public as possible. It should extend beyond the parents eligible to vote because their decision will affect local school provision for future parents. To be credible, the proportion of parents voting should be high and governors should not only make use of the school's PA/PTA as a forum for debate, but should publicise the issues through local media.

Other aspects relevant to parents are that the school cannot alter its character, size or age range initially after changing grant status, but after a period of time may make a public proposal to do so; places will be available to local children; they will be entitled to LEA help with transport.

School Boards (Scotland) Act, 1988

Scotland's legislation has followed a somewhat different path from that of England and Wales but heading in the same general direction. Some curricular cohesion has already happened and more is planned in Scotland, while the Scottish Standard Grade came into existence before the English GCSE. Open enrolment was introduced in 1981 for Scotland and the system, slightly different in detail but not in spirit from the English, has generally worked satisfactorily (see chapter 5) and the English 1988 adaptations of the 1980 Act in regard to open enrolment may be seen as bringing England and Wales closer to the Scottish pattern. In some other respects Scotland lags behind England. Since several of the English reforms depend upon the existence of a governing body for each school, the fact that Scotland has had an unsatisfactory system of school councils associated with groups of schools (see Macbeth, MacKenzie and Breckenridge, 1980) has prevented 'opting-out' and local financial management from being considered until recently. The central feature of the Scottish 1988 Act is the creation of a school board for every school.

Although parents are a *voting majority* on school boards, they are an *attending minority*. The parental dimension is seen as important and the Act requires boards to 'promote contact between the school, parents of pupils in attendance at the school and the community' and in particular to 'encourage the formation of parent–teacher or parents' associations'. Not only can a board call a meeting of parents with children at the school but, if 30 such parents demand it, then a meeting must be held. Such parental meetings may 'make resolutions', thereby making school boards more accountable.

The initial powers of school boards are not great. There is no control over the curriculum – only the right to advise. There is little in the way of local financial management – only the power to approve expenditure on books and materials. And with regard to staffing, their role will be contributory rather than determinant. Yet an interesting feature is the potential not only for the Government to change their powers through subsequent legislation ('opting-out' being the next formal measure) but boards themselves can request increased powers when and if they feel ready individually to take them on. We therefore see a Scottish System in the process of evolution. As with lizards in the Galapagos, isolation is producing its own mutations.

Numbers and Quality of Parent-governors

A fear has been expressed in England that not enough parents will come forward to act as governors and that some who do may be unsuitable. In Scotland where the number needed per school will be higher, the anxiety has also been expressed. The DES has published leaflets entitled *Shouldn't you become a School Governor?* and *School Governors: A New Role* and a Labour Party spokesman, following a Labour survey which suggested that nearly two-thirds of LEAs were experiencing problems recruiting parents, called for recruiting commercials on television.

Part of the problem seems to be in the increased powers of governors. There appear to be two aspects to this: the burden of responsibility accompanying such powers, and the time taken in a voluntary activity. Little can be done about the seriousness of the responsibilities other than the provision of highly professional back-up, advice and information, but action could be taken by governors themselves to ensure that parent-governors are not expected to waste time on the trivial and the menial. Their efforts could be directed to the two main reasons for their presence on governing bodies: the nature of education provided and the quality of educational liaison between parents and teachers. Others – especially co-opted members – can deal with (and be recruited to deal with) delegated financial management, buildings maintenance problems, individual cases of truancy and indiscipline, and so on. Some parents, of course, may feel more confident when dealing with leaking roofs or breaches of school rules about dress, but they could be discouraged from getting involved in such matters. Above all, parental representatives should see themselves as the protectors and reflectors of the parental dimension of education.

Baron (1981) has traced the historical decline of the parental role in school matters until it became 'that of supporting the work of the schools in ways acceptable to politicians, administrators and teachers,' (p.15.) That may be changing. Beattie (1985) suggests that two conflicting movements may be at work: clarification of central control, in which the government's aim may be legitimation, and a more liberal distribution of the authority around the system (pp.229–30). However, the contrasting experiences of European countries which Beattie analyses leave him unsure how to predict the likely success or failure of parental involvement.

9 HOME–SCHOOL LIAISON AND DISADVANTAGED FAMILIES

Deprivation and Disadvantage

Disadvantaged families may be a minority but they present a challenge in the field of home–school relations. If it is true that home-learning contributes to or impedes the effectiveness of schooling and if it is true that the nature of home-learning can be influenced for the better, then presumably education authorities and schools should try to influence the nature of home-learning experienced in disadvantaged families and the relationship those families have with school.

There are difficulties in identifying precisely how education in general, and schooling in particular, can act most effectively within the complex web of forces which contribute towards the condition which we label 'deprivation' or 'disadvantage'. Brown and Madge (1982), having looked at the usage of the word 'deprivation', argue:

> What emerges from this is a highly fragmented notion of deprivation. The term is used in so many ways that it has become almost meaningless. (p.35.)

Yet Brown and Madge themselves go some way to providing the delineations needed for the term. In their book *Despite the Welfare State* they pick two essential features leading towards analysis.

1 *Deprivation or disadvantage must be regarded as relative rather than absolute.* Nisbet and Watt (1984, p.3) refer to 'the gap between the less favoured and the more favoured'.
2 *There is no single state of deprivation or disadvantage.* It can apply to any of various aspects of social life. Brown and Madge especially analyse disadvantage with regard to income and poverty, occupation and employment, housing, educational attainment, physical and mental health, crime and delinquency and, finally, family life.

With regard to each of these (or any other) identifiable elements of social life it should be possible to recognise the gap between the less favoured and the more favoured and to identify in a general way the level below which the condition is unacceptable at any given point in our society's development. From there it is possible to refer to 'multiple deprivation' (when an individual suffers on several counts), 'cumulative deprivation' (when one disadvantage causes or reinforces others) and 'persisting deprivation' (when family and community circumstances make deprivation difficult or impossible to escape).

Mortimore and Blackstone (1982) prefer, and use, the term 'disadvantage' in their book *Disadvantage and Education*. They suggest (p.3) that when it is used with regard to education, three main groups may be described as disadvantaged:

(i)   Those who are denied equal access to educational opportunity in terms of type of school, resources, teachers or curriculum.

(ii) Those who, despite performing well in school, leave at the earliest opportunity.

(iii) Those who underachieve or who perform less well than they might because a variety of social and environmental factors result in their being unable to take advantage of educational opportunities.

These categories help us to focus action, though (perhaps necessarily) they suffer from reliance on the vague and equivocal words 'equal' and 'opportunity'. Also, it is not easy to say what is meant by 'perform less well than they might'. Arguably that applies to all children. Alternatively, reference to what a child might attain suggests a capacity to **assess** what a child might attain, but there is then a danger of ascribing intellectual ceilings to children, and the effects of the national testing schemes have yet to be evaluated. Despite these problems, the categories offered by Mortimore and Blackstone seem helpful, especially when placed in the broader setting of disadvantage being relative and multi-faceted.

We may ask which groups of children are most likely to suffer from any of these three modes of educational disadvantage. In the UK we tend to think mostly of the impoverished and that is appropriate. Yet other groups of children may suffer particular features of disadvantage. Ethnic minorities, girls (relative to boys) and physically or mentally handicapped children have attracted concern and action. It has been argued (e.g. Taylor, 1987) that lesbian and gay pupils ought to be included. The limitations of this book prevent me from reflecting the special arguments applicable to these groups and each has its own literature. As Tomlinson (1984) says in *Home and School in Multicultural Britain*, when referring to racial and cultural features, such differences add an extra dimension to problems of home–school relations. So do the circumstances of any other non-standard group of children such as those whose families are constantly on the move, those who are exceptionally gifted or those who live in remote rural areas. In the present chapter 'disadvantaged' will be taken potentially to embrace all such categories, but because each special sub-group has a distinct range of problems requiring particular home–school cooperative action, I shall adopt two approaches simultaneously. The first is to generalise where it seems that action broadly applies to all these categories. The second is to slant my comments towards children who suffer multiple deprivation in urban areas.

I justify this last stance in terms of the size of the problem. As Quinton (1980) wrote:

> The statistics persistently and consistently point out that there are higher concentrations of adverse living conditions in urban areas. There is more crime, vandalism and delinquency; there are more low-status and single-parent families; there is more psychiatric disorder, and so on. (p.45.)

But it is not just a question of numbers. It is one of cumulative and persistent interaction of kinds of disadvantage. In Marland's (1980) words:

> This intensity of problems becomes, as it were, a change in quality, not merely quantity, and creates a pattern of problems that can fairly be called 'inner-city', and which require addressing with a unified approach.'

One unified approach concerns collaboration between the welfare services. Another concerns collaboration between parents and professionals. The latter is the focus of this chapter.

Uniting Home and School in Conditions of Disadvantage

My sub-title uses the words 'in conditions of disadvantage' rather than (say) 'to counteract disadvantage' since it is clear that neither schools nor even schools and families operating in partnership can counteract deprivation as a generality. Yet it would seem that, united, they can play a part in reducing *educational* disadvantage.

In discussing practical steps, three points should be kept in mind:

1 The reasons for parent–teacher partnership *other than* counteracting educational disadvantage still apply, especially that parents are legally responsible for their child's education and may be regarded as the school's legal clients, and that much learning (for good or for ill) will continue to happen in the home whether schools attempt to influence it or not.
2 The techniques for establishing liaison which have been outlined in earlier chapters also apply in disadvantaged areas. Special action to assist less fortunate families does not replace the basics, but needs to be added to basics, such as the 12 points listed in chapter 2.
3 The steps advocated presuppose the provision of additional resources.

I shall consider practical actions under four headings:
   The value of an area policy,
   School initiatives,
   Influencing the nature of learning in the home,
   The home–school liaison teacher.

The Value of an Area Policy

I have already referred to collaboration between the welfare services and there would seem to be a place for what Marland (1980, p.178) has called 'a new professional synthesis, in which health, education and social services are seen as different but related, and are available as co-ordinated, complementary services from birth.' That, ideally, would be the setting for an area policy to combat educational disadvantage. The Glasgow Eastern Area Renewal Scheme (GEAR), initiated in 1976, sought to tackle the problems of the East End of Glasgow by bringing together housing, health and other services, including various educational objectives, but a report on the social aspects (Donnison, 1983) was unenthusiastic about current school provision and sought non-school means to provide information and learning resources as part of the composite scheme. Nisbet and Watt (1984, p. 37) comment that 'while retaining a belief in education, the report seems to imply that present provision is *not* seen as of genuine value to local people.'

Marland (1980, pp.163–211), by contrast, argued for an area approach combining welfare services in which a 'community of schools' would be a focal point. Recognising a tension between the freedom of the teacher and the need for coherent planning in the inner city areas, he suggests that funding must be drawn from a large region, but that within it control should be local enough to be sensitive to neighbourhood needs while still retaining cohesion.

> If that decision-making is taken too far away from the classroom, it lacks reality; it lacks responsiveness from the teachers; it lacks vigour. However, if it is left too near to the classroom, it becomes bitty. The fragmented nature of educational planning in Britain is appalling.

Advocating his local-area 'community of schools', Marland quotes Rutter's evidence of how schools differ from each other as part of the case for greater coordination, but unlike the GEAR project approach, he sees schools as being central to the process.

Schools in an area setting were also central to the successful (and continuing) Coventry initiatives launched in the early 1970s. Speaking at the EEC School and Family Conference in Luxembourg in 1983, Coventry's Director of Education, Robert Aitken, described the first experimental area for the Community Education Development Project, 'The Hillfields Triangle', as that part of the city which had emerged as the worst on a survey of the elements of deprivation. In 1974 the scheme was extended to four more areas in the city where there was also deprivation. It may be noted that several small areas were created rather than an expansion of the original small area to a large area. The headteachers of the schools in each area formed a policy committee but had the support and guidance of a team of specialists, while the schools themselves were granted resources in staff and other support amounting to 20 per cent above normal funding.

One advantage of a small-area approach is that a team of specialists can advise and coordinate, in a way which could be uneconomic if the strategy is implemented on a single-school basis. Thus in Coventry the initial team, under the leadership of John Rennie as Director, consisted of an adult educator, a language advisor and a home–school liaison specialist. As the project grew, so did the team. The Community Education Development Centre, based in Coventry, was able to extend its field of operations into various parts of England and even into Wales, Scotland and overseas, while its publications gained an ever-growing circulation. Yet the small area approach remains integral to many of its initiatives. Reflecting on its impact, Widlake and Macleod (1988) have written:

> ... a tradition of parental involvement has been established in Coventry such that most primary schools take the presence of parents for granted, and they are included in many activities. In some parts of the City, two generations of parents have now worked in partnership with teachers. Through support from schools, parents have been encouraged to take direct action in relation to their own lives as well as making a positive contribution toward the psychological and educational development of their children. In short, children have been socialized into a school system where there are few barriers between the home and the school. (p.110.)

School Initiatives

There is a danger in putting too much emphasis on an area approach and on education authority policies. Schools or individual teachers may conclude that absence of a central initiative would prevent or absolve them from taking comparable school-based steps. Compared with most educational systems, those of Britain devolve a high degree of autonomy to the individual school even after allowance is made for the centralising effects of the National Curriculum. Worthwhile parent–teacher initiatives can be taken by a school whose staff are determined to do so.

An important consideration is funding and that must involve local government. In disadvantaged areas some of the extra facilities which are valuable – such as language specialists where there is a high proportion of ethnic minority families, or guidance from adult educa-tion tutors – do cost money. Yet these are precisely the schools which find the raising of funds by their own initiatives most difficult. I have already argued against the use of PTAs for fund-raising and it is doubly important that home–school relations in impoverished areas should not be equated in the minds of parents with attempts to prise open their wallets. Most cities which have areas of deprivation do already grant additional finance or advisory assistance to schools in those areas, but even without them a school can do much, given commitment on the part of the teachers.

Bastiani (1988) has drawn attention to the way the national government, the DES, LEAs and training institutions can contribute towards improved home–school relations, but he goes on to comment as a preface to discussion of inner city initiatives:

> By contrast, schools are capable of enjoying special relationships with the neighbourhoods they serve, and operate through the interaction between individual families and the school system. (p. 100.)

The Hargreaves Report (1984) on secondary schools in the ILEA, having referred to parental commitment as 'the cornerstone of the school's success', went on:

> If parents are interested in their children's schooling, if they are supportive of the school's endeavours, if they act in partnership with teachers, then the children will achieve more in school. (see 3.1.3).

This message was especially directed at areas of disadvantage and impoverished families, and the report argued:

> There is very little the school can do towards removing poverty or improving the adverse social conditions in which many such parents live. Yet if we want children to achieve more, especially working class children, then improved home–school liaison and increased parental involvement must be a top priority. Co-operative home–school relations will enhance everything the school does. No school, however good its pastoral care, can be a substitute for the home. The school must complement and work with the home. (para. 3.1.4).

Further, a number of publications provide detailed ideas and guidance upon which a school can build. Widlake's (1986) *Reducing Educational Disadvantage* contains descriptions of actions taken by numerous schools in areas of deprivation, as well as practical checklists of actions. The publications of the Community Education Development Centre in Coventry offer a wealth of practical actions based on experience, including videotapes designed for use by parents. An advisory booklet for parents whose children are about to start school has been published by the Welsh Consumer Council (1988), and more sources of information appear in published form.

Some, however, would go much further than the informing and exhortatory actions designed to encourage parents to understand the schools' objectives and to cooperate with them. Instead they see the need to generate a sense of community confidence in disadvantaged areas by which those living in them can feel a capacity for determining the nature of their own lives and of influencing events. Among those events could be the nature of local schooling itself. For instance, the fostering of residents' commitment, confidence and even competitiveness were among the broad objectives for the Glasgow Eastern Area Renewal Project. In Coventry, Aitken (1983) envisaged as part of the next stage a 'family curriculum' created jointly by parents and teachers, with parents being regarded as having equal status with the teachers, and schemes comparable to that can be found in Denmark. The idea that a neighbourhood should influence the aims and content of schooling is built into the concept of governing bodies, but that presumes a small number of well-informed and motivated representatives. The vision of disadvantaged families not only getting involved in local formalised education, but influencing its nature can be traced back to the Halsey Report (1972) and earlier, but only now is sufficient experience being amassed both in the UK and elsewhere to implement it.

Influencing the Nature of Learning in the Home

Home-learning is constantly happening whenever a child is at home and is awake. (See chapters 1 and 4.) It is not a question of introducing home-learning but of influencing its nature. The long-recognised correlation between home-background and in-school attainment and the presumption of a causal link have increasingly led to the hope that schools might harness home-learning, both informational and attitudinal, for the child's benefit. Of the two, attitudinal learning poses the greater problem. As indicated earlier in the book, parental attitudes may affect a child's motivation to learn and his/her aspirations, and they can be powerful because they are learned from adults with strong affective links with the child. At one level attitudes could be fostered by mechanistic means; persuading parents to engage in paired reading with their child, for instance, may engender a recognition that the home is as important as school in this process and, perhaps, that schooling in general deserves cooperation. Yet, at another level, attitudes must be generated through understanding on the part of parents, for instance that children's approach to life can be affected in the home by emulation of adults as 'reference leaders'. While the Victorian preacher could inveigh against the evils of strong drink or language, it is rarely seen as part of modern teachers' tasks to tell their clients how to live their lives. Yet if schools are to influence home-learning, teachers may have to become preachers to adults as well as teachers of children. The challenge is not just one of imparting routine techniques but also of creating an awareness that home and all that happens in it are as educational as is school, and perhaps more so.

A slight cloud of doubt was cast on belief in the effectiveness of home-teaching by working-class parents by the findings of the study by Tizard et al. (1988). Yet to some degree their report *Young Children at School in the Inner City* has been misrepresented. This valuable study of 277 working-class children in 33 London primary schools found that factors in the home were strongly associated with children's pre-school attainments and, thus, their attainments at age seven, but that more generally school variables and teacher variables were more closely related to pupils' progress than were home variables, except with regard to the amount and complexity of writing at home. This finding appeared even though parents asserted that they helped children with reading, maths and writing.

It would be wrong to leap to the conclusion that this means that even if working-class parents help their children educationally at home it will have no effect. First, the finding that school-teaching does make a difference is in keeping with other research results (e.g. by Rutter *et al.*). Secondly, the recorded non-significance of reading and maths in the home is a statistical statement which does not disclose causes. Thirdly, as the authors point out, other studies in which home-learning has emerged as significant, such as the Haringey reading project, involved professional coordination and guidance of the home-reading process, whereas the 1988 study did not, so that school help to parents might be important. Indeed, it recorded that the amount of parental contact with, and knowledge of, the school *was* significantly associated with children's progress. And finally, this was a study of *schools*, not of homes. The home-learning element was measured by retrospective interviews with mothers and not direct observation of the home-learning process. The measurement is therefore as good as the memory and accuracy of the mothers' comments.

It is thus important to stress the conclusion of the researchers' that more home–school liaison, especially about reading, but also in sharing curricular information, is the way forward (p.178) and that 'a very high level of parent–teacher cooperation is possible if teachers set out to seek and organise it.' Of their study of liaison with a working-class sample of parents, they concluded:

> Undoubtedly teachers are handicapped by the fact that they are not trained to work with parents, and not allocated time in which to do so. Yet parents are potentially the teachers' best allies; as we discovered, most parents, especially black parents, value schools and teachers highly, are anxious to help their children, and welcome opportunities to cooperate with teachers to this end.' (p. 180.)

The evidence, therefore, continues to grow that working-class parents from disadvantaged areas can enhance their children's learning, that such parents are generally not apathetic but keen to assist, and that efforts by professionals can have impact.

One approach used by the Partnership Project in Priesthill in Glasgow has been to hold what it calls 'family nights' in its wing of a primary school. The setting is informal, with arm-chairs, curtains and tea-making facilities; it is deliberately un-school-like and adult in its atmosphere, and parents soon learn that it is not only a place where they are welcome but is, in a sense, *their* centre. Although the focal point of a family night may ostensibly be to impart a teaching technique to the parents of young children – making glove puppets from paper bags, perhaps, or paired reading methods – the analysis of *why* that type of activity is valuable in the home is also stressed.

A typical evening might be in three parts. While the children are looked after in an adjacent room (by other parents who have been trained as play-leaders) the first stage is devoted not only to demonstrating a teaching technique to parents, but to explaining the educational aims of the activity. At first parents are impatient to get on with the activity with their children, but in time they come to recognise the value of understanding the *reasons* for the activity. The second stage brings back the children, and the parents then try out the technique with them. The final stage involves consolidation for the parents and constructive criticism. While the children disappear again – perhaps to be told a story in a group – parents and professionals discuss the practicalities of the experience and how they might build on it in other ways at home.

Aitken (1983) considers that there are four elements to such development of partnership in an area of disadvantage. The first concerns the creation of trust, what Aitken refers to as 'building bridges into houses' with the implication that bridges can be crossed from either side. This is important for every school, but is especially so for families to whom institutions are places to be regarded with awe and suspicion and in which parents themselves may have felt a sense of failure in childhood. Not just an open door policy, but an invitation and welcome policy, given atmosphere by parents' rooms, cups of tea and personal greeting, and given publicity in shops, pubs, doctors' waiting rooms and buses; classes can be, and have been, held in department stores, and street festivals can demonstrate the human warmth of all concerned.

Developing skills is the second stage, teachers' skills in handling parents being as important as skills for parents in home-teaching. In Coventry workshops were run for each category separately, and then together. 'These were critical developments' says Aitken 'because this was where ideas and attitudes were formed and where anxieties were massaged; where confidence was born and security in new roles was established. It was a deliberate, patient, slow policy'. The third element is the developing of materials; books, projects and maths schemes based on local examples and created by parents and teachers jointly. That leads to the fourth element, the sharing of teaching, and this is the aspect which involves home-learning as much as school-learning. The guided homework, the parental awareness of skills (finding information, recording information, following written instructions, working things out from clues, finding a compromise, etc.) and their encouragement and implementation in the home.

Some schools produce booklets to help parents with clear, simple guidance. One school (Davies, 1986) has a series with such titles as *Welcome to Whitehill Infant School, Contact Points, Handy Hints for Helping with Reading, Alphabetical Order, Writing Skills Progression, Good Books on Reading, Water Play, Sand is Fun, Lunch Time, The Story of Whitehill School.*

These are just part of a more personal and welcoming policy of parental involvement, but the essential message which they convey is that learning happens at home and can be both structured and fun; but most important of all, they apply to all families.

Finally, let us not pretend that home-learning is easy to launch in areas of deprivation. Widlake (1986, p.67) offers a list of problems including over-anxiety, illiterate parents, shortages of books to go round, domestic crises and adverse criticisms of the school. He also offers some remedies which can go some way to meeting these difficulties, but perhaps the most essential step is to recognise that there will be problems in a minority of cases, but that this is not a reason to discourage the majority.

The Home–School Liaison Teacher

Several education authorities have introduced in various guises and with different titles personnel commonly referred to as Home–School Liaison Teachers (HSLTs). Views differ about the wisdom of creating such posts. Widlake (1986) warns of the dangers of expecting too much of the HSLT and presents a double-page chart (pp.34–5) of tasks which might befall him/her. He cites cautionary tales of a HSLT being shared between schools and warns of overlap with the work of outside agencies and remedial teachers. Bailey (1980) points to the diversity of expectations from various sponsoring bodies, isolation of practitioners, deficiencies in support systems, the short-term nature of some appointments, and lack of supervision and of training and career structure. Simpson (1983) warns of the HSLT being seen as an 'outsider' by fellow-teachers and a trespasser by other welfare agencies, and of the headteacher who regards the HSLT as a spare teacher to stand in for others. He also notes that if the HSLT is too readily associated in the minds of parents with trouble and problem-solving 'he may find it difficult to achieve more general attitudes of liaison in his "image-setting" role. Perhaps accentuating this difficulty is the fact that the HSLT system has only been established in areas known to have difficulties, and the question arises whether *every* school should have a HSLT.'

Much of the confusion, it seems to me, can be overcome by a clearer analysis of what the task entails and some ambassadorial work to ensure good relations with other professionals who may feel that 'their' territory is being threatened. Given these precautions the HSLT post appears to have special attractions in disadvantaged areas. However, one overriding point of principle must be made clear to all staff of a school employing a HSLT. This is that his presence does not diminish in any way the continuing obligation of *all* teachers to have regular educational contact with parents. The HSLT supplements and assists but does not replace educational partnership between parent(s) and teacher(s).

Bailey focuses on two main aims of the HSLT: 'firstly to increase the social understanding of the teacher; secondly, to increase the educational understanding of the parent' (p.261). Simpson, while embodying these aims, offers a clear and compact structure to the HSLT's work (pp.1–2):

A *Problem-solving*

(i) To act on behalf of the school in contacting parents whose children have problems, either meeting them in the school or meeting them in their homes.

(ii) To establish relationships with other welfare agencies in helping to alleviate these problems.

(iii) To be a specialist in such matters to whom other teachers may turn for assistance in the event of problems, or anticipated problems, hopefully prior to the crises.

B *Image-making*

(i) To encourage parent–teacher liaison more generally in the school, especially in recognition that such liaison can contribute to pupils' attainment levels. In this respect the HSLT does not replace normal parent–teacher relationships but augments and facilitates them.

(ii) To create extra mechanisms to increase liaison such as multilingual brochures, parent–teacher meetings, standing in for class teachers to enable them to meet parents, etc.

(iii) To encourage a community image for the school and to emphasize to parents that it is both their right and their responsibility to visit the school.

C *Specialist Resource*

(i) To be a centre of specialist knowledge about the cultural background of categories of pupils to whom fellow teachers may turn for information and guidance.

(ii) To be a means by which the school may use parental skills in the school for educational purposes.

To prevent or to minimise the problems listed earlier, Simpson urges not only clarity of remit but also a thorough understanding with the headteacher about it. Although a case can be advanced for having a non-teacher in the post (see Widlake, 1986, p.91), Simpson argues that, as a teacher, not only can the HSLT stand in for colleagues to allow them to talk to parents, but his status in the school is more assured if he is recognised as a fellow professional. One may add that the post of HSLT should not be a dumping ground for failed teachers. Simpson also sees the value of HSLTs meeting to develop their own specialist expertise through comparison of experience and training and to decrease the sense of isolation which some HSLTs can experience. In Northern Ireland regular reporting-in and role-defining sessions characterised the growth of their specialisation in the 1970s.

Some HSLT work has been especially effective in helping to build bridges between schools and ethnic minority families. There is a danger in including reference to any minority group in a chapter on educational disadvantage since it might be misinterpreted as suggesting that there is a necessary link between being a member of that group and disadvantage. However, cultural and linguistic differences from those of a school may result in difficulties for children in terms of success in that school and many disadvantaged areas do include ethnic minority families. Such a statement does not imply that the school is right and the family wrong, but rather that a problem exists. As Tomlinson (1984, p.118) has written:

> In the literature of home–school relations minority homes are invisible, are conceptualised as 'problems', or are subsumed under a wider group – that of the 'disadvantaged'.... the stereotype of the 'disadvantaged' parent, who is in need of organisation by professionals and whose children are in need of 'compensation' for their background, is inappropriate when applied to minority communities. Indeed, the model adds further stigmatisation to groups already at a disadvantage in society.'

For this reason I am not discussing links with ethnic minority families in this chapter on educational disadvantage, but placing it in the next chapter. However, it may be worth noting that it has been in the context of links with such families that the work of the HSLT has been especially valuable.

In brief, the HSLT – by whatever name – can be an enabler in a variety of ways. As the multiple strands of initiatives which are developing in different areas become publicised and best practice becomes better known, so the HSLT could be an essential change agent. Yet his position must be seen in the wider perspective, one which sees the problems of deprivation and disadvantage approached on an area basis with recognition that education is only one part of the solution and that schools only provide one part of education.

10 A WHOLE-SCHOOL APPROACH

The Need for a Whole-school Policy on Liaison

Current practice with regard to home–school relations is sometimes fragmented, uncoordinated and left to the initiatives of individuals. Tizard (1987) can write, 'We found that it was rarely possible to speak of a *school's* parent involvement policy, as practices varied from year to year, depending on the views of the particular class teacher.' The arguments would seem to be strong for every school to develop a consistent policy of parental involvement. The present chapter considers how this might be done.

One obvious source of a coherent policy is the headteacher. As chief executive, senior professional and the person in whom responsibility is predominantly entrusted by the education authority in our substantially decentralised system, it is to the head that one would look for such impetus. Yet the attitudes and professional assumptions of many heads were consolidated in previous decades when parents were not seen as integral to schooling, and schools can function superficially, in the sense of daily routines being completed, without any parental involvement. With other administrative pressures abounding, one is unlikely to encounter consistency of enthusiasm among headteachers for anything involving additional work. Those who have tried to increase home–school partnership may have been disheartened by meagre responses from both parents and teachers. Further, the tradition lingers that it is the headteacher, rather than staff, who should be the point of contact with parents, perhaps reflecting an assumption that a school only needs to consult with parents at a time of crisis. For these reasons it may be inappropriate to expect all headteachers simultaneously to initiate whole-school policies of parental involvement. Despite these impediments, many headteachers are taking a constructive lead and we may expect the trend to continue. Indeed, it may be precisely at a time of change that schools most need to consult with their clients and to enlist their support.

Yet there is as much onus on the governing body (in Scotland, school board) to take the lead, especially with its newly-defined role and membership. It is difficult to think of a more obvious area for governing body initiative. In chapter 8, I suggested that the governing body:

(i)   should be concerned with all major, especially educational, decisions made at the school level;
(ii) should concentrate on an 'ensuring' or accountability function;
(iii) could have a 'Parents in Education' sub-committee to ensure that the parental dimension of every issue is considered; and
(iv) could monitor the mechanisms for liaison between home and school.

The responsibility of governors to keep constantly in mind their obligation to parents as the school's clients can scarcely be over-stressed. One of the purposes of a governing body is to check that perspectives other than those of the professionals are brought to bear. Hopefully the headteacher and staff will originate a parental policy, but if they do not then governors can. There is now a requirement for the governing body to make an annual statement and to hold a meeting for parents. The structures and processes of home–school liaison could be a regular feature of these.

In turn, the PA or PTA can develop its own views on appropriate steps and can convey these through parental representatives to the governing body. The 12-point basic programme listed in chapter 2 could be the starting-point for any head, governing body or PA, but it is not intended as an exhaustive list. However, all items on the list can (and in my view should) be implemented by a school without the necessity to wait for an education authority or central government edict.

The objection would probably be raised that some of the 12 points would require extra resources – not much, but some. This is true, both in terms of staff time and in terms of direct costs. When the Secretary of State for Scotland made his announcement in April 1987 that every Scottish school should have a school board (i.e. governing body), he suggested that one of its tasks might be to 'generate additional money from the community.' If he had added 'according to its means', with an assurance of government subsidy for disadvantaged communities, the suggestion might perhaps have been easily defensible. But if the quality of parent–teacher partnership – as well as other facets of governance – is to depend upon the capacity and willingness of local people to pay, this could discriminate against poorer communities and there would appear to be a departure from the principle of free education which has been part of our system's foundation. In the chapter on voluntary parental organisations I similarly argued that fund-raising by PAs or PTAs should generally be avoided. In brief, the issue of resources provides a useful test of whether the teaching profession and education authority do or do not regard parents as integral to schooling. Yet the costs in terms of time and money are so relatively small that a school and its governors need not be deterred from action even if no additional funding is on offer.

Various mechanisms for parent–teacher cooperation in the education of children have been discussed in detail in previous chapters. It is possible to argue for a whole-school policy for each. Yet there are other whole-school actions which can be taken and it is to those that I now turn. For the school as a corporate body can also take initiatives which reach out not only to parents as clients, but to the wider community also.

Welcome

The past decade or so has witnessed a small revolution in the extent to which schools convey to parents and others a sense of welcome. An encouraging tone in school handbooks, circular letters, reports and other publications has become evident, and schools have made an effort to ensure that the entrance halls to schools are pleasant and colourful. Not only have forbidding notices instructing parents to report to the headteacher been replaced with friendly, often imaginatively decorated, messages, but they may appear in more than one language according to the nature of the local population. I know one primary school which has transformed a bleak, traditional hall into a mock lounge of an airport, with a bubbling fountain in the centre, easy chairs and even flight departure information. If the helpfulness of airline ground staff could also be replicated in schools throughout the country, entering a school could always be a pleasure.

Practical assistance such as clear signposts to different parts of the school, a note of regular bus-routes to the school during day-time and in the evenings, adequate car-parking space, perhaps a creche for small children when evening meetings are arranged and, ideally, a comfortable parents' room with the facility for a cup of tea, are all techniques which we can encounter in Britain. Perhaps especially important is the provision of a private meeting-place where the parents of a child can meet his/her teacher(s) with the assurance that their child's problems are not being overheard. Discussions in crowded corridors, classrooms or halls where other parents are standing by, or in the playground always cause a sense of unease, even if, in fact, nobody can overhear.

The headteacher has a special problem to overcome: the ingrained traditional image of the awesome head. At times one has the feeling that some headteachers enjoy the sense of power, or even need the defence of status-symbols and an imperious manner. It may be difficult for the head, under the pressures of the moment, to devote the time or to convey the concern which he would like; yet evidence from our study of parental choice of school indicates that many people categorise a school according to the image which the headteacher has created. Further, a head who conveys a sense of commitment to parents is more able to ask the same of the rest of the staff.

It is possible for a school to go through the formalities of partnership grudgingly and without conviction, thereby transmitting the opposite message to that intended by the procedures. I remember a particular scene from an old film about the Second World War. A German civilian, disenchanted with the Nazi regime, had business in a government office and, exasperated by an official, murmured bitterly under his breath, 'This wonderful Third Reich!' The official, sensing heresy, challenged him to repeat out loud the mumbled sentiment. 'This *wonderful* Third Reich' said the man radiantly. How something is said or done often conveys the real message. No matter how much the printed words of school handbooks or report forms extol the virtues of educational collaboration, they will have little impact if parents are only reluctantly allowed into the school, face stern notices on entry, have no comfortable place to go nor privacy in discussing the problems of their child, get abrupt and offhand attention from whoever is answering the query, have no encouragement to drop in even when there is no problem, and so on. The way in which a head or teacher summons a parent can be friendly and respectful, or curt and overbearing; teachers may either convey recognition that a child's parents know more about him/her than do the teachers (though probably less objectively) and can make important contributions to the child's education, or staff can pose as the sources of all knowledge, wisdom and influence. It may be difficult for a busy teacher always to remember this, but tone and atmosphere, whether in writing or in speech, can be vitally important and can be the result of a deliberate policy agreed to be applied throughout the school.

Behaviour and Discipline in School

The HM Inspectors' *Good behaviour and discipline in schools* issued in 1987 by the DES had a short section entitled *Parents* (pp.22–3). This drew attention to good relations with parents, home–school links and a climate of trust. It went on to discuss the involvement of parents when a disciplinary incident has occurred, referred to possible feelings of guilt and/or powerlessness of parents and ways by which teachers can devise a joint plan with parents (and pupils) to rectify the situation. It also suggested that the annual parents' meeting required by the 1986 Act might be used to discuss disciplinary issues.

Is it possible to go further than this? Perhaps. First, the legal position may need some clarification. The term *in loco parentis* does not mean that teachers can do what they like, but that they should take such care of the children in their charge as a careful parent would (Barrell and Partington, 1985, pp.372, 438 and 474). Teachers have a general right to inflict punishment (p.444) but within prescribed limits (pp.444–79). That, however, would not seem to be the central point with regard to the parental dimension of school discipline. Parents are legally responsible for their child's education. When the child truants, it is the parents who are called to account. When a pupil is expelled from school, it is parents who become responsible for ensuring the child's continuing education. LEAs may feel a moral obligation to make alternative provision, but as Barrell and Partington state (p.461):

If a pupil is then expelled lawfully from that [LEA-provided school] place, no duty to find a place reverts to the local education authority. In law, the duty to educate falls back on the parent at that stage . . .

Thus, it is more than just a courtesy for a school to inform parents of the indiscipline of their child. What seems to remain unclear is whether parents can be held legally responsible for their child's behaviour in school, as they are for attendance. Probably not. A change in the law may be necessary to confirm it. Atherton *et al.* (1987) have suggested that there may be different legal grounds for parents to have the right to be involved in the in-school discipline of their children. They advise parents:

> In providing education for your child, the education authority must have regard to your wishes. This could include paying attention to the way you want your child to be disciplined in school. (p.82.)

Whatever the legal arguments, it makes good professional sense to inform parents immediately of any problems. Parents have grounds to be upset if the first they hear of persistent difficulties is when problems have reached crisis stage. Informing parents may also have a useful deterrent effect on the pupil. In a study of discipline in Scottish secondary schools, Cumming *et al.* (1981, pp.38–9) conclude:

> It is clear that the likelihood of parental involvement in a school discipline matter is not at all welcome by the vast majority of pupils, and that the threat of informing their parents is likely to deter many from indiscipline.

Similarly, the Scottish enquiry into truancy and indiscipline (Pack Report, 1977) made frequent reference to parents, not only because of the need for schools to inform parents, as clients, but because of the potential influence of the home on school behaviour. This leads to consideration of *group* parental involvement in disciplinary matters and to whole-school policies.

Behaviour and discipline depend upon the preparedness of pupils to conform to arrangements made by adults and to exercise self-discipline. The necessary attitudes are influenced by parents as well as by the arrangements made by schools. In as far as parents do have some impact upon the state of mind which we call discipline, it is sensible not only to inform them what is expected of pupils, but to enable them to influence the disciplinary measures through their representatives on governing bodies. In particular, school rules and codes of discipline should be subject to governing body discussion and determination. One of the undertakings which was suggested in chapter 2 as part of the parents' signed understanding was '(f) to support school rules', while another was '(g) to abide by decisions made by the headteacher and the governing body [in Scotland, school board] with regard to the school's management.'

An additional influence is that of the peer group. If there is some consistency of attitudes among families it is more likely, though not certain, that peer group conformity will be enhanced. Thus, it is appropriate that disciplinary questions be discussed in class meetings (see chapter 6). By these means, greater legitimation of the school's rules and arrangements is likely to be achieved.

School Handbooks and Other Publications

In chapter 5 I referred to the requirement upon schools to make information available to parents. This is commonly achieved through handbooks which can vary considerably in aims, content and tone. Booklets of guidance for parents may also be produced by the DES or SED; by education authorities; by parents' or teachers' organisations; by churches; or by a range of other bodies. A school may choose to make these available to members of the governing body, the PA/PTA or parents more generally. However, the present section is concerned with publications created in the school for the parents of that school.

A school handbook may serve several functions: as a prospectus for potential clients, as a reference document for parents with children already in the school, as a means to lay down expectations of parental and pupil cooperation, as a medium to show off achievements or to convey an image (real or false), as a means to explain procedures or as a tone-setter for relationships. Its compilation can be an important activity and logic suggests that if it is intended to be of assistance to parents and pupils, then those groups or their representatives should play a part in its construction. More specifically, the task can be shared with the PA/PTA.

Handbooks are generally intended to be retained as reference documents for at least a year, sometimes longer, but they are often supplemented by more ephemeral materials giving guidance at particular stages of children's schooling or announcing forthcoming events. Newspapers, sometimes of substantial sophistication, printed on the presses of the local paper and financed by advertisements, or bulletins produced on increasingly accessible desktop publishing computers, may be designed specifically to enhance parent–teacher relations, as distinct from school magazines which report pupils' events. (I know of one newspaper produced by a PTA which appears termly, is fully-printed and illustrated, and is entering its eighth successive year. Its costs are covered by advertisements from local firms and it goes free of charge to all parents and teachers.) These and other publications ranging from glossy magazines to three-lined duplicated notes all contribute to the rich variety of written communication open to schools.

Yet there is a basic minimum of information which schools are required to make available to parents in writing. In both England (1981) and Scotland (1982) regulations prescribed that minimum. For England these include the name, address and telephone number of the school, the names of the headteacher and chairperson of the governing body, the type of school, visiting arrangements, curricular policy, subject choices and the levels to which those subjects are taught, arrangements for careers guidance and pastoral care, RE (including any religious affiliation), streaming, setting and homework policies, discipline and uniform regulations, policy for entering pupils for public examinations, and recent examination results. There are additional requirements for special schools. The Scottish list is similar, but adjusted to the Scottish system. (Parents are also entitled to request information about a range of additional topics which do not have to appear in published form.) Since such information usually appears in the school handbook, one would expect a degree of uniformity to emerge, especially since education authorities may prescribe exact wording to be used about some topics. But some schools have demonstrated ingenuity in putting a distinctive stamp on their handbooks both in what extra information appears, how it is expressed and how the text is supported by diagrams and illustrations.

Writing before the 1980 and 1981 legislation, Bastiani (1978) suggested that school brochures could be categorised into four models. The Basic Information Model has as its main feature 'the transmission of a rather limited range of information to parents'. The Public Relations Model projects an image of the school, often seeking to convey an impression of high standards rather than to inform. The Parental Involvement Model encourages parents to become actively involved in both the education of their children and the life and work of the school. Finally, the Developmental Model concentrates on explanations and support during the process of entry or transfer from one stage of education to another. The researchers were critical of the tone, presentation and content of many brochures, drawing special attention to confusion of purpose, a tendency to be prescriptive and negative (Thou shalt not . . .), too little attention to the process of education itself and a tendency to verbosity. However, they drew attention to the potential for the future use of the Parental Involvement approach.

In analysing brochures sent to us from nine countries in our EEC study we found that most of our sample were of the Basic Information type, but with occasional imaginative departures. In terms of conveying a sense of welcome, the Dutch, Danish and English booklets tended to be the most encouragingly friendly, and we encountered some helpful examples of the Developmental type. Disappointingly, however, only a few were clearly categorisable as having the Parental Involvement approach.

We also received from 1737 headteachers in the nine countries answers to the question: 'Does your school send information brochures to parents of children *before* their children become pupils at your school?' Germany (87 per cent), the Netherlands (81 per cent) and the UK (76 per cent) recorded the highest rates of 'Yes' responses compared with an EEC average of 63 per cent. More secondary than primary schools took this action.

Phrasing a suitable question for EEC headteachers about other school publications for parents posed problems because practice varied so widely. In some cases schools issued booklets prepared by education authorities, some of a very high standard; in others key information was incorporated in individual report forms or *carnets de liaison*; and we gathered a rich harvest of other modes of presentation, including information calendars with pictures of the schools for parents to hang on their kitchen walls. In the end we settled for asking heads about frequency:

> How often do parents of children at your school receive information brochures or newsletters from all sources, including the Ministry, the school, class teachers, etc.? About . . . times a year.

The highest average estimate was 12.07 items a year per family in the Netherlands and the lowest was 3.22 in the Republic of Ireland, the EEC average being 7.93. The UK figure was a respectable 9.27 items per family a year. Broken down by territory the results for the UK were:

	No. schools in sample	Av. publications per family
Eng. and Wales	175	11.4
Scotland	99	8.6
N. Ireland	75	5.1

Thus, although the UK emerged poorly compared with other European countries with regard to modes of liaison about the individual child (see chapter 3), its schools fared rather better in terms of *numbers* of school-level publications designed to keep parents informed. But there is evidence to add to Bastiani's that the *quality* could be improved. Atherton (1982) analysed 83 Scottish handbooks and concluded that there was 'considerable scope for improvement in both presentation and content' particularly criticising them for providing what teachers thought parents *ought* to know rather than what parents really wanted to know. Like Bastiani he found that much space was devoted to rules and regulations, but little about the content of courses or assessment methods used.

The University of Glasgow study of parental choice of school (1986) reported an analysis of 206 secondary school handbooks by Cathlin Macaulay who criticised their formal and impersonal tone, the use of unexplained technical terms, inflated wordy styles of writing and 'almost Orwellian inversions of meaning' such as the word 'discipline' used to mean indiscipline and 'attendance' to refer to non-attendance. The report concluded, 'Most, but not all handbooks contained the full range of information required by regulations ... Some handbooks seemed more concerned with laying down the school's requirements than with encouraging a friendly sense of educational partnership with parents.'

The Glasgow University study, which received handbooks from all over Scotland, also noted that none of the sample handbooks sent by schools had been translated into the languages of ethnic minority groups in the areas. However, excellent examples from some English urban education authorities do exist. Translation and publication costs can be high, especially in districts with several language groups, and it is difficult for individual schools to create such special handbooks without additional grants.

Minority Ethnic Families

> Many black people prefer the term *minority ethnic* to *ethnic minority*. Ethnicity, we argue, is not just limited to minority groups in Britain or wherever, but can be used to define any group, large or small. (Foster, 1987).

Corner (1988) reinforces this point by reminding us that a multiplicity of races and cultures have constantly shifted and related to each other throughout the history of Europe and that what we now tend to perceive as minority ethnic groups are simply a continuation of that centuries-old process. However, Corner makes a distinction between 'regional' or 'indigenous' minorities (such as the Scots Gaels) on the one hand, and more recent European settlers. It is important to note, he writes 'that many of the educational problems which we now see as "ethnic minority problems" are in fact longer term problems which many Europeans have suffered for centuries, and that the problems themselves often lie with the educational system(s) at least as much as with any given minority.'

There is a danger equating minority ethnic families with disadvantages. As with majority ethnic families, varying degrees of disadvantage can be found among minorities. As Tizard *et al.* (1988, p.5) state, 'Most studies have found that children in certain ethnic groups on average achieve as well as, or better than, white British children, whilst others do worse.' They go on to quote examples, such as an ILEA study of 1986 which showed that while among 7–11 year-olds, those of Caribbean and Cypriot origin had lower reading attainments than white children, Gujerati speakers and children of Chinese origin had above average reading scores. Other examples could be cited, but the general point is that minority ethnicity need not necessarily lead to educational disadvantage.

Yet there are problems. Macleod (1985), discussing the involvement of Muslim parents in their children's education, picks out three main difficulties. First, that the parents' first language is often not English which makes home–school communication difficult. Second, that there is a shortage of teachers from minority groups. And third, that parents from different cultural, linguistic and religious backgrounds often regard schools quite differently from indigenous parents. Tizard, Mortimore and Burchell (1988, pp. 80–1) especially take up this last point, suggesting that particular issues giving rise to difficulty are expectations about the role of punishment and the amount of emphasis that should be given to formal teaching. They advocate:

We do not underestimate the difficulty of explaining modern teaching aims and methods to parents from a very different culture. Nor do we suggest that teachers should – or indeed would – accede to parental wishes which were totally at variance with their own approach. But unless schools are prepared to discuss such issues with parents, explain their approach, listen to parents' points of view, and go some way towards meeting them, they cannot hope to enlist parental support for their work.

They suggest four aims for home–school relations with regard to minority group parents (p.77):

- To facilitate the contribution of minority group parents to the life of the school by adopting a multi-cultural approach.
- To enable minority group parents to contribute their knowledge of their children and their culture to the teachers.
- To enable teachers to consult minority group parents about their children's education, and to discuss educational issues with them.
- To help teachers to explain their aims and methods to minority group parents.

In approaching such aims, it is necessary to remove some impediments which seem common to schools and teachers. One is to assume that minority ethnic parents are apathetic. The evidence is the reverse. To quote Tizard, Mortimore and Burchell again:

In general, truancy rates are lower, and the proportion of children staying on at school after 16 higher, among minority group children, and their parents tend to have high aspirations for them. (p.74.)

Marland (1983, p.2 and 1988, p.233) notes the frequent finding that minority parents 'include a rather high proportion of non-visitors to the school', often taken by teachers to be a sign of apathy, but refutes that assumption:

The reasons, however, were *not* those of the apathetic; rather they are largely the practical problems of shift hours, language difficulties, and the fact that school is often the only major 'white' institution with which an Asian in an English city has to relate ... These factors combine with an attitude to schooling that leads them deliberately not to wish to 'interfere'. Rex and Tomlinson found, as I find weekly, *no* signs of apathy indeed considerable evidence in most families of extreme concern.

Linked to teachers' imprecise assumptions about apathy are assumptions about disadvantage. As pointed out above, any ethnic group may have a disadvantaged element, but as Tomlinson (1984, p.118) argues:

Models of disadvantage may also be ethnocentric, and professionals from white middle-class backgrounds may denigrate minority child-rearing patterns and parental behaviour. Teachers working within the disadvantage model may come to view their work more in a social-pastoral care context than an examination-oriented or skill-oriented one: schools for the disadvantaged are not places where high academic achievement is expected. Teachers' views may thus clash with the expectations of minority parents, who do expect their children to achieve examination passes or acquire skills that will be vocationally useful.

The Swann Report on the education of children from ethnic minority groups asserted that society is not according equality to minority ethnic groups and saw anti-racist teaching in a multi-cultural society as something applicable to all schools, irrespective of the proportions of minority groups on the school rolls. Language is generally recognised as a key factor. While the Swann Report preferred specialist help to be given in mainstream school rather withdrawing children for ESL help, others would not agree, and an accompanying controversy is whether the school should undertake some teaching in the pupils' mother tongues. Corner (1988, p.7) asserts that 'the overall evidence from modern research is that bilingual and bicultural children, if they are encouraged to attain a reasonable degree of balance between the languages and cultures, develop an enhanced intellect.' Yet this does not necessarily mean that the school should be bilingual and we may return to arguments in chapters 1 and 4 that home-learning is as important as, perhaps more important than, school-learning and that the bilingualism and biculturalism can be learnt in the home with the informed support of the school.

The use of home–school liaison teachers and the role of pastoral care staff are discussed in chapter 9, and the place for interpreters in schools with high proportions of minority ethnic pupils is of obvious value, as is the need to prepare all handbooks and written communications from the school in the relevant languages. Home visiting, involvement of parents both in school events and in the classroom, parent education, guidance on homework, videos showing children at work, parental assistance with reading and other initiatives can be of value when carried out with an awareness of the minorities' perspectives (see Macleod, 1985; Tomlinson, 1980). However, the central dilemma may be this: if, among other purposes, a school should be transmitting society's values, then whose values? The pat answer is to say that the National Curriculum will provide common material for 70 per cent of the content of what is taught and that teaching methods and others should be multicultural.

However, that does not really confront the practical problems which arise. These can be about specific issues such as mixed-sex swimming or the nature of food served in the school, and about the content and methods of the proportion of the syllabus not concerned by the National Curriculum and the internal allocation of resources in favour of minority children. Should there be choices within the curriculum, for instance of different types of religious and moral instruction or special classes for cultural groups? Such issues require a whole-school approach and the governing body is the obvious forum in which to determine local policies and initiatives.

Both Tomlinson (1980, p.121) and Tizard, Mortimore and Burchell (1988, p.80) advocate the setting up of groups of parents representing minority interests. These can either represent particular cultural groups or represent a movement towards greater multiculturalism. In chapter 7 I argued that parental interest groups projecting a parental dimension should be regarded as a normal part of local democracy and not sinister 'interference', but that they should operate within an agreed procedure focused on an accepted forum to reconcile their wishes to the wishes of those of others. The governing body is the obvious forum, though the PA/PTA might have sectional groups as part of its structure. Sectional groups are often equated with conflict, on the parliamentary party pattern, but this need not be the case and respect both for each other and for the mechanisms of reconciliation of viewpoints can be integral to this type of approach. Such action not only shows that the school is sensitive to needs and wishes, but it helps to protect a sense of identity for minority groups. It also enables local problems to be settled locally according to the perceptions of those involved rather than by national or regional prescription.

Home–school Liaison: a Specialist or a Generalist Function?

Should contact with parents be a specialist or a generalist function? There is some evidence that parents want to have direct contact with their child's teacher(s) rather than communicate through an intermediary (e.g. Goacher and Reid, 1983, p.115). There is also seemingly contrasting evidence that at secondary level, at least, many parents hold the view 'that it was better not to intervene in the developing relationship between the pupil and his secondary school.' (Johnson and Ransom, 1983, p.117.) Yet perhaps what parents **want** is not here the only issue, despite the law's requirement that education should be in accordance with parents' wishes. Should we not also be asking what is best for the child's education? After all, what some non-involved parents may want is simply to be relieved of educational responsibility, and that would not seem to be in the child's interests. We may therefore consider the specialist/generalist issue in terms of potential effectiveness as well as in terms of generalisations about supposed parental preferences.

The arguments for links with parents being a generalist responsibility (that is, the responsibility of *all* teachers as part of their daily work) are easy to express and are powerful. If the education of the child is to be a partnership, then the partners must collaborate. Only the class or subject teacher knows how the child is progressing in that class or subject, and the parents are in the best position to describe his/her personality, actions and development in the home. If the endeavours of both are to be mutually supporting, the obvious contact is between teacher(s) and parent(s). An intermediary is bound to dilute the immediacy, the detailed knowledge and sometimes the effectiveness of liaison. Further, if a specialist service exists, even if only to deal with exceptional circumstances, there will be a temptation for busy teachers to regard it as absolving them from liaison with parents so that the very presence of a home–school liaison teacher or pastoral care staff may be a barrier to genuine educational partnership. There is much to be said for regular contact with parents being a contractual obligation for **all** teachers, accompanied by enabling mechanisms such as private consultations, liaison booklets, phone-in surgeries, etc., in the school week (especially in evenings), so that teachers do not come to assume that parents are someone else's problem. Parents, too, must come to see contact with their child's teachers as an obligation: I mentioned the signed understanding in chapter 2.

However, there are also some arguments for specialists. In this context I shall group together pastoral care, guidance and home–school liaison teachers. A specialist can get to know families well especially if, as in the Danish system and in some UK schools, a class teacher with pastoral responsibilities 'moves up' the school with one class and therefore retains contact with the families of that one class over several years. Further, guidance which spans subjects (such as for course options or careers advice, as well as providing parents with an overview assessment of a pupil's progress) ought to be the responsibility of someone in the school who can provide that composite picture. Particular and difficult situations, such as truancy or cultural adjustment problems, often require expertise and demands on time which a teacher may not have. It is therefore not difficult to conclude that home–school liaison must be both a generalist and a specialist function, and most schools do operate a combination but with differing degrees of emphasis on the one or the other, and the issue becomes one of extent.

The specialist's role is not just one of dealing with exceptional cases and crises, but one of stimulating rather than replacing contact between teachers and parents. The specialist should be an 'animateur' of liaison, not a substitute for it. Thus, the problem is not just one of structures and systems, but also of attitudinal frameworks. Quite apart from the tendency for education systems, the Inspectorate and schools themselves to view pastoral care and links with parents as being peripheral functions and the literature being relatively sparse (see Ribbins and Best, 1985), there appears to be some confusion over what pastoral care aims to do. I have pointed out elsewhere (Macbeth, 1985) that school-based guidance staff often fail to recognise that families are offering pastoral care systems in parallel to that of the school and that

> ... when we examine the published definitions of pastoral care, guidance and counselling, most of them could apply to the parental function if the word 'child' replaces 'pupil'. Consider, for

instance, 'looking after the total welfare of the pupil' (Marland, 1974, pp.8–9), 'taking of that personal interest in pupils as individuals which makes it possible to assist them in making choices or decisions' (Scottish Education Department, 1968), 'the kind of work which is done to promote the personal development of pupils' (Dooley, 1980, p.24) and the notion of a 'child agency' to assist the child to greater autonomy (Freeman, 1983) . . . and considering the whole child, understanding him as an individual, assisting him in times of need, emphasising prevention rather than correcting maladjustment, use of persuasion rather than coercion, assisting his talents to flourish and provision of information (Auld and Stein, 1965, pp.9–10), the description can still apply to caring parents, and Dooley (1980, p.16) draws our attention to the "fatherly" nature of pastoral care.'

Best *et al.* (1983, p.272) have analysed the relationship of pastoral care to other school services in terms of three overlapping circles representing the academic, pastoral and disciplinary functions (education, welfare and order). While finding that helpful, I have suggested (Macbeth, 1985, p.121) that the complementary family half of these elements should be added and that focus should move to the points of overlap so that each educational, pastoral and disciplinary contribution will support those of the educational partners.

Another approach has focused on the home–school liaison teacher (HSLT). The theory and practice of the HSLT was discussed more fully in chapter 9. Macleod (1985) concludes her CEDC booklet on partnership with Muslim parents by arguing for specific training for HSLTs to be implemented by experiential rather than didactic methods, including ways of seeking to combat racist attitudes, behaviour and curricular content. She argues for clearer job descriptions for HSLTs, refusal to reduce their number at times of recession, regular meetings between HSLTs, headteachers and advisors for planning purposes, evaluation of HSLTs' work and a greater dissemination about the strategies and approaches developed with relation to ethnic minority parents. Whether located to assist disadvantaged families, minority ethnic families or families in general, the functions of a HSLT are clearly related to the school as a whole.

A whole-school approach to liaison with parents might therefore start with a recognition that in parallel to the school's pastoral educational and disciplinary systems are operating counterpart family systems, also dealing with pastoral, educational and disciplinary facets, but often in different ways. Overlap between school and family systems is a matter for professional action by all teachers, but there is a particular role for the specialist (whether pastoral care or HSLT), not to replace the generalist but to assist him. In the words of the 1986 Report of the Scottish Central Committee on Guidance (p.55), 'We believe that parents, or guardians, and teachers should work together in a partnership based on mutual respect, cooperation and trust to ensure that each child's personal curricular and vocational needs are met as fully as possible.'

The Question of Time

Parent–teacher liaison takes up time. Winkley (1985, p.79) points out that to talk to each parent privately for half-an-hour in a primary school of 500 pupils would be 250 teacher hours, or the equivalent of the full-time employment of a teacher for ten weeks. Goacher and Reid (1985, p.45) reported that a secondary teacher could spend 28.5 hours a year writing reports: the equivalent of 43 school periods.

Such figures seem awesome when they are presented as 'extras'. The problem arises from seeing parents as being 'outside' the school. 'Parents', writes Winkley (1985, p.74), 'as outsiders, are untidy and inconvenient'. There would seem to be two steps towards solving the question of time. The first is to persuade everyone concerned, from the Secretary of State to the probationer, to see parents as part of the school community and liaison with them as part of teachers' normal work. The second is to build that into teachers' contracts. In Denmark there is an assumption that teachers will spend two hours a week on contact with parents. If we transfer that figure to a 40-week working year for British teachers we would have a total of 80 hours a year per teacher. In that context, the Goacher and Reid figure of 28.5 hours for reports falls into proportion.

In-service Training

Long (1986) has advocated the use of in-school workshops not only to inform teachers but to change their attitudes towards relationships with parents. He argues:

> If parents are to be successfully involved in the education of their children, teachers must first be convinced that the extra effort and time taken are worthwhile. They must be given the opportunity to explore the issues and express their doubts and reservations freely, otherwise any parental involvement programme will be much less likely to prove satisfying or successful. (p.10)

This hints that the nature and extent of collaboration with parents should be a matter for individual professional judgement while an alternative perspective would be that all teachers should be required to do it. In either case it is advantageous if teachers believe in what they are doing. Long's little book is a practical guide to parent–teacher liaison for primary teachers. The benefits and difficulties for both parents and teachers are exposed through discussion and ways of getting teachers to suggest and consider schemes of parental involvement are outlined. The scheme moves on to parental meetings and workshops and, finally, a timetable for a programme of parental involvement. A similar approach could be devised for secondary school teachers.

An advantage of this method is that it seeks to obtain commitment through conversion. The danger is that, the outcome being voluntary, a persuasive group of staff-room 'baddies and traddies' could consolidate a minimalist approach and thereby defer progress for a number of years. If home–school partnership were integral to teachers' contracts, as suggested in chapter 2, or a normal requirement of the education authority, then such workshops would be a means for fulfilling a pre-established general obligation. Similarly, the head and governing body of an individual school could establish such partnership as one of the major aims of the school, the workshops then becoming a means to fulfil that aim.

Just as the commitment of teachers can be enhanced by their involvement in developing schemes of liaison, so the same incentive might apply to parents. While there is value in the governing body initiating and monitoring the development of new parent–teacher initiatives, and in the PTA/PA coordinating the collection of views and ideas, the need is to involve *as many parents as possible* and not just their representatives on committees. With this in mind, the use of class meetings of parents (discussed more fully in chapter 6) would not only help to initiate schemes but to perpetuate and refine them.

A possible way to initiate a whole-school approach to the development of parent–teacher partnership in education could be for the headteacher to propose to the governing body (or *vice versa* in the absence of a headteacher's move) that the 12-point plan advanced as a basic professional minimum in chapter 2 be considered critically as an initial agenda. In that process there could be consultation with the PA/PTA, and systems of progress and reassessment instituted for the following years. Thereby, hopefully, a whole-school approach to liaison with parents may both be constructed and implemented.

11 POLICY AND THE FUTURE

Assumptions about the nature of education condition how the system operates. Pervasive misconceptions are that education is merely what happens in schools, that schools alone are responsible for the child's education and that schools can educate 'the whole child'. In reality most learning happens outside school, parents are legally responsible for their child's education and if 'educating the whole child' has any meaning, it must include inculcating attitudes, influencing moral standards and providing social experience, none of which is readily achieved in school since schools provide a restricted range of largely cognitive teaching in somewhat artificial circumstances. This is not a prelude to a de-schooling argument. I believe that schools have a vital role to play, but that they can only achieve it if the limitations of schooling are admitted and if schools reorientate their work to collaborate with (and even to lead) other educational forces, the most obvious and accessible of which are parents.

In the first chapter I suggested that we, as teachers, had hi-jacked the word 'education'. We equate it with institutional provision. Curtis (1978, p.ix) offers in a wider perspective:

> The child's education, as a general process of change from baby to adult, is to a large extent going on *remorselessly*, and our problems and responsibilities as educators are to see how it goes on and how we might and ought to try to affect it.

I like that word 'remorselessly' since it not only suggests that educational forces are constantly at work irrespective of school efforts, but it also hints that they may not always be benign. In policy terms there has been a failure to adjust to the recognition that most education happens outside institutions. However, the central point which Curtis is making is that instead of asserting that we provide all education, we professional educators ought to be analysing and harnessing as much as possible the non-school educational forces.

Unfortunately, it suits most adults to equate schooling with education. As teachers we reasonably regard our efforts as indispensable for children's learning and it is easy for us to forget the other forces influencing it. It is convenient to administrators to limit their work to definable and substantially controllable group processes, while politicians like to be able to point to tangible results, and schools are certainly tangible. The most serious element of this distortion is that it also suits many parents to shrug off the educational duty imposed upon them by law and, as they might see it, to 'leave it to the experts.' If teachers have hi-jacked the word 'education', the public has generally acquiesced.

An appropriate attack has been made by FitzHerbert (1985, p.97) on the claim that schools, unaided, educate 'the whole child', a notion which she describes as 'an ideal, not a practical objecctive.' She quotes evidence of the persistence of this idea among teachers and educationists. One could add many more. For instance, the influential Scottish Munn Report (1977) not only led to important changes in the Scottish secondary school system, but may have had impact upon curricular planning in both England and the Republic of Ireland. It expected schools to aim to provide for young people the development of knowledge and understanding, both of the self and of the social and physical environment (para. 4.3), to develop cognitive, interpersonal and psychomotor skills (para. 4.4) and to help develop a daunting list of laudable but complex attitudes (para. 4.5). Then, finally, comes the all-embracing assertion that 'schools have an inescapable duty to ensure that young people are equipped to perform the various roles which life in their society entails' (para. 4.6). Had these been the aims of education generally they might have been acceptable. But they are offered as the aims of the school curriculum. The committee states 'We are deliberately emphasising the part played by the formal curriculum in the achievement of all the aims of the school.' And later, 'We consider that all of them must be provided for in the deliberately planned series of learning experiences which make up the formal curriculum.' In that small fraction of a child's waking life allocated to schooling (about 15 per cent from birth to 16) teachers are being expected to provide not only the skills and knowledge for all aspects of adult life, but social and moral attitudes also. Further, the report contained only fleeting references to parents and to home background, some blaming them for undesirable influences.

The dangers of making such claims for schools would seem to be twofold. First they lead the public (and teachers) to think that schools can achieve such objectives, thereby encouraging parents to neglect their own educational influence. Secondly, when schools fail to achieve these objectives fully, as fail they must, they may be blamed. How much more sensible is the Danish approach which not only recognises that schools can do no more than make facilities available, but sees partnership with parents as integral to the process. The second sentence of their Basic School Law of 1975 reads:

The task of the Basic School is, in cooperation with the parents, to offer possibilities for the pupils to acquire knowledge, skills, working methods and forms of expression which will contribute to each individual's versatile development.

Note also that there are no claims to 'equip' pupils with social and moral attitudes. There is little evidence to lead us to suppose that teachers can compete with home, community and media in equipping pupils with attitudes. And note the words 'in cooperation with the parents.'

Besides persuading teachers that parents are educationally important, there is also a need to persuade parents that they have a central role in education. It is not enough to hold a few extra open days, and to revamp the school handbook, and then blame parents for not responding. For so many decades has the school system cultivated the ethos of parental irrelevance by both word and action that the reversal will require effort. Assumptions have to be unlearnt. Governments, education authorities, the Inspectorate, school governors, headteachers, pastoral care staff, home–school liaison teachers, teachers' unions and parental organisations all have a part to play in such a process of conversion, but surely the most essential feature must be for the teaching occupation as a whole to recognise parents as integral to its professional performance.

That centrality of parents does not depend upon research evidence, even though research evidence strongly points towards their importance in the education of their children. The correlation between home background and children's in-school attainment has given new impetus to professional concern for parents. However, it may also have performed a dis-service in two senses. First, it appeared to imply that so long as there was any uncertainty about either the validity of the research measures or the precise nature of causal factors or the most efficacious practical steps to be taken, for that long could the profession continue to regard the parental dimension of education as unproven and therefore a side-issue. Secondly, emphasis upon research tended to distract us from the other, and possibly more fundamental, reasons for educational partnership with parents. As outlined in chapter one, these are:

1 that parents are, by law, responsible for their child's education and therefore the school's legal clients;
2 that most education happens outside school, especially in the home;
3 that teachers, as agents of the state, should be concerned about and to a limited extent should check on parental support of formal provision; and
4 that parents have a democratic right to influence decisions affecting their children in the school and in the class.

Thus, *even without the research evidence*, grounds for partnership with parents exist. The strong indicators in a multitude of studies from all over the world that home background, including parental attitudes and actions, correlates with and probably substantially causes differences in attainment by pupils in schools and therefore inequality of educational opportunity, add powerfully to an already-potent argument for teachers to seek partnership with parents. That initiative best comes from teachers, not only because teachers can have direct contact with parents, but because they will lose professional status in the eyes of the public if partnership with parents has to be forced on them.

Yet there are policy steps which could assist. The first could be the adoption by all education authorities of the *basic professional minimum* suggested in chapter 2. Its 12 points were:

1   A system of **welcome** at all times for parents.
2   A termly, **two-way written report** exchanged between teachers and parents as an agenda for . . .
3   . . . **a private consultation** at least twice a year.
4   A **termly class meeting** of parents with children in the same class to explain the approaching curriculum and how they can reinforce it in the home.
5   **A parents' association**, with class units.
6   **A governing body** (in Scotland **a school board**) for each school which makes **accountability** its main function.
7   **Publications** by the school.
8   **Parental right of access to see all official records** held on their child.
9   Education according **to parental wishes** (with reservations about suitability and cost).
10 A system of **home-visiting**.
11 **Teaching as a service to parents** and a partnership with them.
12 A degree of **accountability of parents** to teachers.

In support of such a basic programme, there appears to be a need for a professional code of practice for teachers. This should take as its starting-points a recognition that schooling is only part of education and that while the pupil may be the *consumer* of schooling, parents are the *clients*, society (including commerce and industry) are the *beneficiaries* and education authorities are *agents for its implementation*. By emphasising these distinctions we may retain the fundamental philosophy that schooling exists primarily for the development of the individual child and only secondarily (though importantly) to provide a skilled workforce or certain kinds of citizens. If such a code of practice were accepted, it could be monitored by governing bodies and could be a specific element of HMI inspections.

The 'basic professional minimum' and a code of practice for teachers might be boosted by a deliberate government policy to heighten public awareness of the educational responsibilities of parents and the mechanisms for partnership between parents and teachers. It could be that a publicity drive comparable to those associated with dental care, anti-smoking and AIDS campaigns could be mounted to increase awareness of the parental role in education. The analogy with preventive medicine may not be apt in all respects, but parents are responsible for their child's health as well as their education. Active home tuition is something which dentists have long relied upon for the maintenance of healthy teeth among children. Their success substantially depends on the motivation of parents and the extent to which dentists can press home their preventive message. Doctors are increasingly recognising that theirs has been a Sickness Service, not a Health Service, and preventive medicine is acknowledging that parents have an important contributory role, for habits of life are learnt in the home.

An element of publicity about home-learning might be a 'preventive education' campaign aiming to counteract those negative features which may be harmful to good learning. Some of these could be attitudinal, such as the damaging assumption that education is 'best left to the professionals' or that parents would be 'interfering' if they took an active interest in the details of schooling. We know that parents are generally concerned for their own children's welfare and parental apathy may not be the problem which it was once supposed to be, but could some parents be under-ambitious for their children? Roberts (1980), having considered social class values and differing images of society, suggests that aspirations are related to the rung on the social ladder to which a child is born and that working-class children must be more ambitious than middle-class children *relative to their respective starting points* if they are to be academically successful.

Television and radio provide means of getting into all homes. Leaflets and booklets, professionally-produced and authoritatively-written, can be a support to teachers in their diverse dealings with parents. Just as the ethos of parental rejection became so embedded in the public's assumptions about schooling in the past, so it will take a determined assault upon public assumptions to replace it with an ethos of educational partnership.

We may pause at this point to recognise that philosophies other than that of educational partnership are theoretically possible. For instance, schools could abandon all claims to educate children socially or morally, leave that to families and the media, and concentrate on practical knowledge and skills. Another approach might be linked to the National Curriculum. The state, not parents, might be made responsible in law for schooling related to it, leaving parents answerable for all non-school education. In such a circumstance the client-status of parents would diminish and some of teachers' obligation to them would thereby be reduced. Yet even if such shifts were espoused, we would still be left with the uncomfortable knowledge that there is a link between home-learning and in-school performance, so that if teachers and politicians are concerned about equality of educational opportunity and optimising the effects of schooling, mechanisms would still have to be devised to recruit parental support for the school. If the state takes to itself total responsibility for schooling (thereby shifting, to that degree, away from the fundamental principle of parental rights to bring up their children) it would not be able to *capitalise on parental obligation* as the means to counteract differential performance in schools.

For concentration upon a sense of parental obligation would seem to be the only way out of the impasse which the school system appears to have reached. If educational fairness to children depends upon active parental cooperation with the school, and if we accept that the current system of patchy exhortation by schools has failed, then the alternative would seem to be a new concentration upon parental obligation in pursuit of cooperation. That, in turn, implies an increased commitment by schools and relevant resources.

It would therefore seem appropriate to add a fourth element to the package of the 'basic professional minimum', a professional code of practice for teachers and the publicity campaign: this would be the implementation of parental duty. I use the word 'implementation' rather than 'introduction' because that duty is already built into the law in section 36 (section 30 for Scotland), albeit vaguely. In chapter 2 I suggested how a *signed understanding* might be completed annually by parents and school. The focus of that understanding would be the commitment of parents, in recognition of their fundamental duty to provide education for their child, to complement the school's work by support and involvement. What the signed understanding would ask of parents would not be onerous and would therefore be within the capacity of virtually all parents to provide. Its main psychological benefit would be to draw the attention of both partners annually to the fact that the prime responsibility for the child's education lies with the parents and that this is a duty, carrying with it obligations.

I consider that such a well-funded policy package should be introduced by government and education authorities, administered by headteachers and senior staff, monitored by governing bodies (including the calling to account of defaulters) and acted upon by parents and teachers. Without some such action, home–school liaison will continue to be rich in rhetoric and exhortation, but patchy in practice; and children will be the losers.

Bibliography

ABRAHAMSSON, B. (1977) *Bureaucracy or Participation.* Sage.

AITKEN, R. (1983) Address given at the EEC School and Family Conference, Luxembourg.

ALLEN, G., BASTIANI, J., MARTIN, I. and RICHARDS, K. (1987) *Community Education: An agenda for educational reform.* Open University Press.

ANDERSON, D. (1982) *Detecting Bad Schools: a Guide for Normal Parents.* The Social Affairs Unit.

ANDERSSON, B. (1986) *Working materials for class meetings,* paper given at EEC/FAES Seminar, Erice, Sicily.

'Astin Report' (1979) Department of Education for Northern Ireland, *Report of the Working Party on the Management of Schools in Northern Ireland.* HMSO.

ATHERTON, G. (1979) *Reaching Out to Parents: an exploratory study of parents and schooling in Scotland.* Scottish Consumer Council.

ATHERTON, G. (1982) *The Book of the School.* Scottish Consumer Council.

ATHERTON, G. assisted by AITKEN, J., BROWN, R., FRASER, A., KREITMAN, S. and MACEWAN, N. (1987) *The Law of the School. A Parent's Guide to Education Law in Scotland.* HMSO/Scottish Consumer Council.

ATKIN, J., BASTIANI and GOODE, J. (1988) *Listening to Parents: An approach to the improvement of home–school relations.* Croom Helm.

AULD, W.H. and Stein, H.L. (1965) *The Guidance Worker,* Gage.

BACH, P. (1988) *A Parental Viewpoint,* pp. 14–16 in Macbeth, A.M. (Ed.) *Written School Reports for Parents in Europe,* European Parents' Association.

BAILEY, R. (1980) 'The Home–School Liaison Teacher', ch. 17 in CRAFT, M., RAYNOR, J. and COHEN, L. (Eds) *Linking Home and School.* Harper and Row.

BARON, G. (Ed.) (1981) *The Politics of School Government.* Pergamon.

BARON, G. and HOWELL, D.A. (1974) *The Government and Management of Schools.* Athlone Press.

BARRELL, G.R. and PARTINGTON, J.A. (1985) *Teachers and the Law,* (Sixth Edition). Methuen.

BARRINGTON, J. (1981) *School Government in New Zealand: Balancing the Interests,* in Baron, G. (Ed.) *The Politics of School Government,* Pergamon.

BASTIANI, J. (1978) *Written Communication Between Home and School.* University of Nottingham.

BASTIANI, J. (Ed.) (1983) *Teacher/Parent Interviews: Some Materials for Teachers.* University of Nottingham School of Education.

179

BASTIANI, J., (Ed.) (1987) *Parents and Teachers 1: Perspectives on Home–School Relations.* NFER-Nelson.

BASTIANI, J., (Ed.) (1988) *Parents and Teachers 2: From Policy to Practice.* NFER-Nelson.

BEATTIE, N. (1985) *Professional Parents: Parent Participation in Four Western European Countries.* Falmer.

BECHER, T. and MACLURE, S. (1978) *Accountability in Education.* NFER-Nelson.

BECHER, T., ERAUT, M. and KNIGHT, J. (1981) *Policies for Educational Accountability.* Heinemann.

BENN, C. and SIMON, B. (1970) *Half Way There: Report on the British Comprehensive School Reform.* Penguin.

BERGER, E. (1981) *Parents as Partners in Education: The school and home working together.* C.V. Mosby.

BEST, R., RIBBINS, R. and JARVIS, C. (1983) *Education and Care.* Heinemann.

'Black Report' (1987) *Report of the Task Group on Assessment and Testing: National Curriculum.* DES.

BRENT, LONDON BOROUGH OF (1986) *Parents' Handbooks* (separate primary and secondary school versions).

BROADFOOT, P.(1984) *Pupil Profiles, Research and Policy: A Parable for Our Times,* ch. 2 in DOCKRELL, W.B. (Ed.) *An Attitude of Mind.* Scottish Council for Research in Education.

BROADFOOT, P. (1987) *Introducing Profiling,* Macmillan.

BROWN, I. (1980) *Equality of Educational Opportunity, Diversity and Choice.* Australian Schools Commission.

BROWN, M. and MADGE, N. (1982) *Despite the Welfare State. Studies in Deprivation and Disadvantage.* DHSS/Heinemann.

BROWN S. and BLACK, H. (1988) *Profiles and Records of Achievement,* Ch. 5 in Brown, S. (Ed.) (1988) *Assessment: A Changing Practice.* Scottish Academic Press.

BULLOCK, A. and STALLYBRASS, O. (Eds) (1977) *The Fontana Dictionary of Modern Thought.* Fontana.

BURGESS, T. and ADAMS, E. (1985) *Records of Achievement at 16.* NFER-Nelson.

BURGESS, T. and SOFER, A. (1986) *The School Governors' Handbook and Training Guide* (Second Edition). Kogan Page.

BUSH, T., GLATTER, R., GOODEY, J. and RICHES, C. (Eds) (1980) *Approaches to School Management.* Harper and Row.

CHAMBERS, J.H. (1983) *The Achievement of Education.* Harper and Row.

CORNELIUS, H., RAVN, B. and BINGER, B. (1983) *Focus on Family – School Communications: A Danish Approach,* advance paper for EEC School and Family Conference, Luxembourg.

CORNELIUS, H. (1988) *Access by Parents to Records held by the School or the Education Administration about their Child in Denmark,* in Macbeth, A.M. (Ed.) *Parental Access to School Records,* European Parents' Assn.

CORNER, T. (1988) *Equality of Educational Opportunity for Pupils from Ethnic Minority Families,* paper for European Parents' Association Conference, Strasbourg.

COX, C., DOUGLAS-HOME, J., MARKS, J., NORCROSS, L. and SCRUTTON, R. (1986) *Whose Schools? A Radical Manifesto.* Hillgate Group.

COX, C. and MARKS, J., (1980) *Education and Freedom: The Roots of Diversity,* National Council for Educational Standards.

CNAP (1977) Guide for members, Confédération Nationale des Associations de Parents, Belgium.

CRAFT, M., RAYNOR, J. and COHEN, L. (Eds) (1980) *Linking Home and School.* Harper and Row.

CULLINGFORD, C. (Ed.) (1985) *Parents, Teachers and Schools.* Robert Royce.

CUMMING, C.E., LOWE, T., TULIPS, J. and WAKELING, C. (1981) *Making the change: A study of the process of the abolition of corporal punishment.* Scottish Council for Research in Education.

CURTIS, B. (1978) Introduction to CURTIS, B. and MAYS, W. *Phenomenology and Education: Self-consciousness and its development.* Methuen.

CYSTER, R., CLIFT, P.S. and BATTLE, S. (1979) *Parental Involvement in Primary Schools.* NFER.

DAVIE, C.E., HUTT, S.J., VINCENT, E. and MASON, M. (1984) *The Young Child at Home.* NFER-Nelson.

DAVIE, R., BUTLER, N. and GOLDSTEIN, H. (1972) *From Birth to Seven.* National Children's Bureau/Longman.

DAVIES, E. (1986) Series of handbooks for parents with children at Whitehall Infant School, Uxbridge.

DEPARTMENT of EDUCATION and SCIENCE (see also H.M. INSPECTORS and TASK GROUP ON ASSESSMENT AND TESTING).

DEPARTMENT of EDUCATION and SCIENCE (1985) *The educational system of England and Wales.* HMSO.

DEPARTMENT of EDUCATION and SCIENCE (1985) *Better Schools,* White Paper. HMSO.

DONNISON, D. *et al.* (1983) *GEAR Review: Social Aspects,* quoted in Nisbet, J. and Watt, J. (1984) *Educational Disadvantage: Ten Years On,* HMSO.

DOOLEY, S.K. (1980) *The relationship between the concepts 'pastoral care' and 'authority',* in Best, R., Jarvis, C. and Ribbins, P. (Eds.), *Perspectives on Pastoral Care,* Heinemann.

DOUGLAS, J.W.B. (1964) *The Home and the School.* MacGibbon and Kee.

DOUGLAS, J.W.B., ROSS, J.M. and SIMPSON, H.R. (1968) *All Our Future: A Longitudinal Study of Secondary Education.* Peter Davies.

DOWLING, E. and OSBORNE, E. (1985) *The Family and The School.* Routledge and Kegan Paul.

Education Act (1944). HMSO.

Education (No. 2) Act (1986) ch. 61. HMSO.

Education Reform Act (1988) ch. 40. HMSO.

Education (Scotland) Act (1980) ch. 44. HMSO.

Education (Scotland) Act (1981) ch. 58. HMSO.

ELLIOTT, J., BRIDGES, D., EBBUTT, D., GIBSON, R. and NIAS, J. (1981) *School Accountability: The SSRC Cambridge Accountability Project.* Grant McIntyre.

EPA (1988) *Training of Parents as Class Delegates,* European Parents' Association.

ETZIONI, A. (1964) *Modern Organisations. Foundations of Modern Sociology Series.* Prentice-Hall International.

EULAU, H. and PREWITT, K. (1973) *Labyrinths of Democracy: Adaptations, Linkages, Representation and Policies in Urban Politics.* Bobbs-Merrill.

FEDERAL REPUBLIC OF WEST GERMANY (1949) *Federal Basic Law,* 23rd May 1949.

FITZHERBERT, K. (1985) *Parents, teachers and the 'whole child',* Ch. 6 in Cullingford (Ed.) *Parents, Teachers and Schools,* Royce.

FLOUD, J., HALSEY, A.H. and MARTIN, F.M. (1957) *Social Class and Educational Opportunity.* Heinemann.

FOSTER, E. (1987) personal communication.

FOWLER, W.S. (1988) *Towards the National Curriculum: Discussion and Control in the English Educational System 1985–1988*. Kogan Page.

FRASER, E. (1959) *Home Environment and the School*. University of London Press.

FREEMAN, M.D.A. (1983) *The Rights and Wrongs of Children*. Pinter.

FURNISH, C. (1985) M.Ed. research exercise, University of Glasgow.

GLATTER, R., PREEDY, M., RICHES, C. and MASTERTON, M. (1988) *Understanding School Management*. Open University Press.

GLYNN, T. (1987) *More Power to the Parents: Behavioural Approaches to Remedial Tutoring at Home*, ch. 4 in WHELDALL (Ed.) *The Behaviourist Classroom*. Allen and Unwin.

GOACHER, B. and REID, M.I. (1985) *School Reports to Parents*. NFER-Nelson.

GOULD, R. (1973) 'The Teaching Profession' in Lomax, D.E. (Ed.), *The Education of Teachers in Britain*. Wiley.

GRAY, J., McPHERSON, A.F. and RAFFE, D. (1983) *Reconstructions of Secondary Education: Theory, Myth and Practice since the War*. Routledge and Kegan Paul.

GRIFFITHS, A. and HAMILTON, D. (1987) *Learning at Home: The Parent, Teacher, Child Alliance*. Methuen.

HALL, V., MACKAY, H. and MORGAN, C. (1986) *Head Teachers at Work*, Open University Press.

'Halsey Report' 1972 and 1974, *Educational Priority*, Vols. I and V. HMSO.

HANNON, P. (1987) 'Parent Involvement – a no-score draw?' in *Times Educational Supplement*, 3rd April 1987.

HANNON, P. and JACKSON, A. (1987) *The Banfield Reading Project Final Report*. National Children's Bureau.

'Hargreaves Report' (1984) *Improving secondary schools*. ILEA.

HARRIS, R. (1980) 'Parent–Teacher Contacts: a Case Study', ch. 10 in CRAFT, M., RAYNOR, J. and COHEN, L. (Eds.) *Linking Home and School*. Harper and Row.

HART, D. (1988) *Open Enrolment: Who'll pay to prop the school gates open?* Ch. 6 in Haviland, J., *Take Care, Mr. Baker!*, Fourth Estate.

HAVILAND, J. (Ed.) (1988) *Take Care, Mr. Baker!*. Fourth Estate.

HEWISON, J. (1985) *The evidence of case studies of parents' involvment in schools*, Ch. 3 in Cullingford (Ed.) Parents, Teachers and Schools, Royce.

HITCHCOCK, G. (1986) *Profiles and Profiling: A Practical Introduction*, Longman.

H.M. INSPECTORS (1987a) *Homework, Education Observed 4*. Department of Education and Science.

H.M. INSPECTORS (1987b) *Good behaviour and discipline in schools*. Department of Education and Science.

H.M. INSPECTORS (1988) *Secondary Schools: An appraisal by HMI*. DES/HMSO.

HOLBERG, J. (1976) 'The Parent–Teacher Movement in Sweden' in *Current Sweden*, No. 128.

Houghton Report (1974).

HOYLE, E. (1974) 'Professionality, Professionalism and Control in Teaching' in *London Educ. Rev.*, Vol. 3, Summer 1974.

HUGHES, M. (1985) *Leadership in Professionally Staffed Organizations* Ch. 10 in Hughes, M., Ribbins, P. and Thomas, H. *Managing Education: The System and the Institution*, Holt.

HUGHES, M., RIBBINS, P. and THOMAS, H. (Eds.) (1985) *Managing Education: The System and the Institution*. Holt, Rinehart and Winston.

HURT, J. (1985) 'Parental involvement in schools: a historical perspective', ch. 2 in CULLINGFORD, C. (Ed.) *Parents, Teachers and Schools*. Robert Royce.

ILEA *Examination Results, 1976, 1977, 1978, 1981, 1982.*

IRISH CURRICULUM AND EXAMINATIONS BOARD (1986) *In Our Schools: a framework for curriculum and assessment.* Curriculum and Examination Board.

ISAACS, D. (1986) *Methods of training of class delegates,* paper given to EEC/FAES Seminar, Erice, Sicily.

JACKSON, B. and MARSDEN, D. (1962) *Education and the Working Class.* Routledge and Kegan Paul.

JENCKS, C., SMITH, M., ACLAND, M., BANE, M.J., COHEN, D., GINTIS, H., HEYNS, B. and MICHELSON, S. (1973) *Inequality: a Reassessment of the Effect of Family and Schooling in America.* Allen Lane.

JOHN, D. (1980) *Leadership in Schools.* Heinemann.

JOHNSON, D. (1987) *Private Schools and State Schools: two systems or one?.* Open University Press.

JOHNSON, D., RANSOM, E., PACKWOOD, T., BOWDEN, K. and KOGAN, M. (1980) *Secondary Schools and the Welfare Network.* Allen and Unwin.

JOHNSON, D. and RANSOM, E. (1983) *Family and School.* Croom Helm.

JONES, J. (1987) *The Parental Dimension,* in *Home and School,* Spring 1987, 2, p.5.

KOGAN M. (1978) *The Politics of Educational Change.* Manchester University Press.

KOGAN, M. (Ed.), JOHNSON, D., PACKWOOD, T. and WHITAKER, T. (1984) *School Governing Bodies.* Heinemann.

LACEY, C. and LAWTON, D. (1981) *Issues in Education and Accountability.* Methuen.

LANG, P. and MARLAND, M. (Eds) (1985) *New Directions in Pastoral Care.* Blackwell.

LANGFORD, G. (1978) *Teaching as a profession. An essay in the philosophy of education.* Manchester University Press.

LEES, D.S. (1966) *Economic Consequences of the Professions.* Institute of Economic Affairs.

LE MÉTAIS, J. (1985) *Homework Policy and Practice in Selected European Countries.* EURYDICE.

LIKERT, R. and LIKERT, J.G. (1976) *New Ways of Managing Conflict.* McGraw-Hill.

LINDSAY, C. (1969) *School and Community.* Pergamon.

Local Government (Scotland) Act (1973). HMSO.

LONG, R. (1986) *Developing Parental Involvement in Primary Schools.* MacMillan.

LUCAS, B.G. and LUSTHAUS, C.S. (1981) 'Public Involvement in School Governance in Canada', in BARON, G. (Ed.) *The Politics of School Government.* Pergamon.

LUCAS, J.R. (1976) *Democracy and Participation.* Penguin.

LYNCH, J. and PIMLOTT, J. (1976) *Parents and Teachers.* Schools Council Research Studies/MacMillan.

MACBETH, A.M. (see also UNIVERSITY OF GLASGOW).

MACBETH, A.M. (1981) 'Scottish School Councils: A New Initiative in School–Community Relations?' in BARON, G. (Ed.) *The Politics of School Government.* Pergamon.

MACBETH, A.M., CORNER, T., NISBET, S., NISBET, A., RYAN, D. and STRACHAN, D., (1984) *The Child Between: a report on school–family relations in the countries of the European Community.* Commission of the European Communities, Studies Collection. Education Series, EEC.

MACBETH, A.M. (1985) 'Parents, schools and pastoral care: some research priorities', pp. 114–29 in LANG, P. and MARLAND, M. *New Directions in Pastoral Care*. Blackwell.

MACBETH, A.M. (1986) 'School-Work and Families' (*'Trabajo Escolar y Familia'*), pp. 38–54 in PICK, R., *Familia y Trabajo*. Fest, Barcelona.

MACBETH, A.M. (Ed.) (1987) *Homework in Europe*. European Parents' Association, Brussels.

MACBETH, A.M. (Ed.) (1988) *Parental Access to School Records*. European Parents' Association, Brussels.

MACBETH, A.M. (Ed.) (1988) *Written School Reports for Parents in Europe*. European Parents' Association, Brussels.

MACBETH, A.M. and CORNER, T. (1988) *Parents' Associations and Teachers' Unions in Europe*. European Parents' Association, Brussels.

MACBETH, A.M., MACKENZIE, M.L. and BRECKENRIDGE, I. (1980) *Scottish School Councils: Policy-Making, Participation or Irrelevance?* Scottish Education Department HMSO.

McCLELLAND, D. (1961) *The Achieving Society*. Van Nostrand.

McCONKEY, R. (1985) *Working with Parents. A Practical Guide for Teachers and Therapists*. Croom Helm.

McCORMICK, R. (Ed.) (1982) *Calling Education to Account*. Heinemann.

MACLEOD, F. (1985) *Parents in Partnership: Involving Muslim Parents in their Children's Education*. Community Education Development Centre.

'Main Report' (1986) *Committee of Inquiry report into the pay and conditions of service of school teachers in Scotland*. HMSO.

MARJORIBANKS, K. (1979) *Families and their Learning Environments: An Empirical Analysis*. Routledge and Kegan Paul.

MARJORIBANKS, K. (1983) *Family Learning Environments: An Overview*, advance paper to the EEC School and Family Conference, Luxembourg.

MARLAND, M. (Ed.) (1980) *Education for the Inner City*. Heinemann.

MARLAND, M. (1983) *Parenting, Schooling and Mutual Learning: a Teacher's Viewpoint*, advance paper for the EEC School and Family Conference, Luxembourg, 1983. Also published in BASTIANI, J. (Ed.), (1988) *Parents and Teachers 2: From Policy to Practice*, pp. 232–42. NFER-Nelson.

MARLAND, M. (1985) 'Our needs in schools', pp. 67–91 in LANG, P. and MARLAND, M., *New Directions in Pastoral Care*. Blackwell.

MARLAND, M. (Ed.) (1986) *School Management Skills*. Heinemann.

MAYNARD, A. (1975) *Experiment with Choice in Education*, Hobart Paper, Institute of Economic Affairs.

MAYCHELL, K. (1986) 'LEA Implementation of the 1980 Act' in STILLMAN, A. (Ed.), *The Balancing Act of 1980: parents, politics and education*. NFER.

MAYS, J.B. (1962) *Education and the Urban Child*. University of Liverpool.

MAYS, J.B. (1980) 'The Impact of Neighbourhood Values', ch. 4 in CRAFT, M., RAYNOR, J. and COHEN, L. (Eds) *Linking Home and School*. Harper and Row.

MILLER, G.W. (1971) *Educational Opportunity and the Home*. Longman.

MILLERSON, G. (1973) 'Education in the Professions' in History of Education Society *Education and the Professions*. Methuen.

MITCHELL, C. (1973) *Time for School. A Practical Guide for Parents of Young Children*. Penguin.

MOORE, W.E. (1973) *In Loco Parentis*. Centre for Research in Measurement and Evaluation, Sydney, Australia.

MORTIMORE, J. and BLACKSTONE, T. (1982) *Disadvantage and Education*, DHSS/Heinemann.

'Munn Report' (1977) *The Structure of the Curriculum in the Third and Fourth Years of the Scottish Secondary Schools*. HMSO.

MUSGROVE, F. (1966) *The Family, Education and Society*. Routledge and Kegan Paul.

NIAS, J. (1980) *Leadership Styles and Job-Satisfaction in Primary Schools* Ch. 4.1 in Craft *et al.* (Eds.) *Approaches to School Management*, Harper and Row.

NIAS, J. (1981) *Parent-teacher meetings*, in Elliott *et al.*, *School Accountability*, Grant McIntyre.

NIAS, J. (1981) Parent Associations, in Elliott *et al.*, *School Accountability*, Grant McIntyre.

NILÉHN, K. (1976) *Samspelet mellan Skola och Hem*. Bonniers.

NISBET, J. and WATT, J. (1984) *Educational Disadvantage Ten Years On*. SED/HMSO.

O'CONNOR, D.J. (1957) *An Introduction to the Philosophy of Education*. Routledge and Kegan Paul.

OPCO (1985) *Huiswerk*, Ouderraad Protestants Christelijk Onderwijs.

OSBORNE, A.F. and MILBANK, J.E. (1987) *The Effects of Early Education: A Report from the Child Health and Education Study*. Clarendon Press.

'Pack Report' (1977) *Truancy and Indiscipline in Schools in Scotland*. HMSO.

PATEMAN, C. (1970) *Participation and Democratic Theory*. Cambridge University Press.

PETERS, R.S. (1966) *Ethics and Education*, Allen and Unwin.

PETERSON, L.J., ROSSMILLER, R.A. and VOLZ, M.M. (1978) *The Law and Public School Operation*, (Second Edition). Harper and Row.

PETTIT, D. (1980) *Opening Up Schools: School and Community in Australia*. Penguin.

PETTIT, D. (1982) *Choice and Diversity in Victorian Schools: a Discussion Paper*, Choice and Diversity Project, Australia.

PLEWIS, I., GRAY, J., FOGELMAN, K. and MORTIMORE, P. (1981) *Publishing School Examination Results: a discussion*. University of London Institute of Education.

'Plowden Report' (1967) *Children and their Primary Schools*. HMSO/DES.

POURTOIS, J.-P., *et al.* (1980) *Eduquer les Parents*, Centre de Recherche et d'Innovation en Sociopédagogie familiale et scolaire. Éditions LABOR, Bruxelles.

PUGH, G. and DE'ATH, E. (1984) *The Needs of Parents. Practice and Policy in Parent Education*. MacMillan.

QUINTON, D. (1980) 'Family Life in the Inner City: myth and reality' in MARLAND, M. (Ed.) *Education for the Inner City*. Heinemann.

RAVEN, J. (1980) *Parents, Teachers and Children: A Study of an Educational Home Visiting Scheme*. Hodder and Stoughton.

ROSEN, B.C. (1961) 'Family structure and achievement motivation' in *American Sociological Review*, 26, 574–84.

RUTTER, M., MAUGHAN, B., MORTIMORE, P. and OUSTON, J. (1979) *Fifteen Thousand Hours. Secondary Schools and their effects on Children*. Open Books.

SANDOW, S., STAFFORD, D. and STAFFORD, P. (1987) *An Agreed Understanding? Parent–Professional Communication and the 1981 Education Act*. NFER-Nelson.

SCHOFIELD, H. (1972) *The Philosophy of Education: An Introduction*. Allen and Unwin.

School Boards (Scotland) Act (1988). HMSO.

SCHWEINHART, L.J. and WEIKART, D.P. (1980) *Young Children Grow Up: The Effects of the Perry Preschool Program on Youths Through Age 15*. High Scope Press.

SCOTTISH CENTRAL COMMITTEE ON GUIDANCE (1986) *More than Feelings of*

Concern: Guidance and Scottish Secondary Schools. Consultative Committee on the Curriculum.

SCOTTISH EDUCATION DEPARTMENT (1968) *Guidance in Scottish Secondary Schools*, HMSO.

SCOTTISH EDUCATION DEPARTMENT 1984, *Learning and Training in Scottish Secondary Schools: School Management*, H.M. Inspectors of Schools, H.M.S.O

SCOTTISH EDUCATION DEPARTMENT (1984) *Learning and Teaching in Scottish Secondary Schools: School Management*, H.M. Inspectors of Schools. HMSO.

SCOTTISH PARENT TEACHER COUNCIL (1982) Booklet 10 *Ideas for an Active PTA*.

SHARROCK, A. (1970) *Home/School Relations*. MacMillan.

SHIPMAN, M. 1984, *Education as a Public Service*, Harper.

SIMPSON, P. (1983) *The Role of the Home–School Liaison Teacher in the Birmingham Education Authority: a personal viewpoint*, advance paper for the EEC School and Family Conference, Luxembourg, 1983.

SMITH, M. (1985) 'Clients', ch. 9 in FRITH, D. (Ed.) *School Management in Practice*. Longman.

SOCKETT, H. (Ed.) (1980) *Accountability in the English Educational System*. Hodder and Stoughton.

STILLMAN, A. (Ed.) (1986) *The Balancing Act of 1980: parents, politics and education*. National Foundation for Education Research in England and Wales.

STILLMAN, A. and MAYCHELL, K. (1986) *Choosing Schools: Parents, LEAs and the 1980 Education Act*. NFER-Nelson.

STONE, J. and TAYLOR, F. (1976) *The Parents' Schoolbook*, Penguin.

TAYLOR, B. (1983) *A Parent's guide to Education*. Consumers' Association/ Hodder and Stoughton.

TAYLOR, F. (1981) *Choosing a School*, Advisory Centre for Education, 2nd. ed.

TAYLOR, H. (1987) 'The Redefinition of Equality of Opportunity' in *Educational Management and Administration*, Vol. 15, No. 1., pp. 13–18.

TAYLOR, W. (1980) *Family, School and Society*, Ch. 1 in Craft *et al.* (Eds.) *Linking Home and School*, Harper and Row.

'Taylor Report' (1977) *A New Partnership for our Schools*. HMSO/DES/Welsh Office.

TICKELL, G. (1980) *Choice in Education*, Australian Schools Commission.

TIZARD, B. (1987) 'Parent involvement – a no-score draw?' in *Times Educational Supplement*, 3rd April 1987.

TIZARD, B., BLATCHFORD, P., BURKE, J., FARQUHAR, C. and PLEWIS, I. (1988) *Young Children at School in the Inner City*. Lawrence Earlbaum.

TIZARD, B. and HUGHES, M. (1984) *Young Children Learning, Talking and Thinking at Home and at School*. Fontana.

TIZARD, B., MORTIMORE, J. and BURCHELL, B. (1988) 'Involving Parents from Minority Groups', pp. 72–83 in BASTIANI, J. (Ed.) *Parents and Teachers 2: From Policy to Practice*. NFER-Nelson.

TIZARD, J., SCHOFIELD, W. and HEWISON, J. (1982) 'Collaboration between teachers and parents in assisting children's reading' in *Brit. J. Educ. Psychol.* 52, 1–15.

TOMLINSON, J. (1988) *Curriculum and market: are they compatible?* Ch. 2 in Haviland, J. *Take Care, Mr. Baker!* Fourth Estate.

TOMLINSON, S. (1984) 'Home and School in Multicultural Britain', Batsford Academic.

UNITED NATIONS (1959) *United Nations Declaration of the Rights of the Child*, quoted in total as an appendix in FREEMAN, M.D.A. *The Rights and Wrongs of Children* (1983) Pinter, pp. 283–5.

UNIVERSITY OF GLASGOW (1986) *Parental Choice of School in Scotland*, Parental Choice Project. DES/University of Glasgow.

WARNOCK, M. (1985) Paper given at the Community Education Development Centre Family Education Conference 25–27 Sept. 1985.

'Warnock Report' (1978) *Special Educational Needs: Report of the Committee of Enquiry into the Education of Handicapped Children and Young People.* DES/SED/WO/HMSO.

WATT, J. and FLETT, M. (1985) *Continuity in Early Education: The Role of Parents*, Aberdeen University.

WELSH CONSUMER COUNCIL (1988) *Dear Parent.*

WEST, E.G. (1970) *Education and the State: A Study in Political Economy.* Institute of Economic Affairs.

WIDLAKE, P. (1986) *Reducing Educational Disadvantage.* Open University Press.

WIDLAKE, P. and MACLEOD, F. (1984) *Raising Standards: a report on a sample of primary schools taking part in reading and language programmes.* Community Education Development Centre.

WIDLAKE, P. and MACLEOD, F. (1988) 'Supporting Work with Parents', pp. 104–12 in BASTIANI, J. (Ed.) (1988) *Parents and Teachers 2: From Policy to Practice.* NFER-Nelson.

WINKLEY, D. (1985) *The school's view of parents*, Ch. 5 in Cullingford (Ed.) *Parents, Teachers and Schools*, Royce.

WISEMAN, S. (1964) *Education and Environment.* Manchester University Press.

WOLFENDALE, S. (1983) *Parental Participation in Children's Development and Education.* Gordon and Breach.

WRAGG, E.C. and PORTINGTON, J.A. (1980) *A Handbook for School Governors.* Methuen.

YOUNG, M. and McGEENEY, P. (1968) *Learning begins at home: A Study of a Junior School and its Parents.* Routledge and Kegan Paul.

Index

INDEX